Unreal Engine 5.4

Beginner's User Guide

A Step-by-Step Guide for Building and Developing Engaging Games for your Target Audience using Unreal Engine 5.4 Blueprints

Matt Vic

CONTENTS

INTRODUCTION

In 1998, Epic Games released the first iteration of their 3D computer graphics game engine, known as Unreal Engine (UE). The game was a first-person shooter. Originally intended for PC first-person shooters, the design has subsequently been embraced by the film, and television industries and also employed in a variety of game genres.

Unreal Engine 5 is no longer just for the big players in the industry. This groundbreaking engine, which powers breathtaking next-generation games, is now accessible to everyone. Imagine creating immersive worlds, pushing graphical limits, and bringing your game ideas to life. This book is your gateway to making that dream a reality.

Unreal Engine's Blueprint graphical programming system is a powerful tool that allows designers to create game scripts and enables programmers to develop core elements that designers can expand upon. This book offers an in-depth look at all the features of the Blueprint Editor, complete with expert tips, and shortcuts.

You'll start by learning how to use variables, functions, and macros, and you'll gain an understanding of object-oriented programming (OOP). As you progress, you'll explore the Gameplay Framework and learn how Blueprint Communication enables one Blueprint to access data from another. The book guides you through the process of building a fully functional game, step by step, starting with a basic first-person shooter (FPS) template. Each chapter adds layers to the modeling, growing it into a more complex and polished game. You'll move from simple shooting mechanics to more intricate systems. For example, user interfaces and intelligent enemy behaviors.

Having no experience in Unreal Engine? Do not worry! This easy-to-learn guide is your gateway to mastering Unreal Engine 5. We'll guide you step-by-step, preparing you with the essential skills and knowledge to master programming, and design concepts to build a strong foundation.

This book empowers you to create professional-quality games and overcome the learning curve with clear explanations and practical examples. Learn from the experts, and master skills and practices used by leading game developers.

Stop dreaming about making games and start bringing your ideas to life with step-by-step guidance.

CHAPTER ONE
GETTING STARTED WITH BLUEPRINT EDITOR

As you are getting started with game development using Unreal Engine 5's Blueprint Editor. This book is your gateway to mastering game creation with Unreal Engine's intuitive visual scripting language, designed by Epic Games.

Before diving into Blueprints, it's crucial to set up our development environment. Unreal Engine is readily available for free download. We'll guide you through the installation process and help you create your first project. Once set up, we'll delve into the fundamental concepts of Blueprints and study each section of the Blueprint Editor.

INSTALLING UNREAL ENGINE APPLICATION

To begin using Unreal Engine, you'll need to install the Epic Games Launcher. Follow these steps:

1) Go to the https://www.unrealengine.com. Then Register an account and download the Epic Games Launcher.
2) Install the Epic Game Launcher and open it.

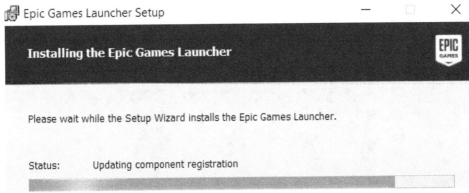

3) click the **Unreal Engine** tab on the left side and then click on the "**Library**" tab at the top.
4) Click the + **button** beside the **ENGINE VERSIONS** to add a version of Unreal Engine to the launcher (preferably the latest version, **5.4.2** in this case).
5) Click "**Install**". The launcher will begin downloading the necessary files for installation, which may take some time.

6) Once installed, click "**Launch**" to start the installed version. You can have multiple versions installed on the same machine; simply designate one as the current version. Use the **Launch** button at the upper right of the launcher to start the current version.

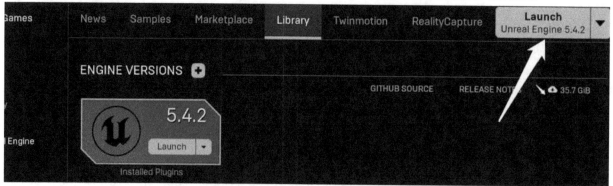

The Blueprint Visual Scripting system is robust and widely used. This book uses version **5.4.2**, and the examples provided should effortlessly work in subsequent versions.

USING TEMPLATES TO CREATE NEW PROJECT

Once you launch the Unreal Engine Editor, the **Unreal Project Browser** will display. Use the **Recent Projects** box on the upper left to access existing projects, and explore different categories of templates on the left to start a new project. The screenshot below illustrates the templates available in the **Games** category.

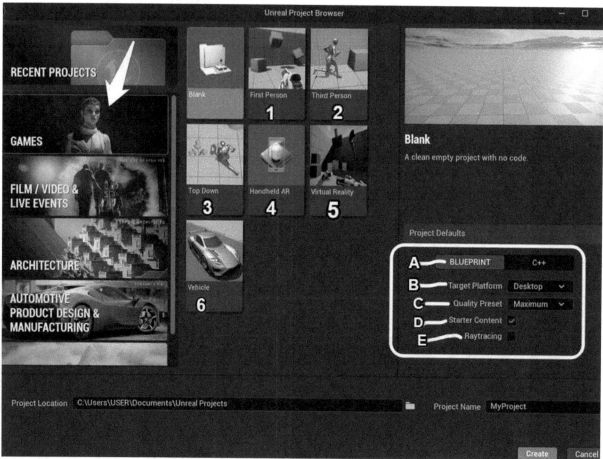

Templates serve as foundational frameworks containing essential files and a level setup, that offers a basic starting point for various project types. They are particularly valuable for quick prototyping or mastering the fundamentals of specific project styles. Though using a template is optional, templates simplify initial setup because all their functionalities can be replicated in the blank template.

Below are descriptions of each template found in the Games category:

1) **First Person**: Designed for games with a first-person perspective. This template includes a player character represented by arms holding a gun that shoots a simple sphere projectile. Players can move the character using a **controller**, **keyboard**, or **virtual joystick** on touch devices.

2) **Third Person:** Features a playable character with a camera positioned behind and slightly above it. The character is equipped with walking, running, and jumping animations, and can be controlled using a controller, keyboard, or virtual joystick on touch devices.

3) **Top Down**: This template features a character controlled by mouse input, viewed with a camera from a high perspective. The player's character is moved with a mouse or touchscreen to click on the required destination and use the navigation system to prevent obstacles. It's commonly utilized in action role-playing games.

4) **Handheld AR**: Tailored for augmented reality applications on Android and iOS devices. This template includes runtime logic to toggle AR mode and includes example code for hit detection and light estimation management.

5) **Virtual Reality**: Designed for virtual reality games, this template includes teleport locomotion, interactive objects, grabbable items, and a VR spectator camera. Players can move within a designated level and interact with various objects.

6) **Vehicle**: This template offers both a standard vehicle and a complex one with suspension. its level includes a straightforward track with obstacles for testing vehicle mechanics.

Located at the bottom right of the Unreal Project Browser, you'll find **Project Defaults** with project configuration options specific to the selected template. Here are the settings used in this book:

A. **Blueprint/C++:** Projects can be created with either Blueprint or C++. This book focuses exclusively on Blueprint, though Unreal Engine supports using both languages interchangeably. You can even add Blueprint code to C++ projects and **C++** to Blueprint projects.

B. **Target Platform**: Choose between Desktop for computers and game consoles or Mobile for mobile devices. This book primarily uses the Desktop option.

C. **Quality Preset**: Select Scalable for optimized performance, which disables some complex features, or Maximum to enable all platform-specific features. The book focuses on the Scalable option.

D. **Starter Content**: If checked, the project includes Starter Content, which provides basic meshes, materials, and particle effects. This book focuses on the Started Content.

E. **Raytracing**: Enable this option for real-time raytracing, a computationally intensive feature. We won't use retracing in this book.

To start creating a project in Unreal Engine using the template, follow these steps:

1) Select the **Third Person** template, specify a location folder using **Project Location**, and enter a name for your project in the **Project Name** field.
2) Choose the **Project Defaults** as described earlier, then click the **Create** button.

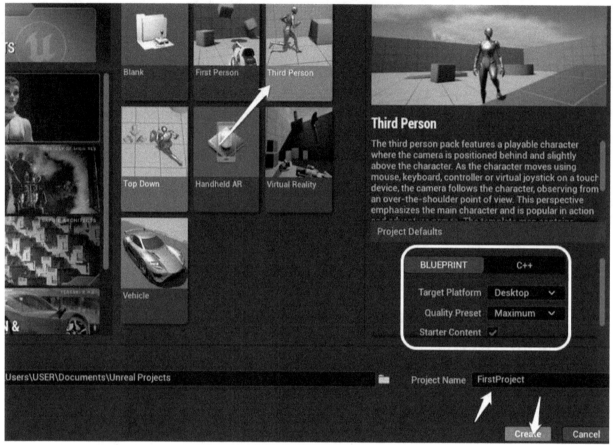

3) Once the project starts, the **Unreal Engine Level** Editor will appear, resembling the layout shown below.

Key panels within the Level Editor include:

A. **Viewport**: Centered within the **Level Editor**, it displays the current Level being constructed. The Viewport allows movement within the Level and adds objects to the level. While pressing down the right mouse button, move the mouse to rotate the camera and use the **WASD** keys to navigate around.

B. **Toolbar**: Positioned at the upper area of the Level Editor, it features buttons grouped for various operations. The first group includes saving work and adding several objects and code to the project, the second group for changing editing modes, the third group for testing the current level, and offers several platform-specific options, and the last group for accessing project settings.

C. **Outliner**: situated at the right of the Level Editor, it lists all objects within the Level to facilitate easy management and selection.

D. **Details**: situated under the Outliner panel, the Details panel displays editable properties of selected objects within the Viewport.

E. **Content Browser**: you can access this via the **Content Drawer** button at the lower-left corner, this panel manages project assets. Assets contain various content types such as

Materials, Static Meshes, and Blueprints. Dragging assets from the Content Drawer to the Level Editor creates duplicates for placement.

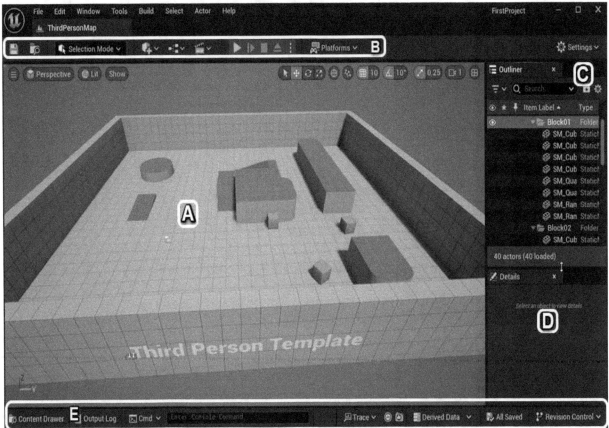

With an understanding of the Unreal Engine Level Editor interface, the focus now shifts to examining Blueprint Visual Scripting. This powerful tool allows developers to create game logic and interactions using a visual programming approach.

BLUEPRINTS VISUAL SCRIPTING

The term "**Blueprint**" carries dual meanings within Unreal Engine. First and foremost, it serves as a visual scripting language crafted by Epic Games specifically for Unreal Engine. Secondly, it denotes a distinct type of game entity generated using this scripting language.

There exist two primary categories of Blueprints:

- **Level Blueprint:** Every game level possesses its own unique Level Blueprint. Unlike Blueprint Classes, Level Blueprints are tied directly to specific levels and cannot be created separately.
- **Blueprint Class:** This type of Blueprint is utilized to construct interactive game objects that can be reused across multiple levels.

ACCESSING THE LEVEL BLUEPRINT EDITOR

Access the **Level Blueprint** Editor by clicking the **Blueprints** button positioned in the leftmost section of the toolbar within Unreal Editor. From the dropdown menu, select "**Open Level Blueprint**".

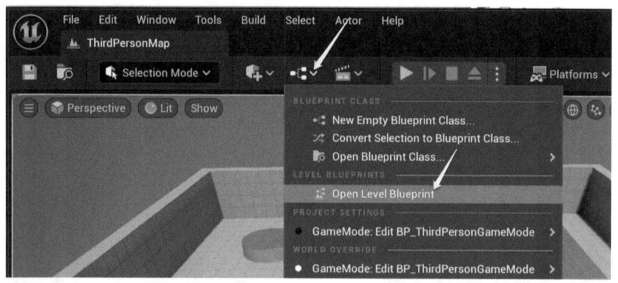

The **Level Blueprint** Editor displays a simplified interface compared to the **Blueprint Class** Editor. It features the **"My Blueprint"** panel, the **Details** panel, and the **Event Graph** Editor, tailored for managing level-specific scripting tasks.

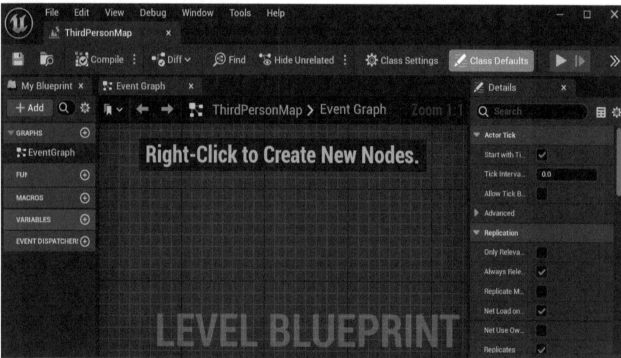

For introductory purposes, we won't be making any adjustments to the **Level Blueprint** Editor at this time. Simply familiarize yourself with its layout and then close it to return to the Level Editor window.

CREATING A BLUEPRINT CLASS

Next, we'll proceed to create a Blueprint Class to dig into the Blueprint Class Editor and explore its comprehensive range of panels and functionalities.

Let's check how to create a Blueprint Class in Unreal Engine through various methods:

USING THE TOOLBAR:

- Click on the **Blueprints** button in the toolbar, the same one used to open the **Level Blueprint.**
- From the dropdown menu, select "**New Empty Blueprint Class**".

USING THE CONTENT BROWSER:

- Click the **Content Drawer** button to summon the **Content Browser**.
- Click the **Add** button and choose "**Blueprint Class**" in the **Create Basic Asset** category.

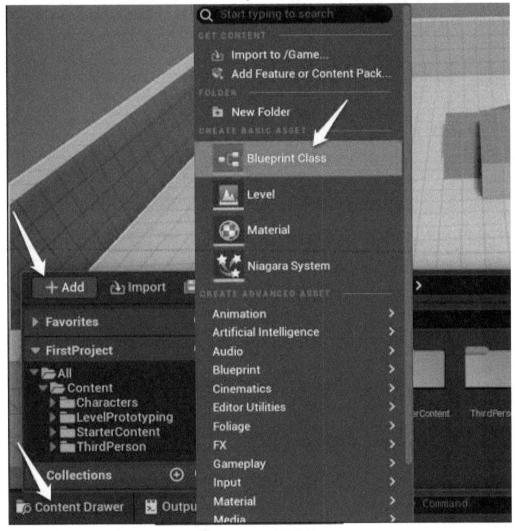

USING THE CONTEXT MENU IN THE CONTENT BROWSER:

- Right-click in the empty space within the **Content Browser**.
- Choose "**Blueprint Class**" from the context menu that appears.

After selecting one of these methods, a window will prompt you to choose the parent class for your new Blueprint. Think of the parent class as the fundamental type of Blueprint you're creating. The window initially displays the most commonly used classes, but you can expand the class to view all available classes by clicking the **ALL CLASSES** button. Once you've chosen the parent class, this window closes, and a new Blueprint asset appears in the **Content Browser**, ready to be renamed.

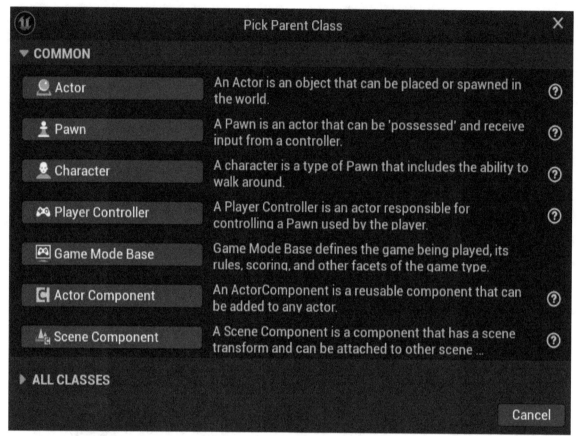

For now, you can click the **Cancel** button during this process as we are focusing on familiarizing ourselves with the steps. Now that we've covered how to open the Level Blueprint and create a Blueprint Class, let's dig into exploring the panels within the Blueprint Class Editor. To open the Blueprint Class Editor, right-click on a Blueprint asset in the **Content Browser** and choose "**Edit**" or simply double-click on the **Blueprint asset** itself.

UNDERSTANDING BLUEPRINT CLASS EDITOR USER INTERFACE

The Blueprint Class Editor, often referred to simply as the Blueprint Editor, features several essential panels, each dedicated to editing specific aspects of a Blueprint. These panels collectively provide a comprehensive environment for creating and modifying game logic and interactions. Here are the main panels found in the Blueprint Editor:

A. Toolbar
B. Components
C. Viewport
D. Event Graph
E. My Blueprint
F. Detail

To illustrate these panels in action, let's use the example of the **BP_ThirdPersonCharacter** Blueprint from the **Third Person** template. You can find this Blueprint in the **ThirdPerson > Blueprints** folder. Simply double-click on **BP_ThirdPersonCharacter** to open it in the Blueprint Class Editor.

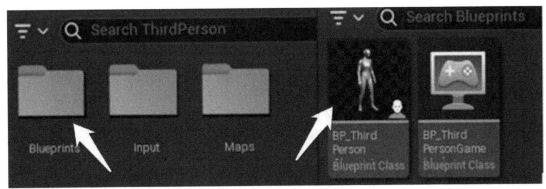

These panels collectively empower developers to design complex gameplay mechanics and interactions using a visual scripting approach to enhance flexibility and efficiency in Unreal Engine development.

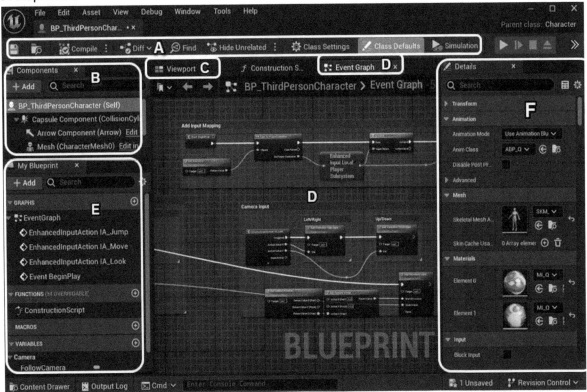

THE TOOLBAR PANEL

At the top of the Blueprint Class Editor lies the Toolbar panel, housing crucial tools for efficiently editing Blueprints. Below is a detailed description of each button:

- ✓ **Compile:** Converts the Blueprint script into an executable format. Before running the game, changes must be compiled to take effect. Clicking this button initiates compilation, indicated by a green check icon if successful.
- ✓ **Save**: Saves all modifications made to the current Blueprint.
- ✓ **Browse**: Opens the Content Browser to display the location of the current Blueprint Class.
- ✓ **Find**: Enables searching within the Blueprint for specific nodes or elements.

- ✓ **Hide Unrelated**: When activated, it hides nodes in the Blueprint that are not directly related to the selected nodes.
- ✓ **Class Settings**: it allows adjustments to the Blueprint's class settings in the Details panel. Settings include Description, Category, and Parent Class configuration.
- ✓ **Class Defaults**: it provides access to modify the initial values (defaults) of variables within the Blueprint, accessible through the Details panel.
- ✓ **Simulation:** it executes the Blueprint within the Blueprint Editor environment, and it facilitates testing and debugging without running the entire game.
- ✓ **Play:** starts gameplay within the current level, it allows real-time interaction and testing of game mechanics.
- ✓ **Advance a single frame/Stop Simulation (Escape)/Toggles the current play session between play in editor and simulation in editor(F8).**
- ✓ **Debug Object**: This dropdown menu enables the selection of an object for debugging purposes within the Blueprint. If no specific object is chosen, it defaults to debugging any instances created from the current Blueprint Class.

THE COMPONENT PANEL

The Components panel within the Blueprint Class Editor displays an overview of all components integrated into the current Blueprint. These components are predefined objects that can be easily incorporated into Blueprints to enhance functionality. To add a component, simply click the "**Add**" button within the **Components** panel.

Each component's properties can be customized and fine-tuned using the **Details** panel. Additionally, some components offer a visual representation within the Viewport panel, providing a preview of how they will appear and behave within the game world.

Examples of components typically found in the Components panel include Static Meshes, lights, sounds, box collisions, particle systems, and cameras.

MY BLUEPRINT PANEL

Moving on to the **My Blueprint** panel, it serves as a workspace for crafting **macros**, **variables**, **functions**, and **graphs** specific to the Blueprint. Clicking the **Add** button at the top of the panel, or the **plus** "**+**" button beside each category facilitates the creation of these elements, each of which can be finely modified via the **Details** panel.

THE DETAIL PANEL

The Details panel enables developers to modify properties of selected elements such as *Variables*, *Components*, *Macros*, or *Functions*. These properties are neatly categorized for easy navigation and editing.

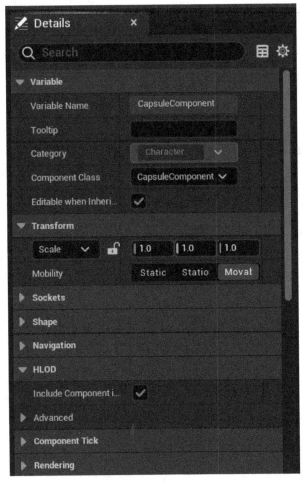

The screenshot above displays the **CapsuleComponent** properties. At the top of the panel, a **Search** box facilitates quick filtering of properties.

THE VIEWPORT PANEL

The Viewport provides a visual representation of the Blueprint and its integrated Components. Its controls resemble controls found in the Level Editor, the Viewport panel enables manipulation of Component features such as position, scale, and rotation directly within a visual context.

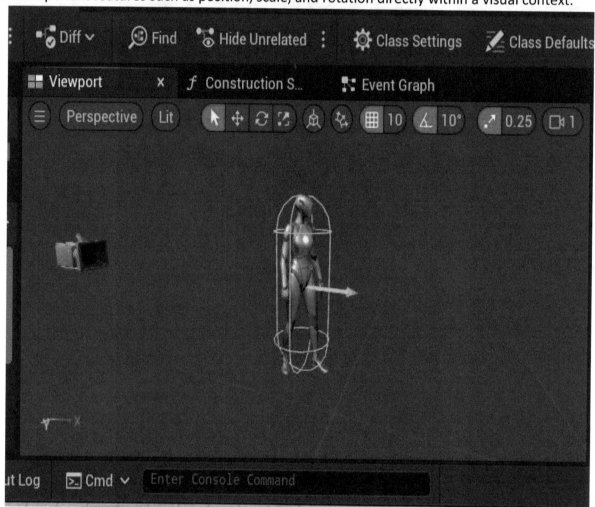

For instance, the Viewport panel screenshot shown above includes a SkeletalMesh component representing the player character, a Camera defining the player's viewpoint, and a Capsule Component used for collision detection.

THE EVENT GRAPH PANEL

The Event Graph panel serves as the core workspace where developers program the behavior of Blueprints. This panel houses a collection of **Events** and **Actions** represented as nodes interconnected by wires.

Events, indicated by red nodes, activate in response to gameplay triggers. Each event can trigger multiple actions, defining the Blueprint's response to various in-game scenarios. For example, events like "**InputAxis TurnRate**" and "**InputAxis LookUpRate**" are shown in the screenshot, highlighting how player input influences gameplay.

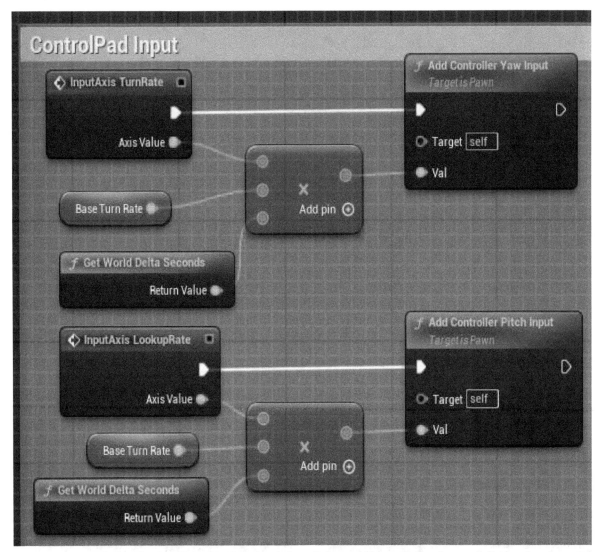

To move around the Event Graph, simply right-click and drag to explore additional events and actions. Beyond events, the graph includes nodes representing functions, operators, and variables. We shall discuss these components in the subsequent chapter.

With this comprehensive overview of the Blueprint Editor panels, we are now prepared to create our first Blueprint. To proceed, close the Blueprint Class Editor and return to the Level Editor where we can continue refining and integrating our Blueprint into the game environment.

CREATING COMPONENTS IN A BLUEPRINT

Next, we will create the first Blueprint, a simple one with just components. We won't be using events or actions for now. Below is a step-by-step guide:

1) Start by clicking the **Content Drawer** button to open the **Content Browser**. Then, click on the **Add** button and choose **Blueprint Class**.
2) In the subsequent window (**Pick Parent Class**), select **Actor** as the parent class.
3) Now, **rename** the Blueprint to **BP_SpinningChair**. Remember, Blueprint names cannot have spaces, and it's customary to begin them with "**BP_**".

4) Double-click on **BP_SpinningChair** to open it in the Blueprint Editor.
5) Go to the **Components** panel, click on the **Add** button, and choose **Static Mesh**. This component will visually represent our Blueprint.

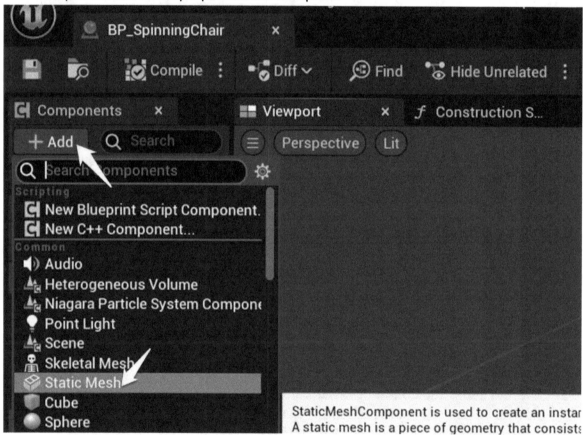

6) Go to the **Details** panel, locate the **Static Mesh** property, and click on the dropdown. Choose the **Static Mesh** named **SM_Chair** from the list. This mesh is part of the starter content.

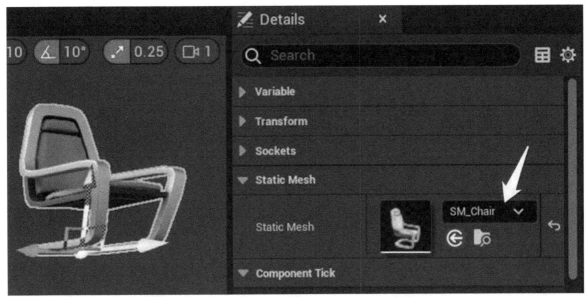

7) Next, we will add another component. Click on the **Add** button in the **Components** panel and type "**rotating**" in the Search box. Select the **Rotating Movement** Component from the results to add it.

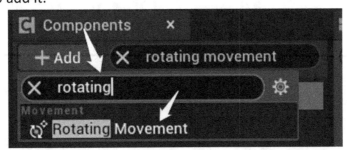

This component will automatically rotate the Blueprint around the z-axis by default, so no further adjustments are necessary.

8) Once added, click on the **Compile** button and then **save** the Blueprint.

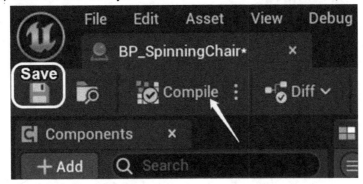

9) Switch to the Level Editor. Drag the **BP_SpinningChair** Blueprint from the **Content Browser** and drop it into your desired location in the Level.

10) To see the rotating chair in action, press the **Play** button in the Level Editor. You can control the character with the **WASD** keys and rotate the camera using the mouse. **Press Esc** to exit the played level. The screenshot below displays the instance of execution.

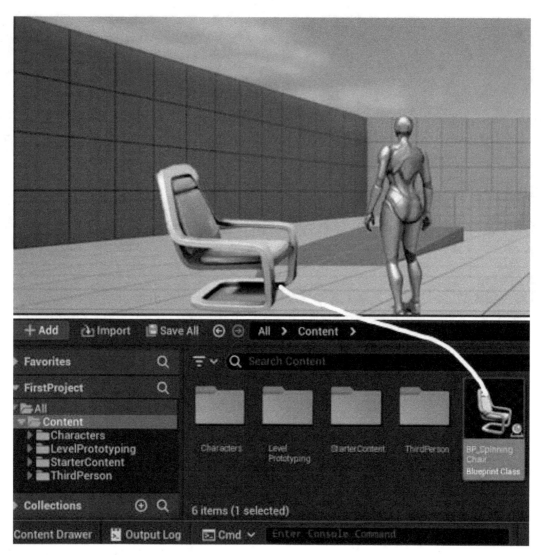

BLUEPRINTS PROGRAMMING

Next, we will be considering fundamental programming concepts specific to Blueprints. Programming involves creating instructions that computers can understand and perform. Unlike traditional text-based languages, Blueprints employs a visual approach using nodes.

Certain programming languages are categorized as scripting languages when they operate within specific environments or serve well-defined purposes. For instance, Blueprints serves as the visual scripting language for Unreal Engine.

STORE YOUR VALUES IN VARIABLES

A variable essentially acts as an identifier that points to a specific memory location where data can be stored. For instance, in a game, a character might have variables to track its health, speed, and ammunition count.

In Blueprints, variables come in different types and can serve various purposes within a Blueprint. These variables are conveniently listed in the "My Blueprint" panel. Adding a new variable is straightforward; simply click the **+** button under the **VARIABLES** category.

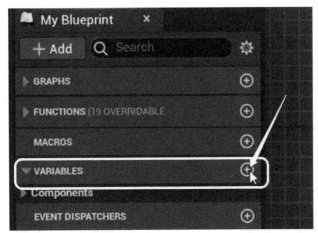

The type of a variable dictates the kind of data it can hold. Blueprint follows a strongly typed approach, meaning you must specify the variable's type when creating it, and this type remains fixed throughout the program's execution.

When you create a variable, its details are displayed in the **Details** panel. The primary features of a variable include its name and type. Common types include:

Each type of variable in Blueprints is visually distinguished by a specific color and serves distinct purposes. In addition to the basic variable types, there are other types related to **Structure**, **Interface**, **Object Types**, and Enum that we will explore in forthcoming chapters.

TYPE OF VARIABLE	DESCRIPTION

Boolean	Holds values of either true or false.
Byte	An 8-bit number capable of storing integer values from 0 to 255.
Integer	A 32-bit number that can store integers ranging from −2,147,483,648 to 2,147,483,647.
Integer64	A 64-bit number capable of storing integers from −9,223,372,036,854,775,808 to 9,223,372,036,854,775,807.
Float	A 32-bit floating-point number for storing values with fractional parts, specific to seven decimal digits.
Double	A 64-bit floating-point number for storing values with fractional parts, specific to 16 decimal digits.
Name	Holds a piece of text used as an identifier for objects.
String	Stores alphanumeric characters and can handle a group of characters.
Text	Used for text intended for localization, facilitating easier translation into different languages.
Vector	Contains X, Y, and Z float values, representing a 3D vector.
Rotator	Holds X (Roll), Y (Pitch), and Z (Yaw) float values, representing a rotation in 3D space.
Transform	Stores information about rotation, location, and scale.

The screenshot below illustrates the Details panel, displaying the customizable attributes of a variable in Blueprints such as **Variable Name, Type, Instance Editable,** and so on:

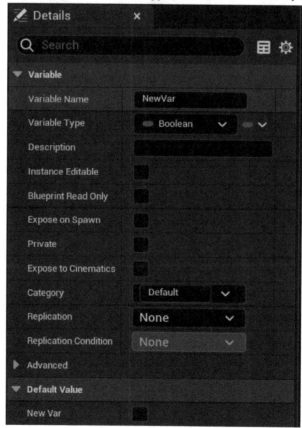

Each feature is explained in the table below:

ATTRIBUTE	DESCRIPTION
Variable Name	This serves as the identifier for the variable.
Variable Type	indicates the kind of data that can be stored in the variable.
Instance Editable	When checked, each instance of the Blueprint placed in the level can store a unique value for this variable. Otherwise, the initial value is shared among all instances.
Blueprint Read Only	If enabled, prevents the variable from being modified by Blueprint nodes.
Tooltip	Provides information displayed when hovering over the variable.
Expose on Spawn	Allows setting the variable when spawning the Blueprint.
Private	When checked, it restricts modification by child Blueprints.
Expose to Cinematics	If enabled, exposes the variable to Sequencer.
Category	Organizes variables within the Blueprint.
Slider Range	Sets the minimum and maximum values for a UI slider that modifies this variable.
Value Range	Specifies the minimum and maximum permissible values for the variable.
Replication and Replication Condition	Used in networked games.
DEFAULT VALUE	Contains the initial value of the variable, which requires Blueprint compilation before setting.

Variables in Blueprints represent the current state of the Blueprint, while its behavior is determined by events and actions, which we'll cover in the next section.

USING EVENTS AND ACTIONS TO DEFINE THE BEHAVIOR OF A BLUEPRINT

To define the behavior of a Blueprint through events and actions, we primarily focus on creating new Actors within Unreal Engine. Actors represent game objects that can be added within a level.

In Unreal Engine, events signify changes in the state of an Actor, while actions dictate how an Actor responds to these events. These events and actions are visualized as nodes within the Event Graph panel.

EVENTS

Events are added via Blueprint's Event Graph panel. To do this, right-click within the **Event Graph** panel to open the **Fly Out** Menu, which lists available events and actions. If more space is needed, the **Event Graph** panel can be expanded by right-clicking and dragging to an empty area. The **Context Menu** includes a **Search** bar for node filtering and a **Context Sensitive** checkbox that are available actions based on the selected node. The screenshot below displays the **Context Menu** featuring various available events:

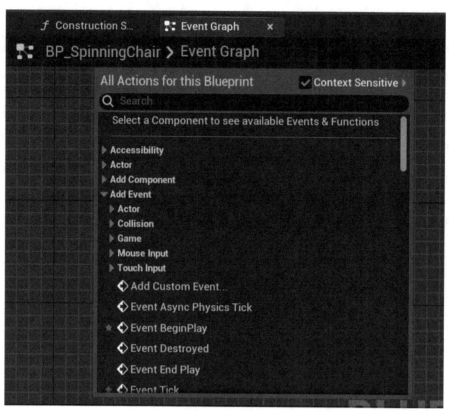

Multiple events can be added to the **Event Graph** panel, but each event can only be added once. Besides built-in events produced by Unreal Engine, custom events can be created by selecting "**Add Custom Event".** The next diagram illustrates a **Custom Event** node and its corresponding **Details** panel, where the custom event can be renamed and configured with input parameters. Detailed exploration of parameters will be covered later in this chapter.

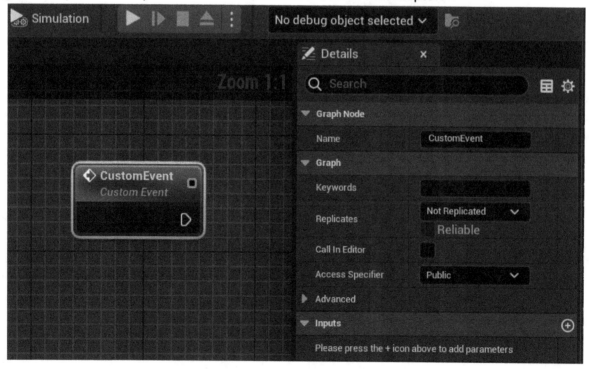

Below are some of the events available within Unreal Engine's Blueprint system:

- ✓ **Event BeginPlay:** it is executed when the game starts for Actors already present in the Level Editor or instantly after an Actor is spawned during runtime.
- ✓ **Collision Events:** These events trigger when two Actors collide or overlap in the game world. Input Events: it is triggered by user input devices such as mouse, keyboard, touch screens, and gamepads.
- ✓ **Input Events:** You can trigger this with input devices such as mouse, keyboard, gamepads, and touch screen.
- ✓ **Event Tick:** Called every frame of the game. For instance, in a game running at 60 frames per second, this event triggers 60 times per second.
- ✓ **Event End Play:** it is executed when an Actor is about to be removed during runtime.

Next, we'll dig deeper by creating actions that link to these events.

ACTIONS

Actions in Blueprints define how a Blueprint responds when triggered by an event. They enable us to set or get values in variables or call functions to alter the Blueprint's state.

The diagram below displays the **Event BeginPlay** event of a Blueprint. In this scenario, the Blueprint includes a **String Variables** called **Bot Name**:

1) **SET Action**: Allocate the value "**Archon**" to a string variable named "**Bot Name**".

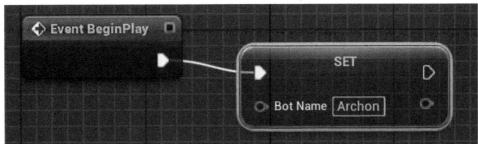

2) **Print String Action:** This displays the value received on the **"In String"** pin on the screen. The values passed into functions like these are referred to as **parameters.**
3) The **"In String"** pin connects to a **GET** node of the "**Bot Name**" variable, which retrieves the current value of the variable and sends it to the **Print String** function.

4) To add **GET** and **SET** actions for a variable in the Event **Graph**, simply drag the variable from the My Blueprint panel and drop it into the **Event Graph** to reveal the **GET** and **SET** options.

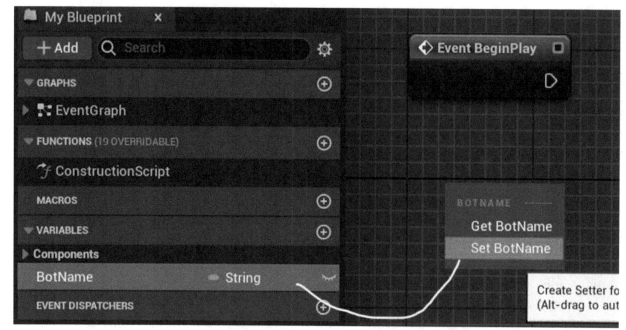

Additional functions such as Print String can be added from the Context Menu accessible by right-clicking within the Event Graph. Both GET and SET actions can also be located using the search feature within the Context Menu.

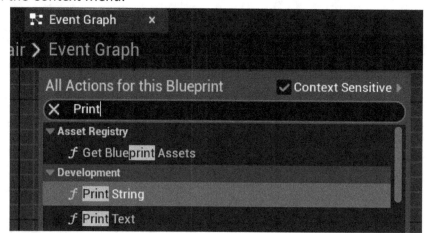

The white lines connecting these actions are otherwise called the execution path

THE EXECUTION PATH

The execution path in a Blueprint involves the flow of operations through nodes, distinguished by their pins. Nodes with white pins are referred to as execution pins and colored pins are the data pins. The sequence begins with a red event node, and execution proceeds along the white wires from left to right until reaching the final node.

Certain nodes within Blueprints control the flow of execution based on specific conditions. A notable example is the **Branch** node, which includes two output execution pins labeled **True** and **False**. The pin that activates depends on the **Boolean** value provided to the **Condition** input parameter. The following screenshot demonstrates the setup of a **Branch** node:

22

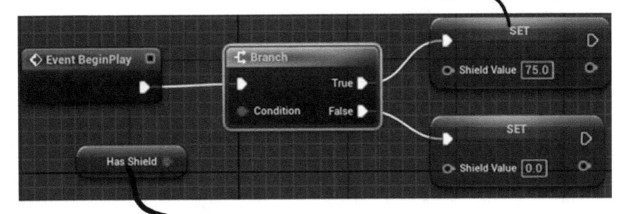

Set Shield Value Variable

Get Has Shield Variable

In this instance, when the **Event BeginPlay** is triggered, the **Branch** node evaluates the **Boolean** value of the **Has Shield** variable. If the value is **true**, the **True** pin executes and assigns a value of **100.0** to the **Shield Value** variable. Conversely, if **false**, the value **0.0** is assigned to the **Shield Value** variable. We've explored how to manipulate variable values using actions. Next, we'll dig into creating expressions utilizing variables.

USING OPERATORS TO CREATE EXPRESSIONS

Creating expressions with operators in Blueprints involves using operators to combine variables and values to perform calculations. These operators are accessible in the **Fly-out** Menu under the **Utilities > Operators** category.

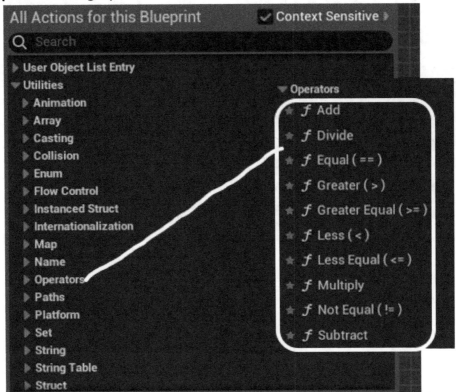

TYPES OF OPERATORS

ARITHMETIC OPERATORS

Arithmetic operators (**+, -, ×, and /**) are used to construct mathematical expressions within Blueprints. These operators take two input values on the left and produce the resulting operation on the right. They can support multiple input parameters; additional input parameters can be added by clicking the "**Add pin**" button on the node. Input values can be acquired via data wires or entered directly into the node.

Tip: In programming languages, the * symbol represents the multiplication operator. In Blueprints, this same *symbol is also identified as a multiplication operator though it uses the letter **X** as the node label. When searching for multiplication nodes in the **Fly-out** Menu, use either the * symbol or type the word "**multiply**".

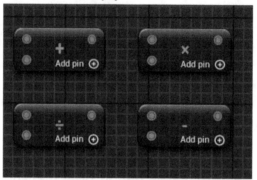

This illustration below is an example of a simple arithmetic expression (the numbers in the diagram indicate the order of completion of the nodes:

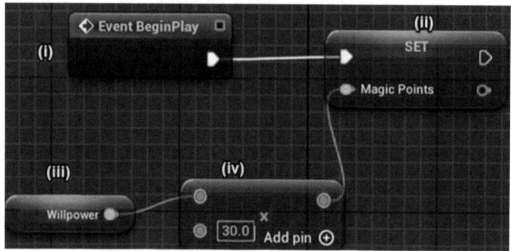

In this scenario:

- ✓ The execution starts with the **Event BeginPlay** event. The **SET** node assigns a new value to the **Magic Points** variable.
- ✓ The value assigned is obtained from the data wire connected to the output of a multiplication node.
- ✓ The **multiplication** node calculates the result by multiplying the value obtained from the Willpower variable (obtained via another data wire) by 30.0.

RELATIONAL OPERATORS

Relational operators in Blueprints facilitate comparisons between two values and then yield a Boolean result (**True** or **False**) based on the outcome of the comparison. These operators are crucial for decision-making within Blueprint scripts.

Relational operators are shown in this diagram

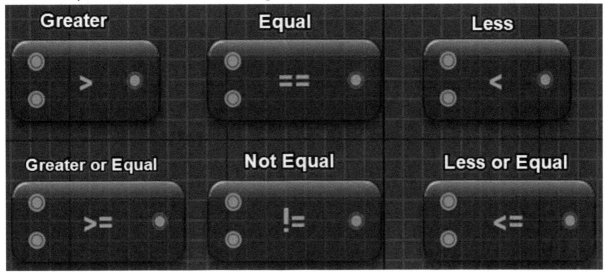

The diagram above illustrates an instance of a relational operator

- ✓ Assume these actions are executed when a game object receives damage, a **Branch** node is used to evaluate whether the value of the **Health** variable is less than or equal to **0.0**.
- ✓ If the condition evaluates to **True**, indicating that the **Health** is at or below zero, the game object is destroyed.
- ✓ If the condition evaluates to **False**, meaning the **Health** is still **positive**, no further actions are taken (as indicated by the lack of connections to the False branch).

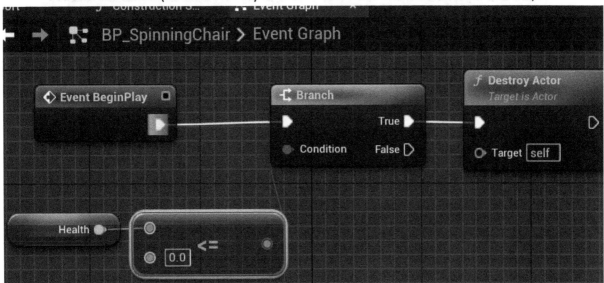

LOGICAL OPERATORS

Logical operators in Blueprints facilitate operations between Boolean values, yielding a Boolean result (**True** or **False**) based on the logic applied. These operators play a crucial role in conditional logic and decision-making within Blueprint scripts. You will find the on the Context menu under **Math > Boolean**.

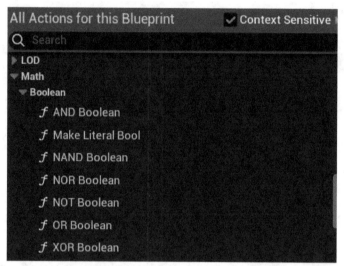

These available the logical operators in Blueprints:

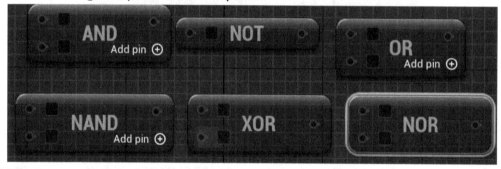

- ✓ **AND:** Returns **True** only if all input values are **True**.
- ✓ **NOT**: Takes a single input value and returns its opposite (True becomes False and vice versa).
- ✓ **OR:** Returns **True** if any of the input values are **True**.
- ✓ **NAND:** Combines the **NOT** and **AND** operators. Returns **False** if both inputs are **True**; else, returns **True**.
- ✓ **XOR (**otherwise called **exclusive OR**): Returns **True** if the two inputs are different (one is **True** and the other is **False**). Returns **False** if both inputs are the same.
- ✓ **NOR:** Combines the **NOT** and **OR** operators. Returns **True** if both inputs are **False**; else, returns **False**.

This is an instance of using the **AND** operator:

- ✓ The **AND** operator is used to check if both the **Health** value is greater than **60.**0 and the **Protection** Value is greater than **40**.0.
- ✓ If both conditions are met (**Health** > **60**.0 and **Protection** Value > **40**.0), the **Print String** node will execute.

26

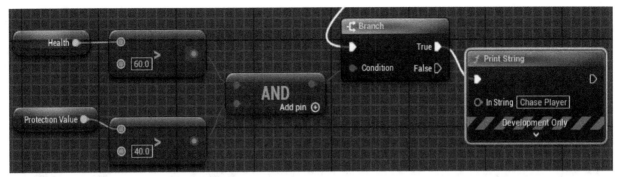

Having covered actions and operators, the next step involves organizing them into macros and functions for more efficient Blueprint scripting.

USING MACROS AND FUNCTIONS TO ARRANGE THE SCRIPT

Organizing Blueprint scripts involves consolidating frequently used groups of actions into macros or functions. This practice enhances script clarity, simplifies maintenance, and facilitates debugging by centralizing changes to a single node rather than scattered instances across the script.

CREATING MACROS

Macros are created within the **My Blueprint** panel by clicking the + button in the **MACROS** category. The panel then displays the newly created macro, such as the example named **"SetUpWave"** shown in the screenshot below:

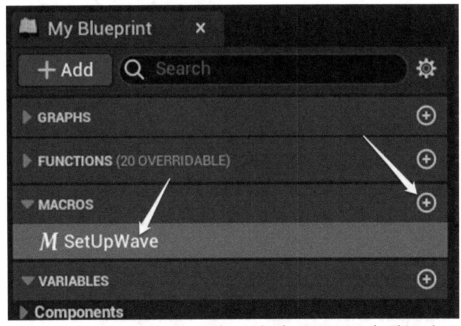

Once a macro is created, a new tab opens alongside the Event Graph. This tab resembles the **Event Graph** but exclusively contains nodes related to the macro's actions. Macro actions can be added in this tab. To revisit or edit the macro after it has been closed, simply double-click its **name** in the **My Blueprint** panel. You can switch back to the Event Graph by clicking its respective tab.

The features of a macro are managed in the **Details** panel, where input and output parameters can be defined. Input parameters are values forwarded into macros or functions, while output parameters are values returned from them.

In the screenshot below, you can see the **Details** panel of the **SetupWave** macro, which features **two input parameters** and **one output parameter**. In macros, the white execution pins are defined as input/output parameters of type **Exec**, allowing you to add as many as needed. In this example, we've added an input execution pin named "**In**" and an output execution pin named "**Out**".

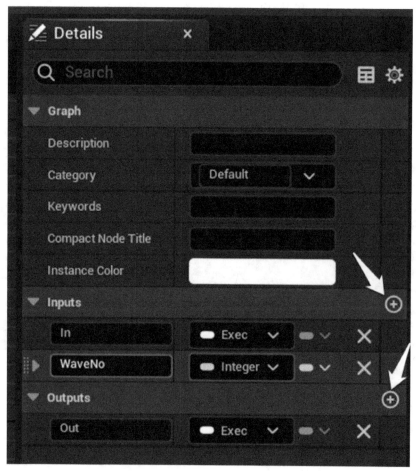

The screenshot below displays the contents of the **SetupWave** macro. This macro is designed to prepare variables for the next wave of enemies in a game. It takes the current Wave No as an input parameter, stores this value in the Current Wave variable, and calculates the number of enemies by multiplying the current Wave No by **10**.

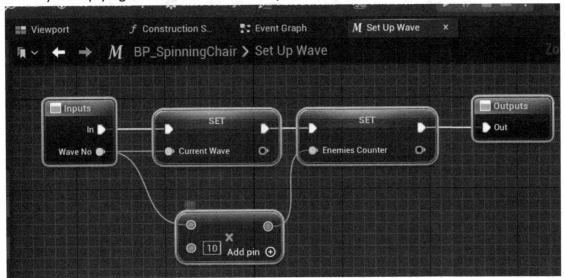

To add the macros to the **Event Graph**, you can either drag its name from the "**My Blueprint**" panel and drop it into the **Event Graph**, or find it in the **Content** Menu. Once the macro is executed, it performs the actions defined within it. The screenshot below demonstrates the **SetupWave** macro being called at the **Event BeginPlay**, with a value of **1** for the **Wave No** input parameter.

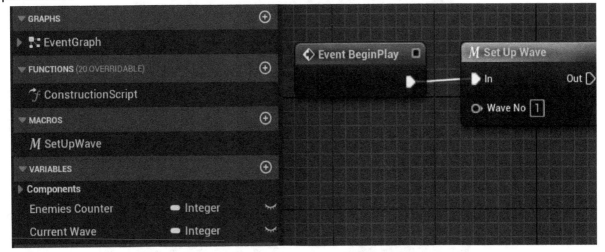

CREATING FUNCTIONS

Functions offer the advantage of reusability across different Blueprints. Functions allow you to encapsulate specific behaviors or calculations that can be called from various parts of your project. To create a function:

1) Go to the **My Blueprint** panel and click the **plus** "**+**" button in the **FUNCTIONS** group.
2) Name your function, such as "**CalculateWavePremium**," as shown in the screenshot below:

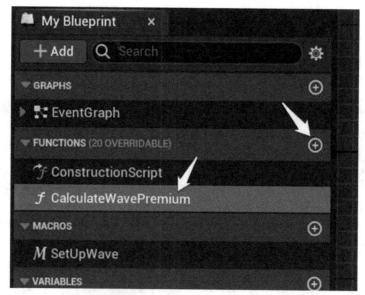

Similar to macros, functions have attributes managed in the Details panel; in this panel, the input and output parameters can be calculated. The screenshot below displays the **Details** panel of the **CalculateWavePremium** Function, with two input parameters and one output parameter.

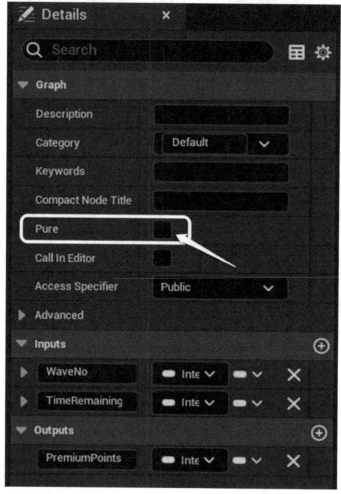

When creating a function, you have the option to define it as **Pure** by checking the **Pure** attribute in the **Details** panel. A Pure function does not have execution pins and is primarily used in expressions. It should not modify the Blueprint's variables but rather serve as a getter function that returns a calculated value or result.

This diagram visually displays that a standard function differs from a **Pure** function in Blueprints:

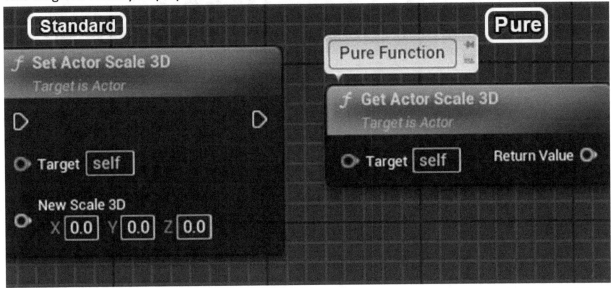

The **CalculateWavePremium** function calculates bonus points for a wave according to the **Wave No** and **Time Remaining** parameters. The calculated bonus points value is then returned through the **Premium Points** output parameter.

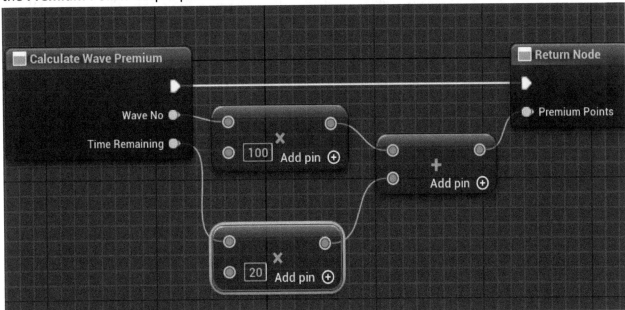

To use the **CalculateWavePremium** function in the Event Graph:
- ✓ You can add it from the **Context** Menu by right-clicking on the **Event Graph**.
- ✓ Alternatively, drag the function name from the **My Blueprint** panel and drop it into the **Event Graph**.

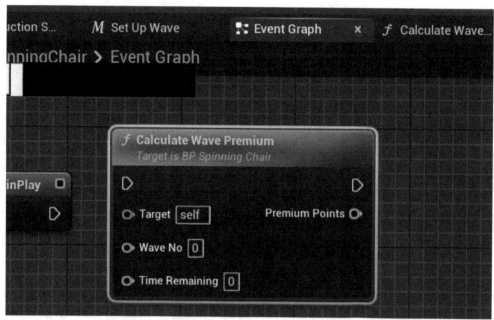

Let's walk through the step-by-step process of creating and executing a function named **CalculateEnergy** in Unreal Engine's Blueprint Editor. This function calculates a player's energy value based on their level using a specific expression, such as "**EnergyValue** = (**Playerlevel** x **6**) + **24**".

1) Click the **Content Drawer** button to open the Content Browser. Next, click the **Add** button and select **Blueprint Class**.

2) Select **Actor** as the parent class and Rename the Blueprint created to "**FunctionIllustration**".

3) Double-click the "**FunctionIllustration**" Blueprint to open the Blueprint Editor.

4) Go to the "**My Blueprint**" panel, and click the plus "**+**" button in the **Functions** group to create a new function. Rename the function to "**CalculateEnergy**".

5) Use the **Details** panel of the **CalculateEnergy** function to create:

✓ An input parameter named "**PlayerLevel**" of Integer type.
✓ An output parameter named "**EnergyValue**" of Integer type.

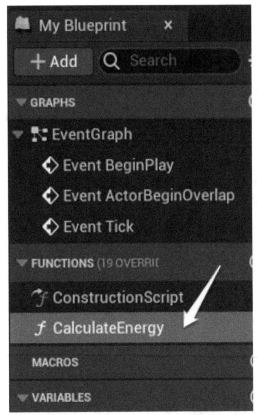

6) Switch to the tab created for the **CalculateEnergy** function in the Blueprint Editor. Construct the calculation expression as shown in the following screenshot:
   ✓ Use the **Context Menu** (right-click on the graph) to add nodes for addition **(+)** and **multiplication** (x).
   ✓ Connect these nodes to compute the expression by clicking one of the **pins**, dragging the mouse, and dropping it on the other pin.
   ✓ Ensure to input the values **6** and **24** into the appropriate nodes. Compile the Blueprint to validate the changes.

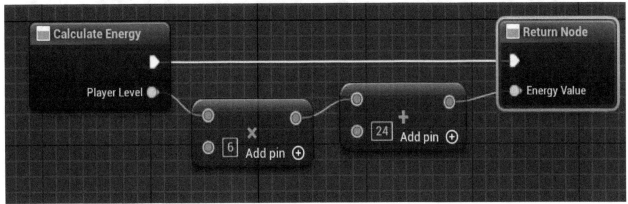

7) Go to the **Event Graph**, and locate the **Event BeginPlay** node (grayed out initially). Connect nodes to this **Event BeginPlay node** as shown below. Set the **Player Level** parameter of the **CalculateEnergy** node to the value **2**.

8) Click the arrow of the **Print String** node to reveal additional input parameters.

Note: The particular **Append** node used here can be found under the **String** group on the **Context** menu.

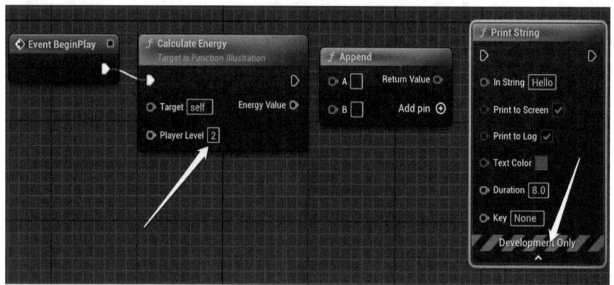

9) Click the **color square** beside the **Text Color** parameter of the **Print String** to open the **Color Picker** panel. Select a **blue color** from the color wheel and click **OK** to apply it.

10) Adjust the **Duration** parameter to **8.0** to control how long the text remains on screen.

11) Connect the **EnergyValue** pin from the **CalculateEnergy** node to the **B** pin of the **Append** node. This instantly creates a **conversion** node from integer to string. In the **A** parameter of the **Append** node, type "**ENERGY:** " followed by a space to format the output correctly.

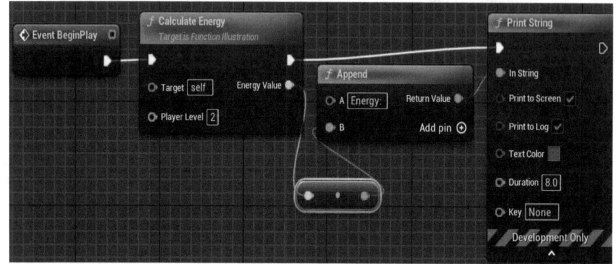

12) Compile the **Blueprint** to apply all changes. Save the Blueprint to retain the modifications made. Drag and drop the **FunctionIllustration** Blueprint into the Level Editor.

13) Play the level to see the calculated **Energy Value** displayed on the screen.

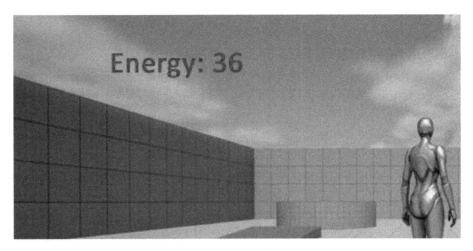

CHOOSING BETWEEN FUNCTIONS, MACROS AND EVENTS

Selecting between functions, macros, and events can be confusing since they share some similarities. The table and description below provide a comparison to help you decide which one best suits your needs:

Functions	Macros	Events	Availability
Yes	Yes	Yes	Input parameters
Yes	Yes	No	Output parameter
Yes	No	Yes	Callable by another Blueprint
No	Yes	No	Multiple execution paths (input/output)
No	No	Yes	Timeline nodes
No	Yes	Yes	Latent actions (for instance, delay)

- ✓ **Macros**: Use when you need a sequence of actions to be reused multiple times within the same Blueprint, providing a straightforward way to manage repetitive tasks.
- ✓ **Functions**: Opt for functions when you require a reusable calculation or action that can be called from any Blueprint, promoting code modularity and reusability across different parts of your project.
- ✓ **Events**: Employ events for triggering specific responses to game events within a single Blueprint, ensuring that actions are executed in response to predefined conditions or player interactions.

CHAPTER TWO
UNDERSTANDING OBJECT-ORIENTED PROGRAMMING

Let's dig into some fundamental concepts of Object-Oriented Programming (OOP), which are essential for understanding Blueprints Visual Scripting.

CLASSES

A class serves as a blueprint for creating objects in OOP. It offers initial values for state (**variables or attributes**) and specifies behaviors (**functions or events**) that objects of that class can exhibit. For example, consider a "**person**" class where attributes like name and height are defined, along with actions such as moving and eating. Using this **class**, we can construct multiple objects, each representing a distinct person with unique values for their attributes.

Each time you create a Blueprint in Unreal Engine, you are essentially creating a new class that can generate objects within the game's levels. A "**Blueprint Class**" option is displayed when you are creating a new Blueprint.

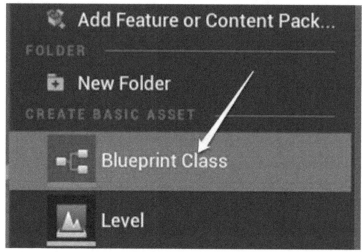

Encapsulation is another crucial concept in OOP. It enables you to hide the intricacy of a class when it is viewed from another class's point of view. Variables and functions within a Blueprint class can be marked as private, restricting access and modification solely to the Blueprint Class where they are created. Conversely, public variables and functions are accessible to other Blueprint Classes.

INSTANCES

An **instance** refers to an object created from a class. When you drag a **Blueprint Class** from the **Content Browser** and place it into the **Level**, you're generating a new instance of that Blueprint Class. All instances are constructed with the default values defined within the Blueprint Class for their variables. However, variables marked as **Instance Editable** can have their values customized individually for each instance within the Level, without impacting the values of other instances.

For instance, consider a scenario where a Blueprint is designed to represent a character type in a game. If four instances of this Blueprint Class are added to the Level, each instance can have unique settings adjusted independently, as illustrated in the screenshot shown below:

INHERITANCE

Inheritance allows classes to inherit variables and functions from other classes in an object-oriented program (OOP). When creating a Blueprint in Unreal Engine, the first step is selecting its parent class. Each Blueprint Class can have only one parent class, known as the **superclass**, but it can serve as the parent to multiple child classes known as subclasses.

For instance, if we're designing Blueprints for different types of weapons in a game, we can create a base Blueprint Class called **Ammunition**. This **Ammunition** class contains attributes and methods common to all ammunitions. Subsequently, individual ammunition Blueprints can be created with Ammunition as their parent class. The hierarchy among these classes is visually represented as shown in this diagram.

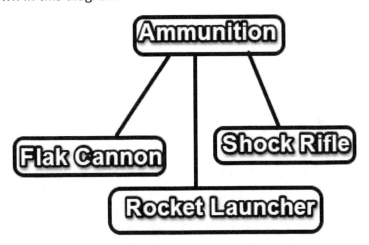

One of the key benefits of inheritance is the ability to override functions defined in the parent class within its subclasses. For instance, if there's a Fire function in the Ammunition class, subclasses like **Rocket Launcher** and **Shock Rifle** can override this function to implement specific behaviors—such as firing an energy beam or launching rockets—unique to each ammunition type. During runtime, if there is a reference to the missile class and call the Fire function, the instance class will be recognized to run its version of the **Fire** function.

Moreover, inheritance helps define the class type hierarchy. An instance of Shock Rifle, for instance, is considered both a Shock Rifle and an Ammunition. This hierarchical relationship allows functions designed to accept inputs of the **Ammunition** class to also handle inputs of any of its subclasses.

These fundamental OOP concepts are crucial for comprehending the Unreal Engine Gameplay Framework. In game development using Unreal Engine, essential classes form part of the Gameplay Framework, with **Actor** being the primary class that encapsulates various functionalities essential for game entities.

HANDLING ACTORS

The Actor class encompasses all the necessary functionality for an object to exist within a Level. Hence, it serves as the superclass for all objects that can be placed or spawned in a Level. Essentially, any object capable of being situated or generated in a Level inherits from the Actor class or its subclasses. This makes the **Actor** class pivotal for the majority of Blueprints that developers create, as they often derive directly from Actor or its descendant classes.

REFERENCING ACTORS

In Unreal Engine, when dealing with objects or Actors, we utilize a specific type of variable known as an object reference. Unlike primitive types such as integers, floats, and Booleans, which store basic values, object references enable communication between different objects in Blueprints. The details of this inter-object communication will be explored in depth in later chapters.

Let's walk through a practical example to illustrate how to create variables in a Blueprint that reference other objects or Actors:

1) From the start screen or go to **File > New Project**, create a new project built on the **First Person** template in Unreal Engine using the starter content.
2) Open the **Content Browser** by clicking on the **Content Drawer** button. Click the "**Add**" button and select **"Blueprint Class"**.
3) Select the **"Actor"** as the parent class for the Blueprint, then name the Blueprint **"BP_Rocket"** and double-click it to open the Blueprint Editor.

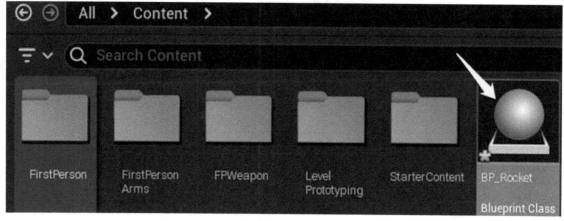

4) Within the **Blueprint** Editor, go to the **Components** panel and click the "**Add**" button. Choose the "**Static Mesh**" Component. Go to the **Details** panel for this component, and select "**Shape_Cylinder**" as the Static Mesh.

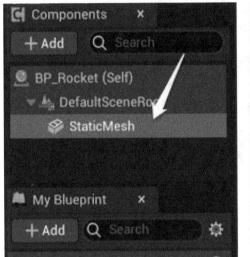 

5) Create a new variable named "**BP_Fire**" within the **My Blueprint** panel. Go to the **Details** panel for this variable, and click the drop-down menu next to the "**Variable Type**" parameter. Under the "**Object Types**" group, you'll find a list of classes available in Unreal Engine. Search for "**fire**", locate "**Blueprint Effect Fire**" and Choose "**Object Reference**" to set the variable type.

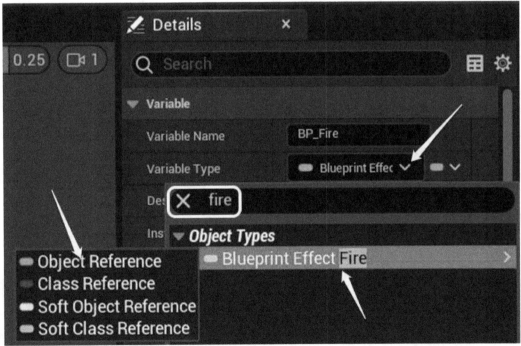

6) By default, the **Object Reference** variable's value is set to **None** (or **null**), indicating it doesn't reference any instances yet. To allow this variable to be set in the Level Editor, check the "**Instance Editable**" feature for the variable.

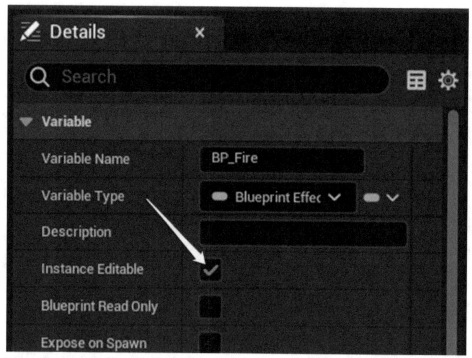

7) Drag the "**BP_Fire**" variable from the **My Blueprint** panel and drop it into the **Event Graph**. Select "**Get BP_Fire**" to create a node. From the blue pin of the "**BP_Fire**" node, drag it onto the graph to open the **Context Menu**. Search for the "**Set Hi**" keyword and select the "**Set Hidden in Game (P_Fire).**"

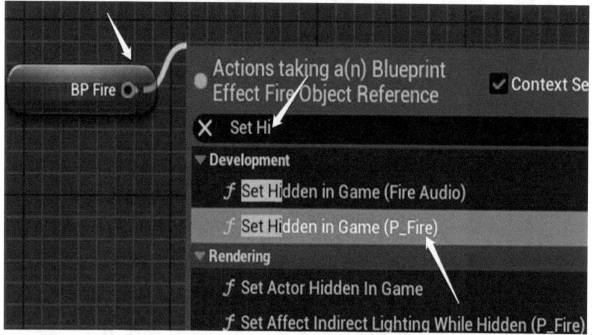

8) Right-click the **Event Graph** within the Blueprint Editor to add an "**Event Hit**" node. Connect the output of the **Event Hit** node to the "**Set Hidden in Game (P_Fire)**" node. Ensure the "**New Hidden**" parameter is unchecked. These actions configure the Blueprint so that when an instance of the **BP_Rocket** Blueprint is hit, it will unhide the particle system component of the instance referenced by **BP_Fire**.

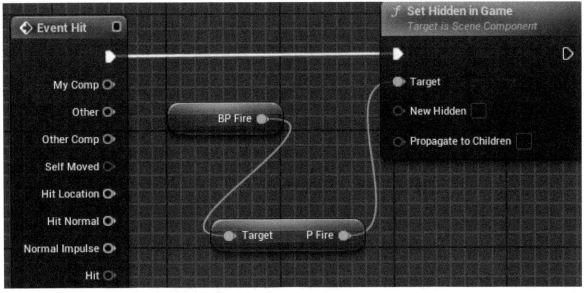

9) **Compile** the Blueprint to **save** your changes. Return to the **Level** Editor, from the **Content Browser**, drag and drop the **BP_Rocket** Blueprint into the Level.

10) Within the **Content Browser**, go to the "**Content > StarterContent > Blueprints**" folder. Drag the **Blueprint_Effect_Fire** and drop it at the top of the **BP_Rocket** Blueprint that you previously added to the Level.

11) Go to the **Details** panel of the **Blueprint_Effect_Fire** instance within the **Level**, and locate the "**P_Fire**" component. Search for the "**hidden**" keyword in the **Details** panel and mark the "**Hidden in Game**" feature.

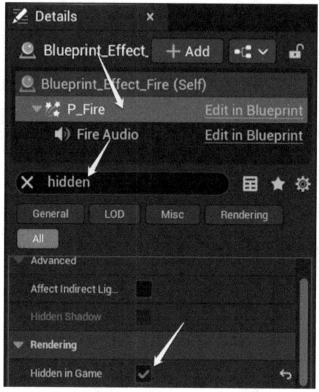

12) Go to the **Details** panel of the **BP_Rocket** instance, and click the drop-down menu of the **BP_Fire** variable. This menu lists the **Actors** in the **Level** that are instances of **Blueprint_Effect_Fire**. Choose the instance of **Blueprint_Effect_Fire** that was dropped on top of the **BP_Rocket** to allocate its instance to the **BP_Fire** variable.

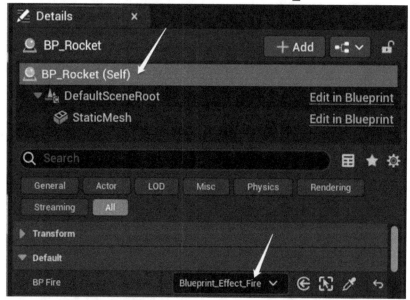

13) Click the "**Play**" button in the Level Editor to examine the Level. Position yourself in front of the BP_Barrel instance placed in the Level. The Blueprint_Effect_Fire instance remains hidden. Use the left mouse button to shoot the **BP_Barrel** instance. After hitting the **BP_Barrel** instance, the Blueprint_Effect_Fire instance will appear, demonstrating the successful interaction between the two Blueprints.

SPAWNING AND DESTROYING ACTORS

Let's explore the process of spawning and destroying Actors in Unreal Engine. Add this function to the **Event Graph** by using practical steps and examples:

1) Right-click on the **Event Graph** panel to access the **Context** Menu. Type "**spawn Ac**" in the search box to filter the results and select "**Spawn Actor from Class**" from the list of functions.

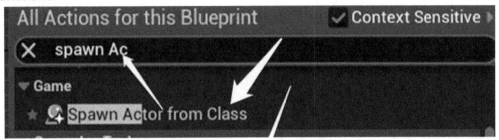

This function accepts two main input parameters: the **class of the Actor** to be spawned and the **Transformation** that defines its initial location, rotation, and scale. Additionally, the **Collision Handling Override** parameter specifies how collisions are managed during creation. A reference to the new instance is accessible in the Return Value output parameter and can be stored in a variable.

To remove an **Actor** instance from the Level, utilize the "**DestroyActor**" function. The Target input parameter specifies which instance should be removed.

The screenshot below displays a scenario using the "**Spawn Actor from Class**" and "**DestroyActor**" functions. Note that the **Is Valid** use in this diagram is found in **Utilities** > **Time Management** on the **Context** menu.

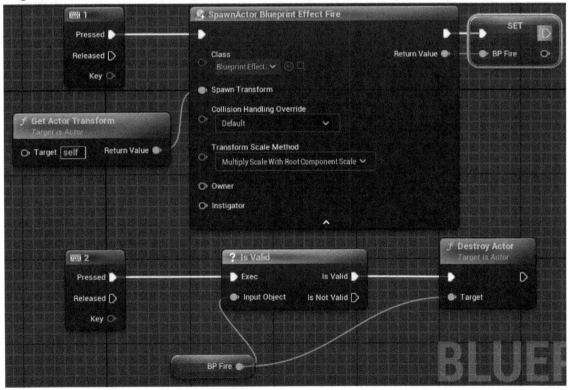

43

To set up an input event that triggers the creation of a fire effect:

✓ Right-click on the **Event Graph** and search for "**1**" in the search box. This locates the "**1**" key Input Event under **Input** > **Keyboard Events**.

✓ Pressing the "**1**" key on the keyboard will create an instance of **Blueprint Effect Fire** by using the Transformation of the Blueprint instance that includes this script. For instance, if this script is part of the **ThirdPersonCharacter Blueprint** found in **Content** > **ThirdPerson** > **Blueprints**, pressing "**1**" during gameplay will create a fire effect at the character's current position.

✓ The instance of the newly created **Blueprint Effect Fire** is stored in the **BPFire** variable. If you haven't yet got this variable, you can easily promote the return value of the **SpawnActor** function to a variable. This automatically assigns it the correct variable type. To do this, drag from the **Return Value** pin and drop it onto the **Event Graph** to access the **Context Menu**. Then, choose "**Promote to variable**" from the **Context** Menu.

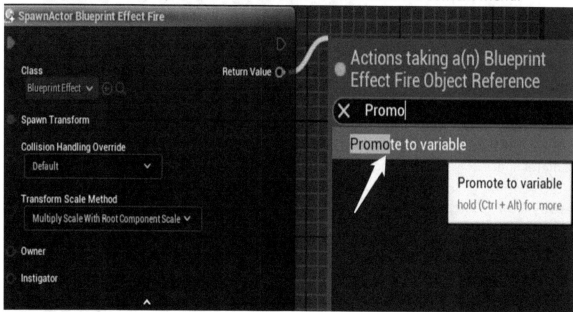

✓ Pressing the "**2**" key triggers a check using the "**Is Valid**" Macro to verify whether the **BPFire** variable references a valid instance. This check ensures that functions are not called with a null reference, preventing potential errors. If **BPFire** holds a value of None, it indicates that no valid instance exists. If BPFire is valid, it proceeds to call the DestroyActor function. This function takes **BPFire** as the Target input parameter, leading to the destruction of the previously created **Blueprint Effect Fire** instance.

✓ Note that pressing the "**2**" key deletes only the most recently created **Blueprint Effect Fire** instance. If multiple fire instances were created before deletion, the others will remain in the Level. This happens because each time a new Blueprint Effect Fire instance is created, BPFire is overridden.

EXPLORING THE CONSTRUCTION SCRIPT

In the Blueprint Editor, one of the essential panels is the Construction Script. This script is automatically executed by all Actor Blueprints under specific circumstances; when the Blueprint is initially added to the Level, when its properties are modified within the Level Editor, or when an instance of this Blueprint is spawned during gameplay.

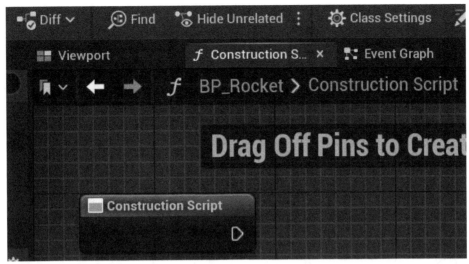

The **Construction Script** plays a vital role in enabling dynamic configuration of Blueprints within the Level Editor. It empowers Level Designers to adjust and customize various features of Blueprint instances directly within the editor environment.

For example, let's create a Blueprint that includes an **Instance Editable Static Mesh** component, that will us to select a different Static Mesh for each instance of this Blueprint placed in the Level:

1) Start by creating a new project or using an existing one that includes starter content.
2) Open the **Content Browser** and click the "**Add**" button. Select "**Blueprint Class**" from the options and select "Actor" as the parent class for this Blueprint.
3) Title the Blueprint as **"BP_Construction"** and double-click it to open the Blueprint Editor.
4) Within the Blueprint Editor, go to the **Components** panel and click the "**Add**" button. Select the "**Static Mesh"** Component Rename this component to "**StaticMeshCom**" for clarity in Blueprint Organization.

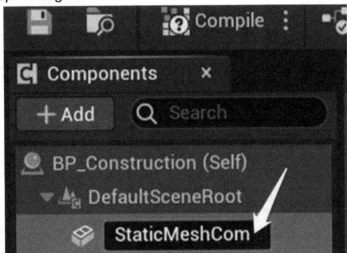

5) Go to the "**My Blueprint**" panel and create a new variable titled **S_Mesh**. To define its type, click on the **Variable Type** drop-down menu and search for "**Static Mesh**". Mouse over the **Static Mesh** and Select "**Object Reference**" from the submenu. Make sure to "**tick**" the "**Instance Editable**" feature for this variable, as illustrated in the screenshot below:

45

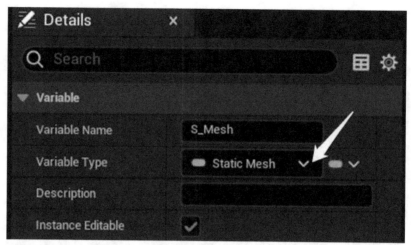

Hint: An **Object Reference** variable can also be termed as an instance created during runtime.

6) Click on the **Compile** button located on the toolbar. Next, we will specify an initial Static Mesh for the **S_Mesh** variable at the lower area of the **Details** panel. Click on the drop-down menu of the **Default value** feature, and select the "**SM_TableRound**" Static Mesh.

7) Go to the **Construction Script** panel. Drag the "**StaticMeshCom**" component from the **Components** panel and drop it into the **Construction Script** graph to create a node.

8) Click the blue pin of the "**StaticMeshCom**" node, then drag it to the graph to open the **Context Menu**. Search for "**set sta**" and select the **Set Static Mesh** function from the options provided, as shown below:

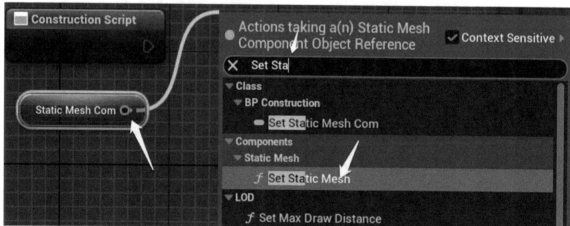

9) Drag the "**S_Mesh**" variable from the **My Blueprint** panel and drop it into the **Construction Script** graph. Select "**Get S_Mesh**" from the displayed menu. Connect the pin of the "**S_Mesh**" node to the "**New Mesh**" pin of the "**Set Static Mesh**" function. The **Construction Script** should now resemble the following screenshot. Once the

Construction Script executes the "**Set Static Mesh**" function, it retrieves the Static Mesh specified in the **S_Mesh** variable and assigns it to the "**StaticMeshCom**" component.

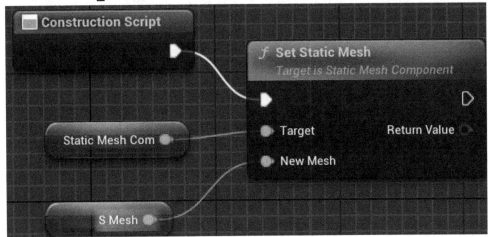

10) After compiling the Blueprint, switch to the **Level** Editor. Drag the **BPConstruction** Blueprint from the **Content Browser** and drop it to the **Level** to create an instance. Repeat this step to create another instance of **BPConstruction**. Select one of these instances in the **Level**, and go to the **Details** panel of the Level Editor. Confirm that the **S_Mesh** variable is visible and editable as displayed in the screenshot below.

11) Click on the drop-down menu of the **S_Mesh** variable and select a different Static Mesh, like **SM_Couch**. Immediately, the Construction Script will execute, updating the selected instance's Static Mesh. The diagram below displays two instances of the **BPConstruction** class: the left instance retains the default Static Mesh, while the right instance has been modified to use **SM_Couch**.

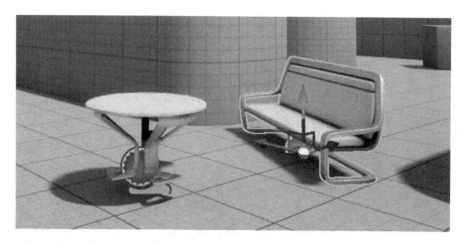

EXAMINING THE OTHER GAMEPLAY FRAMEWORK CLASSES

When creating a new Blueprint, one of the initial steps involves selecting a parent class that serves as a foundational template. The diagram below displays the panel for selecting this parent class. The classes shown on the buttons are called **Common Classes**, which are integral parts of the Gameplay Framework. To choose a different class as the parent, expand the "**All Classes**" category and search for your preferred class.

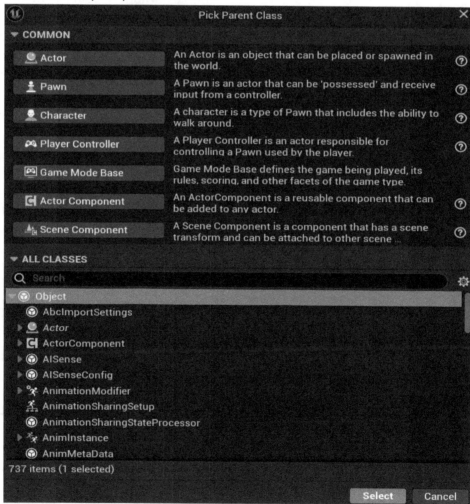

The hierarchy of **Common Classes** in Unreal Engine is shown in the screenshot below. In this hierarchy, classes inherit attributes and functionalities from their parent classes named **Object** in this case. For instance, based on object-oriented programming principles, an instance of the Character class inherits characteristics from the **Character**, **Pawn**, and **Actor** classes.

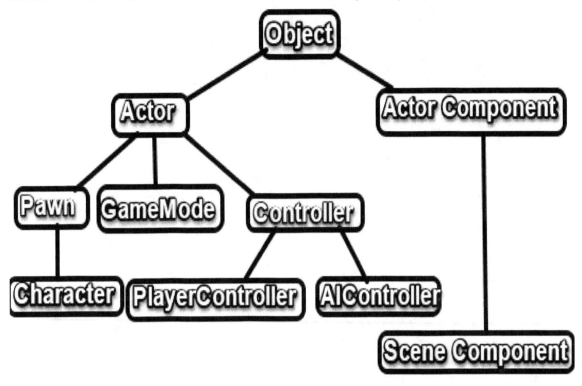

Examining this hierarchy reveals that classes like Actor Component and Scene Component are not Actors themselves. Instead, they are used to create Components that can be added to Actors. Examples of such Component include **Static Mesh** and **Rotating Movement** Components, as demonstrated in previous examples

Let's delve deeper into some of these Common Classes to understand their roles and functionalities within the Unreal Engine Gameplay Framework.

PAWN

In Unreal Engine, the Pawn class is a direct descendant of the Actor. Pawns are specialized Actors that can be controlled by a game's Controller, which can represent either a player or an artificial intelligence (**AI**). Practically, an instance of the Pawn class serves as the physical embodiment or body of a game character within the Level. Meanwhile, the Controller instance that possesses it acts as the cognitive force, enabling the character to navigate the Level and execute various actions.

   ✓ Create a Blueprint built on the **Pawn** class, go to the **Blueprint** Editor, and select the **Class Default**. This populates the **Details** panel with parameters inherited from the **Pawn** class as displayed below.

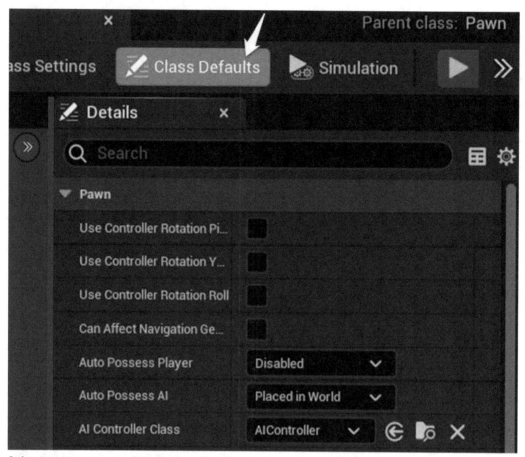

Some of the parameters indicate that the **Pawn** class can utilize values from the **Controller** class that possesses it. Other parameters define how the **Pawn** class interacts with and is controlled by the **Controller** instance.

The Pawn class has two primary child classes: **Character** and **Wheeled Vehicle**.

CHARACTER

The **Character** class extends from the **Pawn** class, allowing instances of **Character** to be controlled by instances of the **Controller** class. This class is designed to symbolize characters capable of performing dynamic movements such as **walking**, jumping, running, swimming, and flying within a game.

A Blueprint based on the Character class inherits several character-specific Components essential for gameplay as listed here:

- ✓ **CapsuleComponent**: This Component is used for collision detection and interaction with the environment.
- ✓ **ArrowComponent**: It specifies the current orientation or direction of the character within the game world.
- ✓ **Mesh**: A Skeletal Mesh Component visually representing the character. The animation of this Mesh is governed by an animation Blueprint.
- ✓ **CharacterMovement**: This Component facilitates various forms of character locomotion, including walking, running, jumping, swimming, and flying.

These components are illustrated in the diagram below:

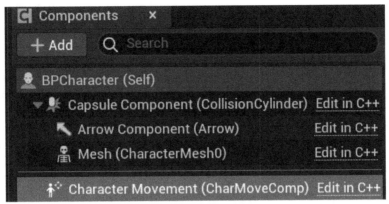

The CharacterMovement Component is important as it manages character movement, replication, and prediction in multiplayer games. It covers a wide range of parameters that define and control the character's diverse movement capabilities across different gameplay scenarios.

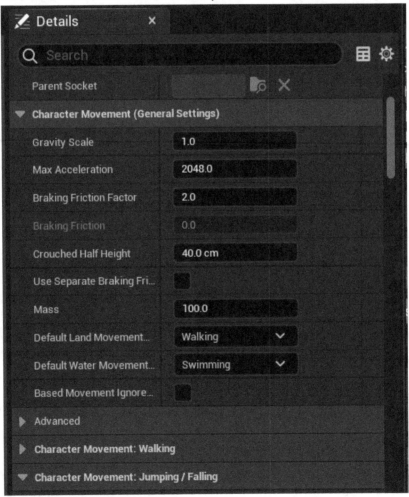

PLAYER CONTROLLER

Within the **Controller** hierarchy in Unreal Engine, the **PlayerController** class and **AIController** class are key subclasses. Human players utilize instances of the **PlayerController** class, whereas **AI-controlled** characters rely on instances of the **AIController** class to handle the **Pawn**.

Instances of both the **Pawn** and **Character** classes can respond to input events only when they are possessed by an instance of **PlayerController**. These input events can be placed either in the **Event Graph** of the **PlayerController** itself or directly within the **Pawn**. Placing input events in the **PlayerController** offers the advantage of decoupling them from the specific Pawn instance, simplifying the process of switching between different **Pawn** classes controlled by the same **PlayerController**. It's essential to maintain consistency in this approach throughout your project for clarity and manageability.

The screenshot below illustrates how to change the **Pawn** possessed by a **PlayerController** during gameplay and demonstrates the use of the **Possess** function. In this scenario, two characters exist in the **Level**, each controllable by the player through pressing the **1** or **2** keys. Commands from the **PlayerController** are directed exclusively to the **Character** instance currently being possessed:

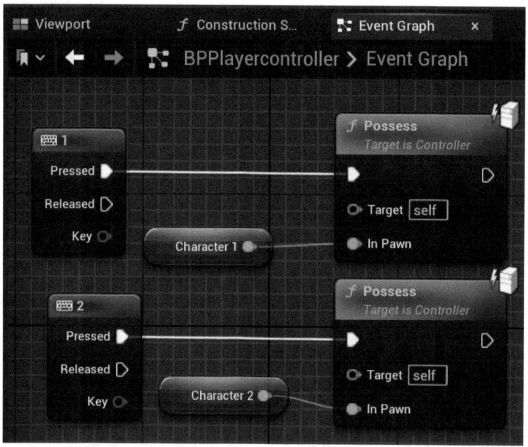

GAME MODE BASE

Game Mode Base serves as the foundational class for defining specific game rules within Unreal Engine. A Game Mode class not only outlines the gameplay rules but also dictates the default classes utilized for creating **PlayerControllers**, **Pawns**, **HUD**, **GameStateBase**, and other essential components of the game architecture.

To customize these default classes within a Game Mode, access the **Class Defaults** section by clicking on the **Class Defaults** button in the **Details** panel of the **Game Mode** class:

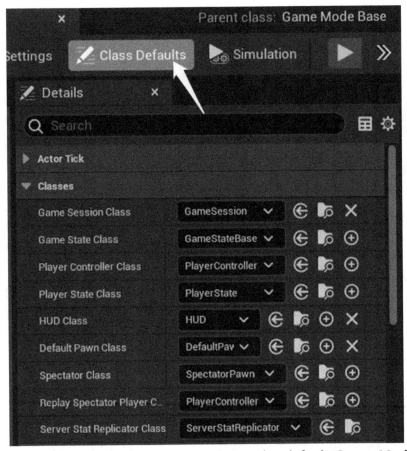

In the Unreal Engine **Level** Editor, you can designate the default **Game Mode** class for your project by:

- ✓ Going to **Edit > Project Settings.**
- ✓ Select **Maps & Modes** under the **Project** category.
- ✓ Select **Game Mode** from the **Default GameMode** dropdown menu.

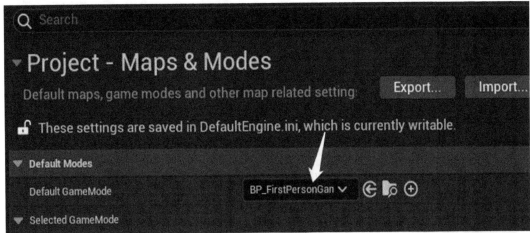

Additionally, each individual **Level** can override the **Default Game Mode** specified for the entire project. To set the **Game Mode** for a specific Level, click the **Settings** button at the top right in the **Level** Editor and select **World Settings**. Within the **GameMode Override** property dropdown, select the **Game Mode** for that Level as shown below.

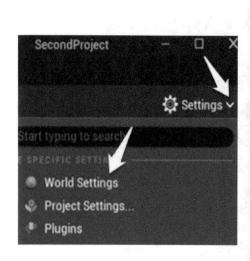

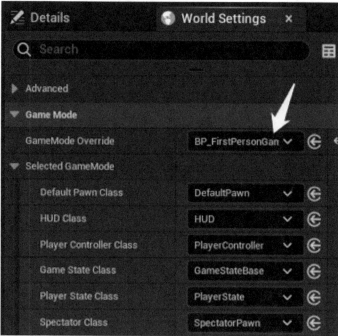

GAME INSTANCE

Understanding the Game Instance class is crucial though it is not categorized under Common Classes. An instance of the Game Instance class persists throughout the game, from its initialization at the start until the game is closed. Unlike Actors and other objects in a Level that are recreated each time the Level is loaded, the Game Instance retains its data across Level transitions.

The Game Instance class is particularly useful for preserving variable values that need to persist between different Levels. This makes it an ideal choice for storing game state information or other persistent data that needs to be accessed globally throughout the game.

To designate the **Game Instance** class for use in your game, adjust the project settings in the **Edit > Project Settings > Maps & Modes** within the Level Editor.

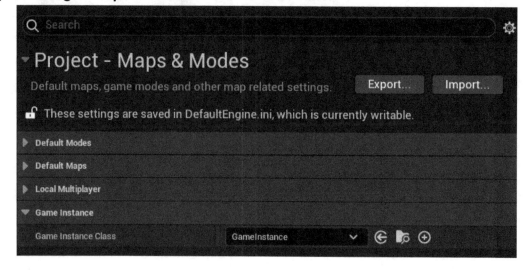

CHAPTER THREE
EXPLORING DIRECT BLUEPRINT COMMUNICATION

Direct Blueprint Communication simplifies communication between different Blueprints or Actors by utilizing object reference variables. These variables store references to other Blueprints or Actors, allowing us to trigger actions on them directly.

For instance, let's consider a practical example with a Blueprint named **BP_LightSwitch**. Within **BP_LightSwitch**, there's an object reference variable designed to hold a reference to a **Point Light** placed somewhere in the Level. When a player overlays with **BP_LightSwitch** in the game world, it switches the visibility of the referenced Point Light.

To create such a Blueprint, follow these step-by-step instructions:

1) Go to **File** > **New Project** and create a new project that includes **Starter Content** using default options as explained in Chapter One.
2) click the **Content Drawer** button to summon the **Content Browser**. Click the **Add** button and choose **Blueprint Class**.
3) Choose **Actor** as the parent class in the subsequent window. Title your Blueprint as **BLP_LightSwitch** and double-click on it to open the **Blueprint** Editor.
4) Go to the **Components** panel and click the **Add** button. Select the **Static Mesh** Component. In the **Details** panel, select the **SM_CornerFrame** Static Mesh for a simple visual representation of the light switch. Adjust the **Collision Presets** to **OverlapAllDynamic** to ensure that the Static Mesh doesn't obstruct the player's movement.

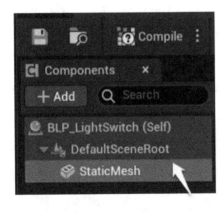

5) Go to the **My Blueprint** panel, and add a new variable titled **Light**.
6) In the **Details** panel, locate the **Variable Type** drop-down menu and search for "**Point Light**". Mouse over the "**Point Light**" to reveal a submenu, then select "**Object Reference**". Ensure the **Instance Editable** feature is checked.

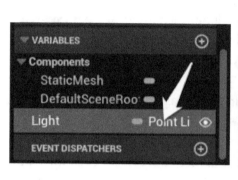
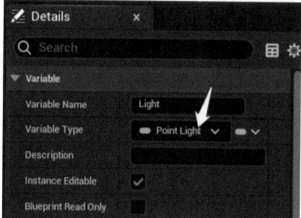

7) Drag the **Light** variable from the **My Blueprint** panel and drop it into the **Event Graph.**
8) Select the "**Get Light**" option to create a node. Drag from the blue pin of the **Light** node onto the graph to open the **Fly-out** menu. Make sure "**Context Sensitive**" is enabled to display **Actions** for a **Point Light** object reference.
9) Search for "**togg**" and choose the function named "**Toggle Visibility (PointLightComponent)**".

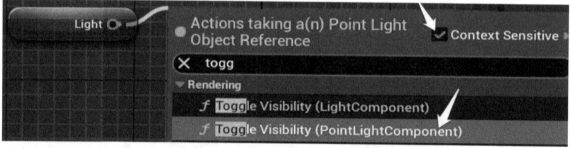

10) Right-click on the **Event Graph** to add an "**Event ActorBeginOverlap**" node. Drag from the blue pin of the **Light** node onto the graph to open the **Fly-out** menu. Add the "**Is Valid**" macro (indicated by a white question mark), which is used to check if the Light variable is referencing an instance. Connect these **nodes** as illustrated below. Remember to **Compile** this Blueprint.

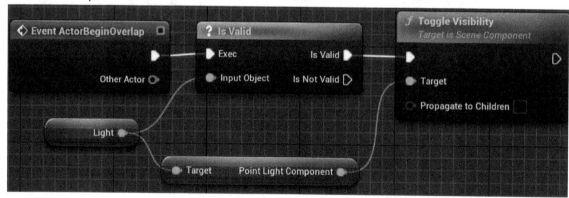

56

Note: Always use the "**Is Valid**" macro before executing a function with an object reference variable. This ensures the variable is valid before performing operations with it. Failing to do so can lead to runtime errors if the variable is invalid for any reason.

11) Go to the **Level** Editor, and click the **Create** button on the toolbar. Mouse over "**Lights**" to reveal a submenu and drag the "**Point Light**" option to a location in the Level to create an instance.

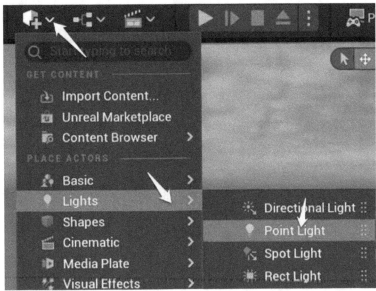

12) Go to the **Details** panel, click on the name of the **Point Light** instance, and rename it to "**Lamp**". Set the **Mobility** feature to "**Movable**" so that you can adjust the light properties during runtime.

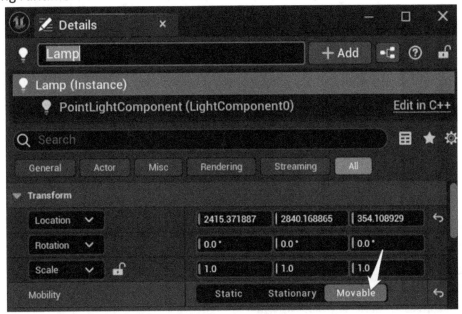

13) Drag the **BLP_LightSwitch** Blueprint class in the **Content Browser** and place it in the **Level** beside the **Point Light** instance you added earlier. The screenshot below displays the **Details** panel of **BLP_LightSwitch**. The "**Light**" variable is visible in the **Details** panel because we enabled the **Instance Editable** feature. Click on the drop-down menu of the

"**Light**" variable to view all **Point Light** instances currently in the Level, and choose the one we renamed to "**Lamp**" in the previous step. This setup establishes Direct Blueprint Communication. **BLP_LightSwitch** now has an object reference to another Actor/Blueprint and can call its actions.

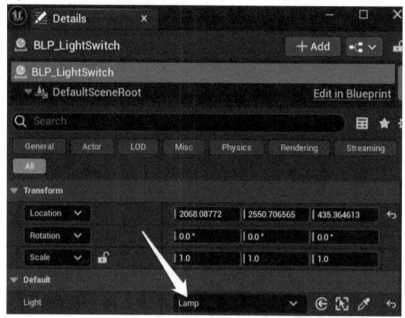

14) Click the **Play** button to observe the **BP_LightSwitch** Blueprint in action. Each time your **character** intersects with the **BP_LightSwitch** instance, it toggles the visibility of the chosen Point Light. The screenshot below displays an instance of the **Third Person** template: the **Point Light** variable is positioned on the wall, while the **BP_LightSwitch** Blueprint is situated on the floor.

In this section, we've explored creating a variable that points to an instance of another Blueprint. However, there are scenarios where we need to access features specific to the subclass of the referenced instance. To achieve this, we will use Cast.

USING CASTING

Casting in Blueprints involves using a node called "**Cast To**" to attempt converting reference variable types to new indicated types. To grasp casting, it's essential to recall the concept of inheritance between classes, which we discussed in Chapter 2, **Actors** and the **Gameplay Framework.**

Consider the Blueprint named **BPGameMode_WithScore** shown in the screenshot below. This Blueprint inherits from **Game Mode Base**, which is its parent class. According to inheritance principles, a variable of type **Game Mode Base** can reference an instance of **BPGameMode_WithScore.** However, such a variable cannot access variables and functions specific to a subclass like those defined **BPGameMode_WithScore** because a Game Mode Base reference is limited to the variables and functions defined in the **Game Mode Base** class.

To access the variables and functions unique to **BPGameMode_WithScore** from a **Game Mode Base** object reference, you can use the "**Cast To BPGameMode_WithScore**" function. This function attempts to cast the reference: if the instance is of **BPGameMode_WithScore** type, the casting operation succeeds. It returns a **BPGameMode_WithScore** object reference that allows us to utilize the **variables** and **functions** defined within **BPGameMode_WithScore.**

Another practical use of the Cast To node is to safely verify whether an object reference matches a desired type. This step-by-step example demonstrates both scenarios:

1) Use an existing project built on the **Third Person** template that includes **starter content**, or create a new project if necessary.
2) Go to the **Content Browser** and click the **Add** button, then select **Blueprint Class** from the fly-out menu.
3) Choose **Game Mode Base** as the **parent** class on the following screen.
4) Title the Blueprint as **BPGameMode_WithScore** and double-click it to open the Blueprint Editor.
5) Go to the "**My Blueprint**" panel of **BPGameMode_WithScore**, and create a **variable** titled **GameScore** of type **integer**. Also, create a function titled **AddGameScore.**

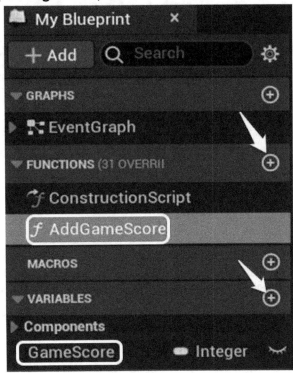

6) Go to the **Details** panel of the **AddGameScore** function, and include an **Input Parameter** named **Score** of Integer variable type. This function is designed to increase the **GameScore** variable by adding points effectively.

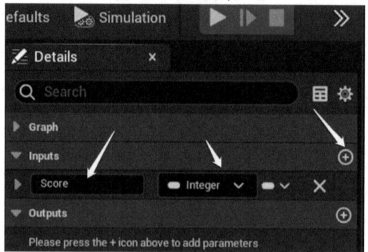

7) Within the function graph, include the **Actions** illustrated in the screenshot below. To add **GET** and **SET** nodes for the **GameScore** variable, simply drag the variable into the graph and select either **GET** or **SET**. The **Print String** function is utilized to display the current value of the **GameScore** variable on the screen.

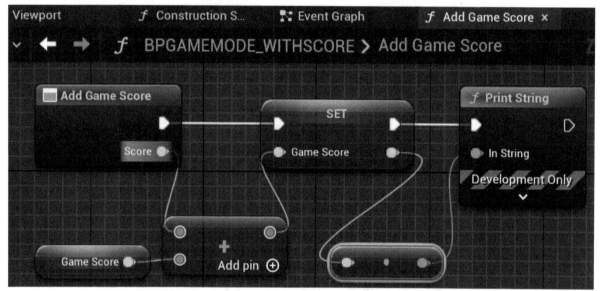

Note: The node positioned between **SET** and **Print String** acts as a converter. It's automatically created when connecting the **SET** output parameter to the **In String** input parameter of Print String. This conversion is necessary because the parameters have different types.

8) After completing the graph, compile and save the **BPGameMode_WithScore** Blueprint. Next, we will configure the **Level** to utilize **BPGameMode_WithScore** as its Game Mode.

9) Go to the **Level** Editor, click the **Settings** button located on the top right side of the Editor, and select **World Settings**.

10) Within **World Settings**, go to the **GameMode Override** feature. Click the **drop-down menu** and select **BPGameMode_WithScore**, as shown below.

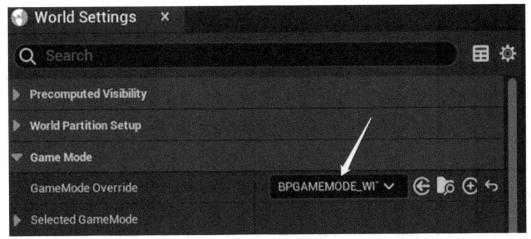

11) Continue by creating a new Blueprint with **Actor** selected as the parent class. Title this Blueprint **BP_Collectable** and open it in the Blueprint Editor.

12) Click the **Add** button within the **Components** panel. Select the **Static Mesh** Component. Configure the **Details** panel by choosing **SM_Statue** as the Static Mesh and selecting **M_Metal_Gold** in the **Materials** section. Also, adjust the **Collision Presets to OverlapAllDynamic**.

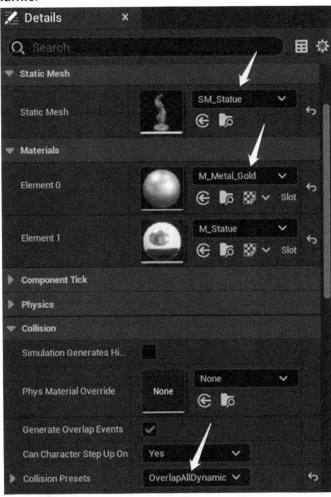

13) Right-click on the **Event Graph** and select **Event ActorBeginOverlap**. "**Other Actor**" refers to the instance that overlays with the **BP_Collectable** Blueprint. Drag from the blue pin of **Other Actor** onto the graph to open the Fly-out menu.

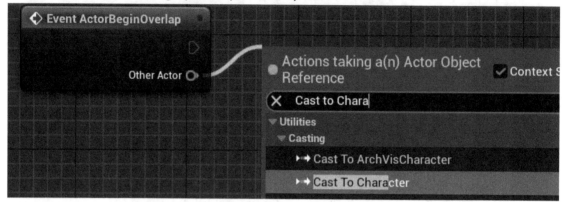

14) Select the **Cast To Character** action from the menu. **The Character** represents the player in the **Third Person** template. This Cast To action verifies whether the instance referenced by the Other Actor is indeed the player.

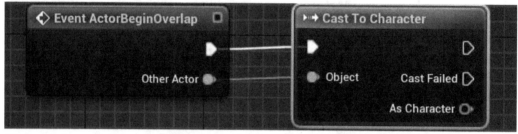

15) Right-click on the **Event Graph** to add the **Get Game Mode** function. Drag from the blue pin of **Return Value** onto the graph to open the **Fly-out** menu. Select the **Cast To BPGameMode_WithScore** action.
16) Drag from the blue pin of **As BP Game Mode With Score**, drop it onto the graph, and select the **Add Game Score** action from the **Fly-out Menu**. Set the **Score** input parameters to 50.
17) Right-click on the **Event Graph** to add the DestroyActor function. Join the white pins of the nodes. The **Event ActorBeginOverlap's** content is illustrated below.

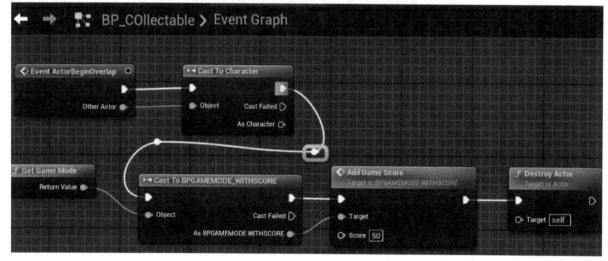

Note: The **Get Game Mode** function yields a reference to the Game Mode used by the current level. But the type of the return value is Game Mode Base. By using a variable of this kind, we were not able to access the **Add Game Score** function, thus, it's essential to use **Cast To BPGameMode_WithScore**.

18) Compile BP-Collectable after making changes. Place some instances of BP_Collectable and drop it in the Level. Click on the **Play** button to examine the Level. Collect the statues with your character to update the score displayed on the screen.

Note: Reroute nodes (white connection pins that show in the earlier screenshot) help organize the Blueprint and streamline connections. You can double-click the connection line to add reroute node

This example illustrates typical uses of the Cast To node in Unreal Engine. it helps to check whether an instance is of a particular type. It also helps to gain access to functions and variables of a subclass. Since you have learned how to use Cast To, it is time to master how to add references and events of Actors in the Level Blueprint.

LEVEL BLUEPRINT COMMUNICATION

Unreal Engine features a specialized Blueprint known as the **Level Blueprint**. Each game level includes a default Level Blueprint, which helps create Events and actions specific to that particular level. To open the **Level Blueprint,** click on the **Blueprints** button in the toolbar of the **Level** Editor and select the **Open Level Blueprint** option.

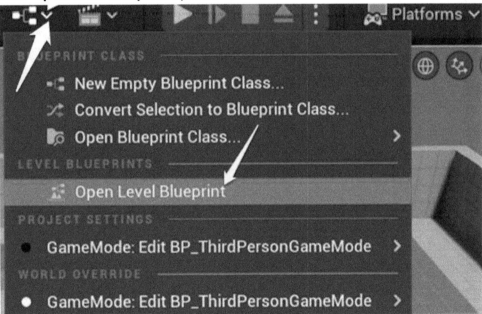

Within the **Level** Blueprint, it's straightforward to establish references to **Actors** that are present within the level itself. To illustrate this capability, let's walk through an example where we add a **Trigger Box** to the Level. When an Actor intersects this trigger, it will activate the **Blueprint_Effect_Sparks**, creating a sparking effect:

1) Use an existing project based on the Third Person template with starter content or create a new project.

2) Within the **Level** Editor, go to the **Create** button on the toolbar. Under the **Basic** category, you'll find a **Trigger Box,** as illustrated in the screenshot below. Drag the **Trigger Box** from the panel and place it within the Level.

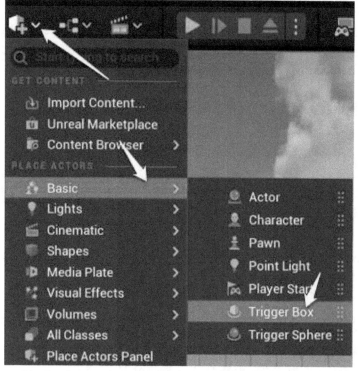 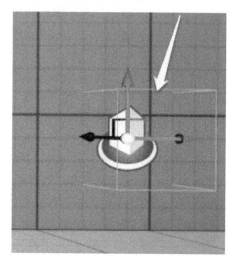

3) Resize and position the **Trigger Box** in a location within the **Level** that the player must pass through. The diagram below shows an instance of this. The **Trigger Box** should be hidden during gameplay.

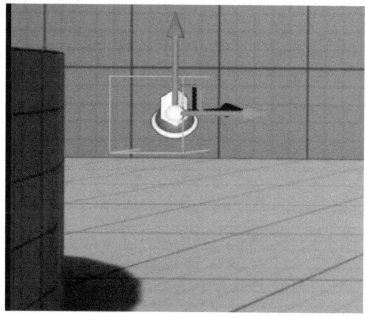

4) Ensure the **Trigger Box** is selected, then access the **Level Blueprint** by clicking on the Blueprints button in the toolbar of the **Level Editor** and selecting **Open Level Blueprint**.

5) Right-click on the **Event Graph** to add the Event labeled **"Add On Actor Begin Overlap"** from the **Add Event for Trigger Box** group.

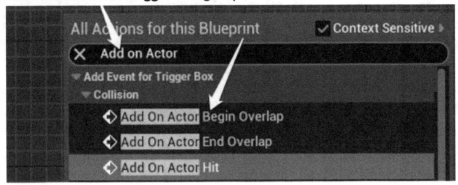

6) Move back to the **Level** Editor. Go to **Content > StarterContent > Blueprints** in the **Content Browser**. Open **Blueprint_Effect_Sparks.**

7) Go to the **Components** tab of **Blueprint_Effect_Sparks**, and select the **Sparks** Component. Go to the **Details** tab, locate the "**auto-activate**" feature, and uncheck it. This step ensures that the Sparks component starts inactive to allow activation during runtime.

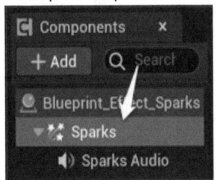 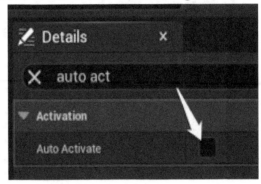

8) Back in the **Level** Editor, drag and drop **Blueprint_Effect_Sparks** from the **Content Browser** into the **Level** beside the **Box Trigger** to create an instance.

9) Ensure **Blueprint_Effect_Sparks** is selected and open the **Level Blueprint**. Right-click the **Event Graph** and choose "**Create a Reference to Blueprint_Effects_Sparks**".

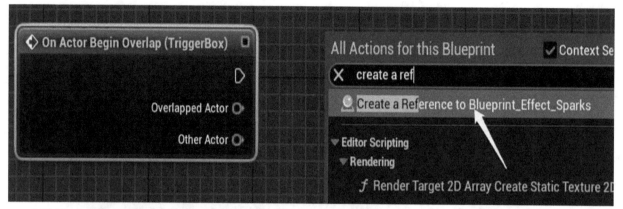

10) From **Blueprint_Effect_Sparks,** drag the blue pin of the node into the **graph** to open the **Fly-out** menu. Search for **"activate"** and select **"Activate (Sparks)"**. Join the white pin of the **OnActorBeginOverlap (TriggerBox)** event to the white pin of the **Activate** function as illustrated below.

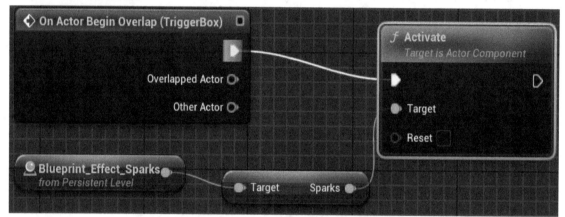

11) Compile the **Level Blueprint** and click the **Play** button in the **Level** Editor to test the Level. Move the character to the position of the **Trigger Box** to activate the sparks.

In this instance, we've learned how to create references and events for Actors within the Level Blueprint. This process forms the basis of **Level Blueprint Communication**. Another method of communication between Blueprints and the Level Blueprint involves using **Event Dispatchers**.

EVENT DISPATCHERS

An Event Dispatcher enables one Blueprint to notify other Blueprints when a specific event occurs. Both the Level Blueprint and other Blueprint classes can listen to these events and execute different actions in response.

Next, we shall illustrate an example of creating event dispatchers.

1) Use an existing project based on the Third Person template with starter content or create a new project.

2) Create a new Blueprint with **Actor** selected as the parent class. Title this Blueprint **BP-Platform** and open it in the Blueprint Editor.

3) Click the **Add** button within the **Components** panel and select the **Static Mesh** Component. In the **Details** panel, select the **Shape_Cylinder** Static Mesh. Adjust the **Scale** feature by setting the **Z** value to **0.1**. Also, modify the **Collision Presets to OverlapAllDynamic**, as demonstrated below.

4) Compile the Blueprint, then go to the **My Blueprint** panel, create an **Event Dispatcher,** and title it **PlatformPressed**. Event Dispatchers can include input parameters. Let's add one to send a reference of the overlapped **BP_Platform** instance. Go to the **Details** panel, under the **Inputs** category, and create a new parameter named **BP_Platform**. Set its type as **BP Platform**, which is an object reference type.

5) Right-click on the **Event Graph** to add **Event ActorBeginOverlap**. Drag the **PlatformPressed** Event Dispatcher from the **My Blueprint** panel and drop it onto the **Event Graph**. Select "**Call**" from the submenu.

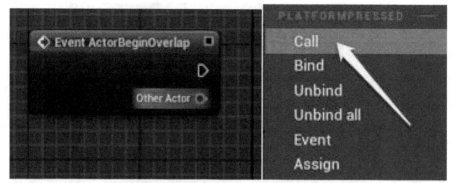

6) Then, right-click on the **Event Graph**, search for "**self**," and choose **"Get a reference to self"**. This retrieves a reference to the current instance. Join these actions together.

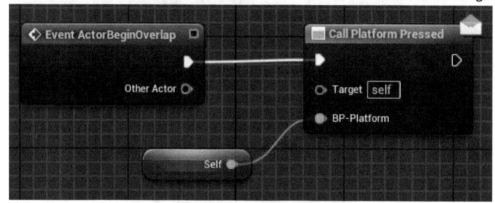

7) Once again, Compile the Blueprint. Go to the **Level** Editor, drag an instance of **BP_Platform** from the **Content Browser,** and place it within the Level to generate an instance.

8) Ensure the **BP_Platform** instance is selected. Click on the **Blueprint** button in the toolbar of the **Level** Editor and select **Open Level Blueprint**. Right-click on the **Event Graph** and choose "**Add Platform Pressed**".

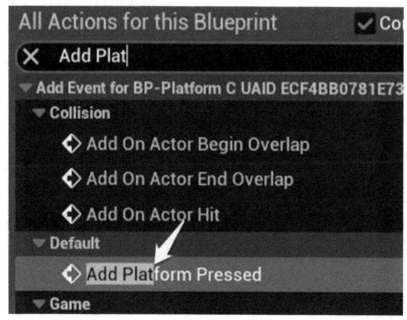

9) Right-click on the **Event Graph**, search for **"spawn"** and choose **"Spawn Actor from Class"** on the drop-down menu, then select **Blueprint Effect Explosion** from the **Class** option menu.

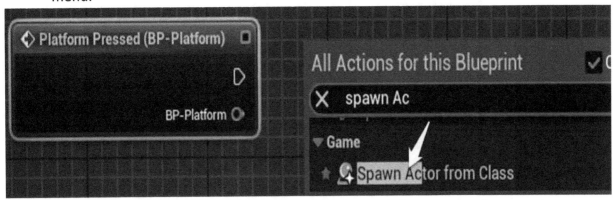

10) Pull a wire from the blue pin of the **PlatformPressed (BP_Platform)** Event, drop it onto the graph to open the **Fly-out** menu, and select the **GetActorTransform** action. Join these nodes together.

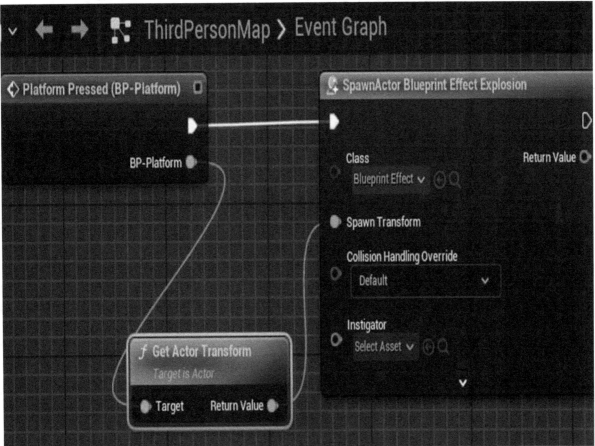

11) compile your **Level** Blueprint, and click the **Play** button in the Level Editor to test your Level. Move your character to the place where **BP_Platform** is positioned. When your character intersects with BP_Platform, the Level Blueprint will trigger and spawn an explosion at that location.

In this example, we've demonstrated how the Level Blueprint can respond to events dispatched from other Blueprints. Additionally, we can also make one Blueprint listen to an Event Dispatcher of another Blueprint by binding events.

BINDING EVENTS

Bind Event node allows one **event** to be linked to another event or an Event Dispatcher, even if they belong to different Blueprints. When an event is called, all bound or linked events are also called.

To illustrate, let's create a child Blueprint Class based on Blueprint_Effect_Sparks. This new Blueprint will bind an event to the **PlatformPressed Event Dispatcher** of the **BP_Platform** Blueprint from our former example:

1) Start by opening the project used in the **Event Dispatcher** example.
2) Create a new Blueprint. Expand the **All Classes** menu and search for **Blueprint_Effect_Sparks**, which we'll use as the parent class. Name this **Blueprint BP_Platform_Sparks** and open it in the Blueprint Editor.
3) Go to the **Components** tab, and choose the **Sparks** Component. Go to the **Details** tab, and verify that the **"auto activate"** feature is unchecked. This should already be the case since we previously adjusted it in **Blueprint_Effect_Sparks**.

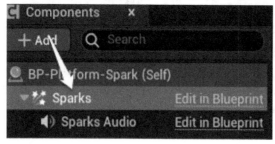
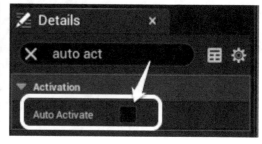

4) Within the **My Blueprint** panel, create a variable named **BP_Platform** of BP_Platform type object reference. Enable the **Instance Editable** feature for this variable in the **Details** panel.

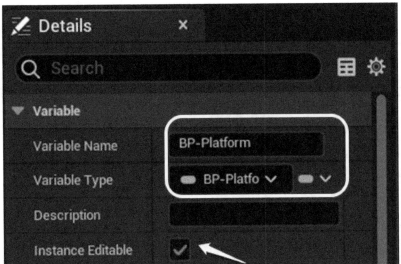

5) Right-click on the **Event Graph** to add **Event BeginPlay**. Drag and drop the **BP_Platform** variable from the **My Blueprint** panel into the **Event Graph**. Select "**Get**" from the options to create a node.

6) To open the **Fly-out** menu, drag from the blue pin of the **BP Platform** node and drop it in the graph. Then, add the "**Is Valid**" macro to check if the **BP Platform** variable references an instance. Join the white pin of the "**Event BeginPlay**" to the **Exec** pin of the "**Is Valid**".

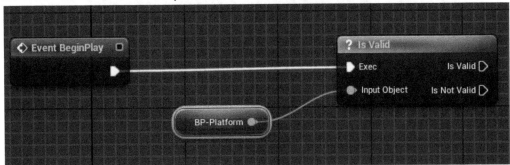

7) Drag once more from the blue pin of the **BP Platform** node to add the "**Bind Event to PlatformPressed**" action. Join the "**Is Valid**" pin to the white pin of the "**Bind Event**" node

8) Drag from the red pin of the "**Bind Event**" node, drop it in the graph, and select **"Add Custom Event"**.

9) From the Components panel, drag and drop the **Sparks** Component into the **graph**. Then, drag from the blue pin of the **Sparks** node, drop it in the **graph**, and select "**Activate**".

10) Join the nodes as shown in the screenshot below and compile BP-Platform_Spark.

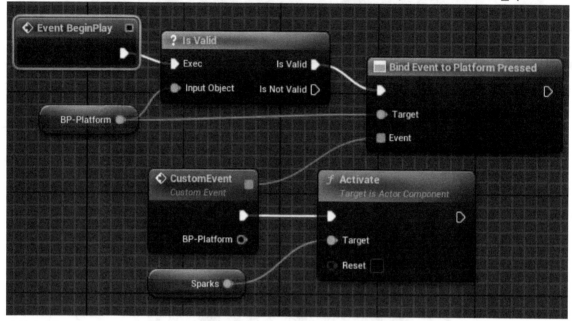

11) Add an instance of **BP_Platform_Sparks** beside the **BP_Platform** instance that is already in the Level. In the **Details** panel of the Level Editor, click the drop-down menu of the **BP_Platform** variable and choose one instance.

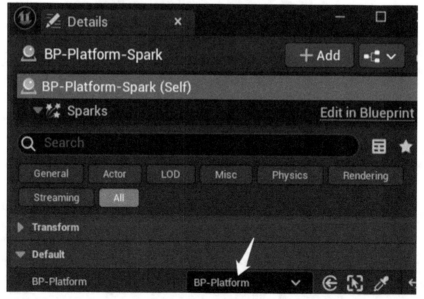

12) Click the **Play** button in the Level Editor to examine the Level. Move your character to the position of the BP_Platform. When your character intersects it, the **PlatformPressed Event Dispatcher** is triggered, executing the Custom Event of BP_Platform_Sparks and activating the sparks.

CHAPTER FOUR
USING BLUEPRINTS TO CONNECT OBJECTS

When developing a game, part of the first step is to create a prototype to explore your ideas. Unreal Engine and Blueprints make this process easier than ever, allowing you to quickly get the vital gameplay functionality up and running so you can start testing your concepts sooner. We'll start by prototyping simple gameplay mechanics using a couple of default assets and some Blueprints.

By the end of this chapter, you'll learn how to create a Blueprint target that alters its material when hit and moves back and forth between two points. Every instance of this Blueprint target in the level can be customized with different speeds, directions, and timing for changing direction.

CREATING THE PROJECT AND THE FIRST LEVEL

We'll start by creating a project using one of Unreal Engine's templates. We'll use the template to see what gameplay elements it provides. Since our game will be a first-person shooter, we'll use the **FIRST PERSON** template from the **Games** category:

Under the game templates, you'll see a folder path field where you can indicate where to store your project. You can use the default folder or select the one you prefer.

The screenshot below displays the project defaults you should use for this chapter project. These options were explained in **Chapter 1**. Then Title this Project "**FourthProject**" using the **Project Name** field.

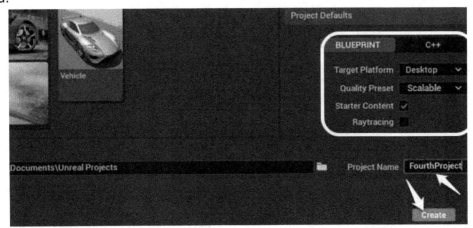

With the template selected and the project settings configured, we can create the project. Follow these steps:

1) Click on the "**Create**" button. Once the engine initializes the assets and sets up your project, the Unreal Editor instantly opens the Level Editor.

2) click the "**Play**" button to try the default gameplay built into the **First Person** template. Click on the viewport for the game to start reacting to input. You can move the player character using the **W, A, S,** and **D** keys and check around by moving the mouse. Fire the projectiles with the **left** mouse button, and observe how the projectiles affect some physics objects in the Level. Try shooting at the white boxes scattered around the Level and watch them move.

3) In Play mode, the **Play** button will be replaced with "**Pause**", "**Stop**", and "**Eject**" buttons. Press "**Shift + F1**" to access the mouse cursor and click the "**Pause**" button to momentarily halt the play session. This can be useful for exploring the properties of an interaction or Actor you encounter during gameplay.

Clicking the "**Stop**" button ends the play session and returns you to editing mode. A click on the "**Eject**" button disconnects the camera from the player, allowing you to move freely through the Level.

try to play the game before proceeding.

ADDING OBJECTS TO OUR LEVEL

Next, we will add our own objects to the Level. We aim to create a simple target Actor that alters color when shot with the included gun and projectile. Follow these steps to create a simple Actor:

1) Go to the **Level** Editor, and click the **Create** button on the toolbar. mouse over **Shapes** to show a submenu, then drag and drop a "**Cylinder**" into the Level to create an instance.

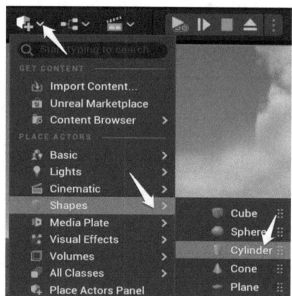

This generates a new **Cylinder** Actor and places it in our Level. You can relocate the **Cylinder** by dragging and dropping it. You'll see the Actor in the **Viewport** and in the **Outliner** panel, where it is named "**Cylinder**" by default:

74

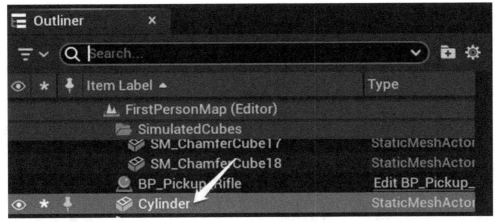

2) Go to the **"Details"** panel, and rename the **Cylinder** instance to **"CylinderTarget"** as illustrated below.

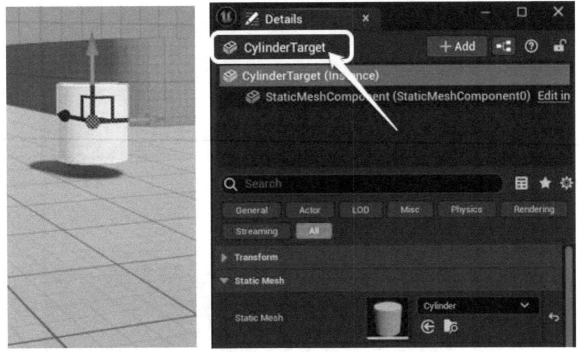

An Actor has been added to the Level that will be used as a target. Next, we'll learn how to create a Material to apply to the Actor.

CREATING AND USING MATERIALS

To change the color of the Cylinder when it's hit by a projectile, we need to modify the Actor's Material. A Material is an asset applied to an Actor's mesh to define its appearance, similar to a coat of paint on a surface. Since an Actor's Material determines its color, one way to alter the color is to replace its Material with another color. Let's create a new Material to make the Actor appear Blue. Create a Material with the following steps:

1) Click the **"Content Drawer"** button to access the content browser. Go to the **FirstPerson** folder. Click the **"Add"** button, choose "New Folder", and title it **"Material"**. Though it is not necessary, it helps keep the project file hierarchy organized.

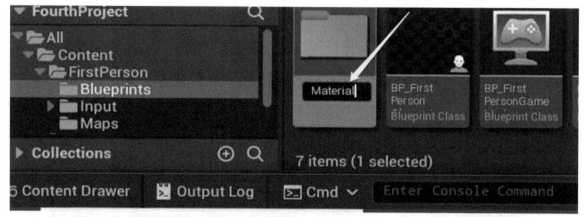

2) Go to the newly created "**Material**" folder. Right-click in a space in the content browser, choose "**Material**", and title it "**M-TargetBlue**".

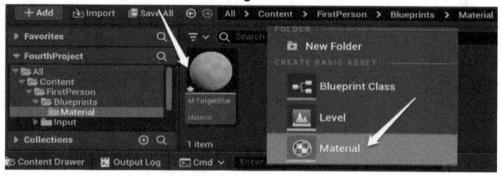

MATERIAL PROPERTIES AND NODES

Next, we will open the Material Editor and study how to use nodes to alter the Material. Design the look of your simple Material using the following steps:

1) Double-click on "**M_TargetBlue**" to open the Material Editor as illustrated here.

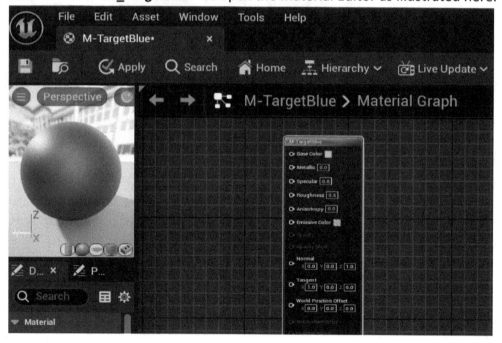

The Material Editor shares many features and conventions with Blueprints. The middle of the screen is called the graph, where we place all the nodes that define our Material's logic. The node you see in the middle of the graph, labeled with the name of the Material, is the result node. This node has a series of input pins that other Material nodes can attach to define the Material's properties.

2) To add a color to the Material, we have to create a node that delivers color information to the input labeled "**Base Color**" on the result node. Right-click in an empty space near the result node. A popup with a search box and a long list of expandable options will appear:

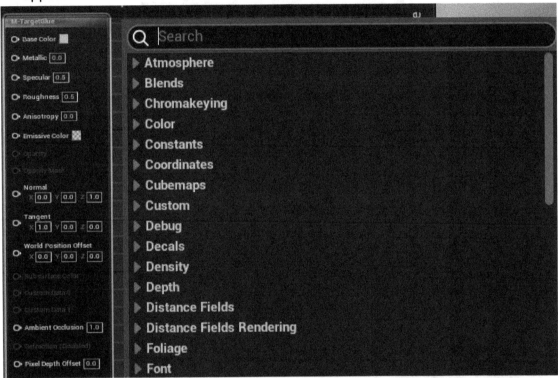

This menu displays all the available Material node options we can add. The search box is context-sensitive, so if you begin to type the first few letters of a valid node name, the list will narrow down to consist of only those nodes. We need a node called "**VectorParameter**". Start typing "**VectorP**" in the search box and click on the **VectorParameter** to add this node to our graph.

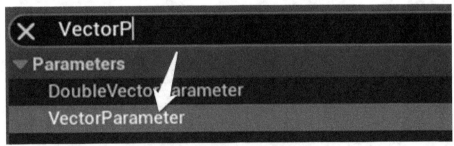

3) Rename the added node to "**Color**" using the **Details** panel on the left side of the Editor. A vector parameter in the Material Editor enables you to define a color, which we can then attach to the **Base Color** input on the long Material definition node.

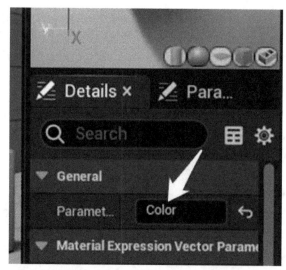

4) To assign a color to the node, double-click the black square in the center of the node to open the **Color Picker**. We want our target to turn bright blue when hit, so either drag the center point in the **color wheel** to the **blue** section or enter the **RGB** or hex values manually. Once you've selected the desired shade of blue, click "**OK**". You will see that the black box in your vector parameter node has turned blue.

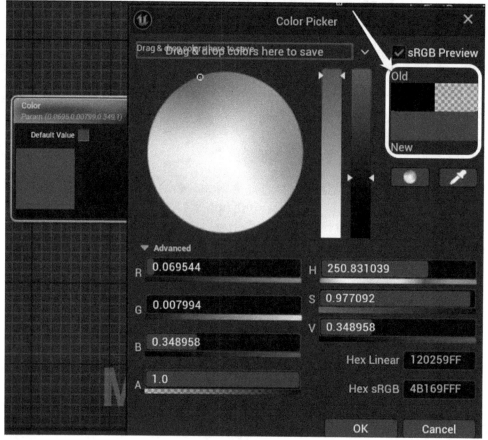

The final stage is to connect our color vector parameter node to the base Material node. Similar to Blueprints, you can join two nodes by clicking and dragging from one node's output pin to another. Input pins are located on the left side of a node, while output pins are on the right side in this case. For our Material, click and Pull a wire from the top output pin of the "**Color**" node to the "**Base Color**" input pin of the Material node as illustrated below.

By using the "**Base Color**" input pin, we've defined a simple Material.

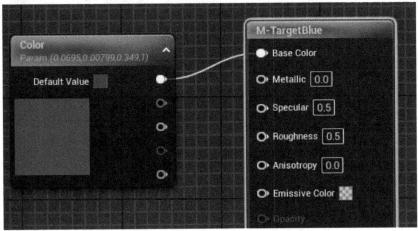

ADDING SUBSTANCE TO OUR MATERIAL

You can enhance your Material by using additional input pins on the **Material definition node**. 3D objects can appear unrealistic with flat, single-color Materials, but adding reflectiveness and depth through the **Metallic** and **Roughness** inputs can improve realism. Follow these steps:

1) Right-click in the empty space in the grid and type "**Scalar**" into the search box. The node we want to use is called "**ScalarParameter**".

2) Choose the **ScalarParameter** and move to the "**Details**" panel. ScalarParameter takes a single float value. Set **0.1** for the **Default Value** to keep any additional effects on our Material subtle.

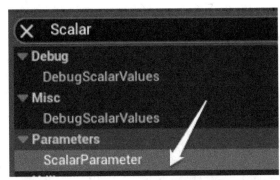 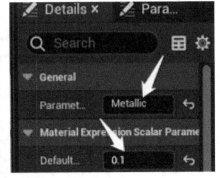

3) Alter the **Parameter Name** to **Metallic**, then click and drag the output pin from the **Metallic** node to the "**Metallic**" input pin of the Material definition node.

4) To add a connection to the Roughness parameter, right-click on the "**Metallic**" node we just created and choose "**Duplicate**". This creates a copy of the node without the wire connection.

5) Choose the duplicated **Metallic** node and adjust the "**Parameter Name**" field in the **Details** panel to "**Roughness**". Keep the default value of **0.1** for this node.

6) Click and drag the output pin from the "**Roughness**" node to the "**Roughness** input pin of the **Material** definition node.

The Material should resemble the screenshot below.

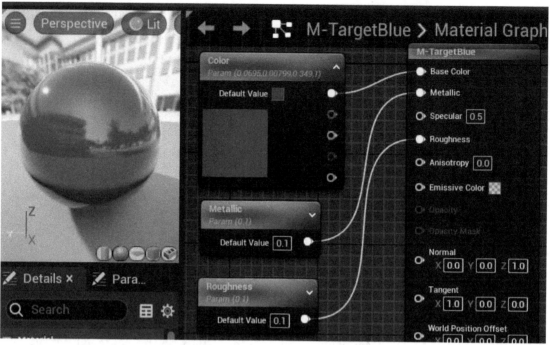

You now have a shiny blue Material that ensures our targets attraction when they are hit. Click the **Save** button at the upper-left corner of the Editor to save the asset. Close the Material Editor to switch back to the Level Editor.

You have mastered how to use the Material Editor to produce a simple Material using the **Base Color**, **Metallic**, and **Roughness** input pins. Next, you will see how to change the Material of an Actor during runtime.

GENERATING THE TARGET BLUEPRINT

You now have a Cylinder in the world and a Material that we want to apply to the Cylinder when it is shot. The last step is to create the game logic that detects when the Cylinder has been hit and changes its Material to the new blue one. To achieve this, you need to convert our Cylinder into a Blueprint. Follow these steps:

1) Confirm that you have the "**CylinderTarget**" object selected in the **Level**. Go to the **Details** panel, and click the icon on the right side of the **Add** button.

2) A "**Create Blueprint From Selection**" pane is opened. Change the Blueprint Name to "**BP-CylinderTarget**". Go to the "**Path field**" and select the "**/Game/FirstPerson/Blueprints**" folder. Use the "**New Subclass**" option for the "**Creation Method**". The **StaticMeshActor** parent class is already selected since it is the parent class of the **Cylinder** Actor. Click the **Select** button to create the Blueprint.

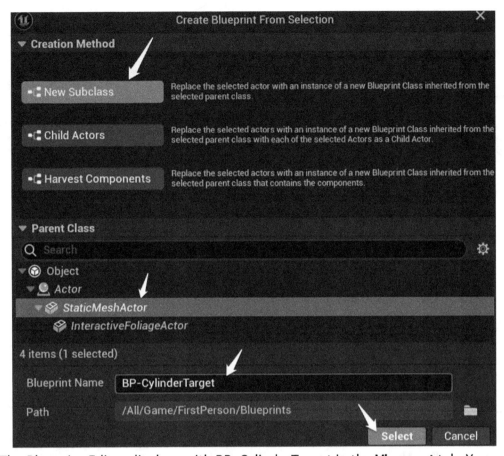

3) The Blueprint Editor displays with BP_CylinderTarget in the **Viewport** tab. You will notice the **Blueprint** already has a **Static Mesh** component with a Cylinder mesh allocated to it.

We will examine the use of components in Chapter 5. Currently, we want to create a simple Blueprint that will respond to a hit. To achieve this, click on the "**Event Graph**" tab.

DISCOVERING A HIT

Follow these steps to create a hit discovery mechanism:

1) **Create the Hit Discovery Event**: Right-click in an empty space of the **Event Graph** and type **"Event hit"** in the search box. Select the **Event Hit** node from the search results. This node is triggered every time another Actor hits the Actor controlled by this Blueprint:

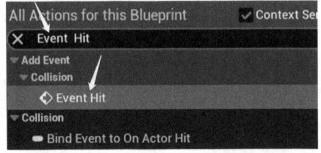

2) **Set the Material on Hit**: Click and Pull a wire from the **white execution** pin of the **Event Hit** node to an empty space to access the context menu. Type "**set material (sta**" in the search box and select the **Set Material (StaticMeshComponent)** node.

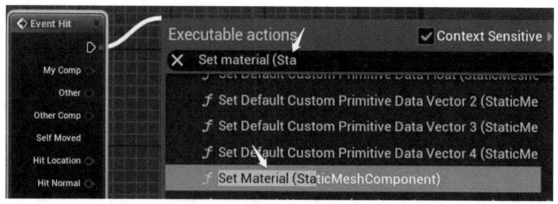

Note: If you were unable to locate the node you are finding in the Context Sensitive search, try unchecking **Context Sensitive** to see the complete list of node options. Even if the node is not found in the **Context Sensitive** search, it might still be compatible with the node you are attempting to attach it to.

With the "**Set Material**" node added, we now need to modify its input parameters.

APPLYING A NEW MATERIAL ON HIT

After placing the "**Set Material**" node, you'll notice it is already connected via its input execution pin to the output execution pin of the "**Event Hit**" node. This Blueprint now triggers the "Set Material" action whenever the Blueprint's Actor collides with another Actor. Nevertheless, we still need to specify the Material that will be applied when this action occurs. Without setting the Material, the action will execute but won't visibly affect the Cylinder target.

1) To specify the **Material** to be used, click on the drop-down field titled "**Select Asset**" under "**Material**" inside the "**Set Material**" node. Go to the asset finder pane that opens, and type "**m-tar**" in the search box to locate the "**M_TargetBlue**" Material that we created previously. Select this asset to attach it to the "Material" field inside the "**Set Material**" node.

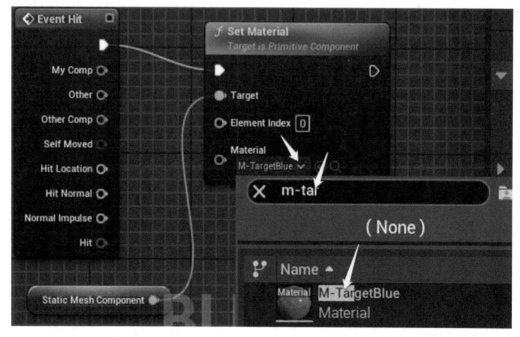

2) With this setup, we've configured the Blueprint to switch the target Cylinder blue when triggered. Remember to "**Compile**" and "**Save**" the Blueprint.

since we've established a basic gameplay interaction, it's important to test the game to confirm that everything functions as intended. Click the **Play** button in the Blueprint Editor to test the game. Try shooting and running into the "**BP_CylinderTarget**" Actor you created.

Next, we will explore ways to enhance the "**BP_CylinderTarget**" Blueprint.

REFINING THE BLUEPRINT

As you run the game, you will observe that the Cylinder target changes colors when hit by a projectile fired from the player's gun. This marks the start of a framework of gameplay by which enemies can be made to respond to player actions. Nevertheless, you might have also observed that the Cylinder changes color even when the player runs to it directly. Our original intention was for the Cylinder to turn blue only when hit by a player projectile, not by any other object collisions. Such unintended outcomes are common during scripting, and the best approach to mitigate them is frequent testing during game construction.

To refine our Blueprint so that the Cylinder target changes color only in response to a player projectile, follow these steps:

✓ Return to the "**BP_CylinderTarget**" tab and examine the "**Event Hit**" node.

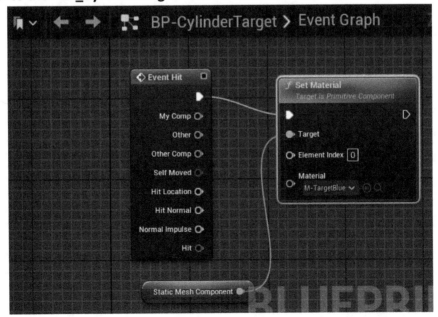

The residual output pins on the "**Event Hit**" node are variables that store data regarding the event that can be passed to other nodes. The color of the pin indicates the type of data variable they pass. Red pins include a Boolean (True or False) variable while the blue pins pass objects like Actors.

The blue output pin titled "**Other**" includes a reference to the other Actor that collided with the Cylinder target. This is helpful to confirm that the Cylinder changes color only when hit by a projectile fired from the player, not by other Actors.

1) To implement this change, drag the "**Event Hit**" node to the left to create space for another node. Click and Pull a wire from the "**Other**" output pin to an empty space to open the context menu. Type "**projectile**" in the search box.

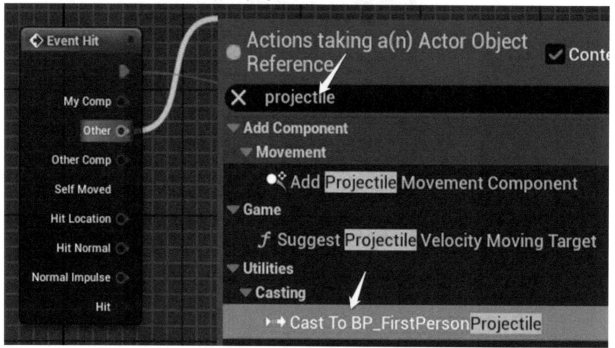

You should have results that include a node called "**Cast To BP- FirstPersonProjectile**". This node allows us to identify if the colliding Actor is a projectile fired from the player.

The "**FirstPersonProjectile**" is a Blueprint included in Unreal Engine 5's **First Person** template, governing the behavior of projectiles fired from your gun. The "**Cast**" node ensures that subsequent actions are executed only if the Actor hitting with the Cylinder target is an instance of "**BP-FirstPersonProjectile**".

When the "node" displays, you'll notice a blue wire already connected between the **Other** output pin of the **Event Hit** node and the "**Object**" pin of the cast node. To complete the setup:

2) Join the white execution pin of the "**Event Hit**" to the execution pin of the "**Cast To BP-FirstPersonProjectile**" node.

3) Join the output execution pin of the "**Cast To BP_FirstPersonProjectile**" node to the execution pin of the "**Set Material**" node.

4) After making these connections, **Compile** and **Save** your Blueprint. Click the **Play** button to test the game again. Now, you'll observe that the Cylinder target holds its default color when you walk up and touch it, but turns blue when you shoot it from a distance.

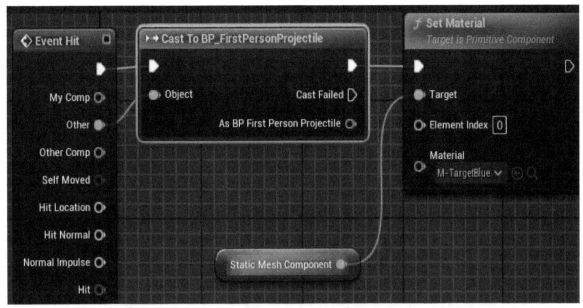

We've effectively used the "**Cast To BP_FirstPersonProjectile**" node to confirm that specific actions are triggered only when interacting with instances of a particular class. Next, we will explore how to cause the Cylinder target to move in the Level

ADDING MOVEMENT

With a target that responds to player shooting, the next step is to introduce a challenge to transform our project into a playable game. An effective approach is to infuse our target with movement. This involves defining our target Actor as a movable object and establishing logic within the Blueprint to govern its motion. Our objective is to create a scenario where the Cylinder target moves back and forth across our Level.

ADJUSTING ACTOR MOBILITY AND COLLISION SETTINGS

To enable movement for our target, we first need to change its **Mobility** setting to "**Movable**". This setting enables the Actor to be manipulated during gameplay. Follow these steps to make these adjustments:

1) Open "**BP-CylinderTarget**" again. Go to the **Components** panel, locate and select the "**Static Mesh Component**" that represents our Cylinder target.
2) Go to the **Details** panel, under the **TRANSFORM** properties, and find the **Mobility** toggle. Switch it from **Static** to **Movable**:

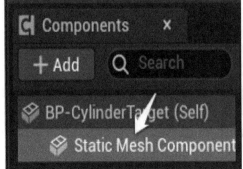 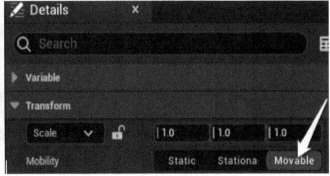

Note: By default, static objects are non-interactive and do not move during gameplay, which optimizes performance by reducing rendering complexity. Changing the Mobility to Movable enables us to animate or move the Cylinder target dynamically.

Additionally, to ensure that the Cylinder target can interact properly with other game elements, such as projectiles from the player's gun, we need to adjust its collision settings.

3) Go to the **Details** panel, and locate the **Collision** category. Look for **Collision Presets** in the drop-down menu. Choose "**Custom**" from the options to fine-tune the collision interactions with various object types. For our specific requirement, set the Collision Presets to "**BlockAllDynamic**".

DEFINING OUR OBJECTIVES

With our target now capable of movement, our next step is to establish actions that dictate how the Cylinder moves across the Level. To achieve this, we need to consider four essential sets of data:

✓ **Current Location**: We must determine where the Cylinder is positioned within the game world at any given time.
✓ **Movement Direction**: Define the intended direction in which the Cylinder should travel.
✓ **Movement Speed:** Specify how quickly the Cylinder should move across the Level.
✓ **Direction Switch Timing**: Determine when the Cylinder should change its movement direction.

To gather the current location of the Cylinder, we'll use a function that retrieves its coordinates in the world. While we can directly provide the speed, direction, and timing values to the Blueprint, we'll also need to perform calculations to transform these values into actionable information that the Blueprint can interpret to move the object effectively. This process ensures that our movement logic is both precise and responsive within the game environment.

Follow these steps to configure the Blueprint for BP_CylinderTarget:

1) Go to the "**My Blueprint**" panel in the Blueprint Editor. Create a new variable titled "**Speed**". This variable will store the speed at which **BP_CylinderTarget** moves.
2) Go to the **Details** panel, change the **Variable Type** to **Float,** and ensure that the "**Instance Editable**" feature is checked.

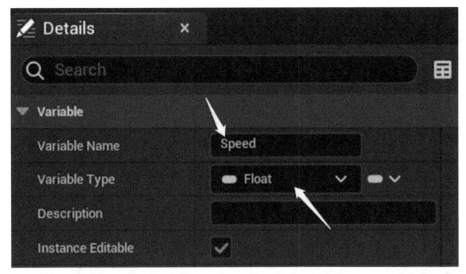

3) Compile the Blueprint to allow for setting the default values. Set the "**DEFAULT VALUE**" of the Speed variable to "**200.0**".

4) Go to the **"My Blueprint"** panel, and create another **Float** variable titled "**ChangeTime**". Tick the "**Instance Editable**" feature. **Compile** the Blueprint. Set the "**DEFAULT VALUE**" of the **"ChangeTime"** variable to "**5.0"**. This indicates that the Cylinder will change its movement direction every 5 seconds.

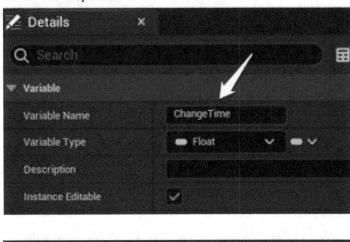

5) Create another variable named "**Direction**" in the "**My Blueprint**" panel. Change the **Variable Type** to "Vector" in the **Details** panel and tick the "**Instance Editable**" feature to allow adjusting the direction for each instance of **BP_CylinderTarget**.

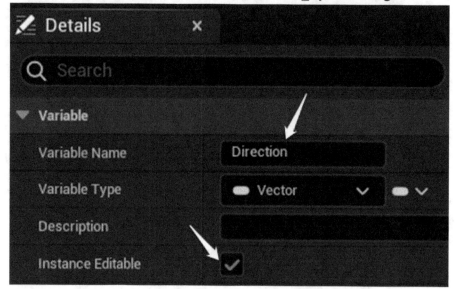

6) **Compile** the Blueprint to and specify **1.0** for the **Default Value** on the Y-axis. The vector includes **X**, **Y,** and **Z** float values, this shows it will move in the positive direction of the **Y**-axis.

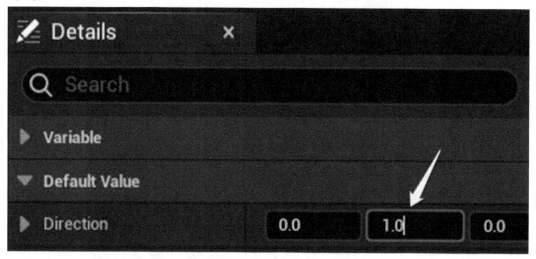

PREPARING DIRECTIONS FOR CALCULATIONS

To ensure our Blueprint can accurately handle movement instructions, we'll walk through the necessary steps. Each step will be broken down to make it more understandable, focusing on how each node contributes to our overall objective.

Normalizing the Direction Vector:

1) Start by dragging the **Direction** variable from the **My Blueprint** panel into the "**Event Graph**". Select "**Get Direction**" to create a node.
2) From the output pin of the **Direction** node, drag in the graph to access the **Context** menu. Search for "**normali**" and locate the **normalized** node under the **vector** category.

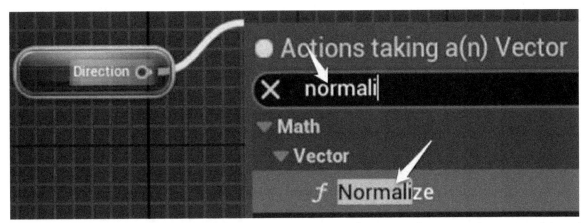

3) This joins **Direction** variables to a node that automatically normalizes our Direction vector.

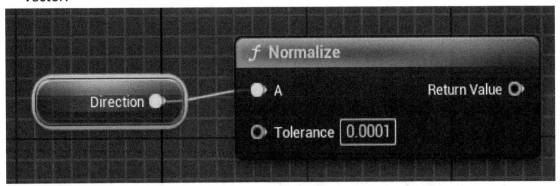

Note: It's beneficial to add comments to your Blueprints as you build them. Comments provide clarity about the purpose and function of different Blueprint sections, especially useful when revisiting or sharing the Blueprint. To add a comment:

✓ Click and drag to select the nodes in the Blueprint that you want to describe.
✓ Right-click on any of the selected **nodes** and choose "**Create Comment from Selection**" from the menu.
✓ Type a descriptive comment that explains the purpose of the selected nodes. This helps in understanding the logic and functionality of the Blueprint at a glance. It is *Normalize Vector Direction* in this case

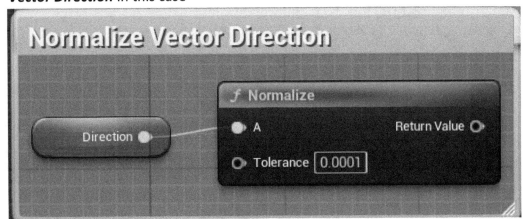

CALCULATING RELATIVE SPEED USING DELTA TIME

Delta time is crucial in game development to ensure consistent movement regardless of frame rate differences. Let's walk through the steps to incorporate delta time into our Blueprint to adjust the speed of our object dynamically.

1) Start by dragging the "**Speed**" variable from the "**My Blueprint**" panel into the **Event Graph**. Select "**Get Speed**" to create a node.
2) Right-click in an empty space of the "**Event Graph**" to open the **Context** menu. Search for delta and choose "**Get World Delta Seconds**".
3) From the output pin of the "**Speed**" node, drag to an empty space. Type an asterisk "*" in the search field to search for the Multiply node and select it.
4) Connect the output pin of the "**Get World Delta Seconds**" node to the second input pin of the "**Multiply**" node. This multiplies the speed value by delta time to calculate the relative speed of our object.

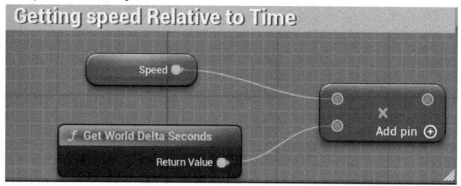

UPDATING LOCATION WITH NORMALIZED DIRECTION AND RELATIVE SPEED

Since we have normalized the direction vector and calculated the relative speed using delta time, let's proceed to update the location of our Cylinder target in the Blueprint. This involves multiplying the normalized direction vector by the relative speed and adding this to the current location of the Cylinder.

1) Drag the output pin of the **Normalize** node (which contains the normalized direction vector) into an empty space in the **Event Graph**. Type an asterisk **(*)** in the search field to search for the **Multiply** node and select it.

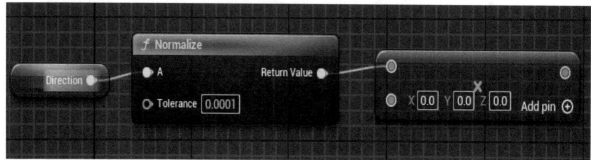

2) This creates a **Vector x Vector** node. However, we need to multiply the vector with a float. Thus, right-click on the second input pin of the **Multiply** node and select "**To Float (single-precision)**".

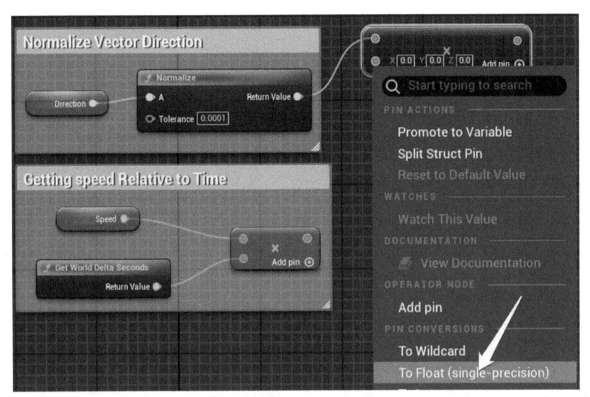

3) Join the output pin of the **Float** x **Float** node to the Float input pin that we transformed.

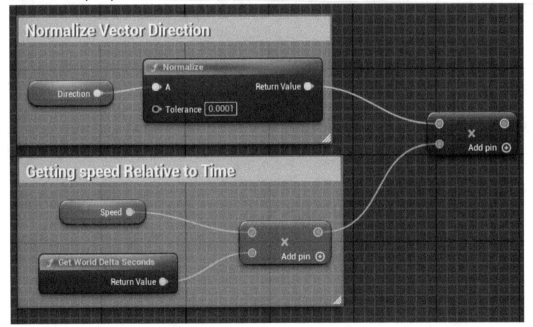

4) To update location with **Event Tick**. Right-click an empty space in the **Event Graph**. Search for "**tick**" and choose **Event Tick** from the options.

5) To move the **Cylinder** target, we will use the **AddActorWorldOffset** node. There is a **Delta Location** input parameter in this node, which is a vector symbolizing the change of location of the Actor. Right-click to open the **Context** menu, and search for "**AddActorWorldOffset**", to add the node to the **Event Graph**. Join the **Event Tick** node to the **AddActorWorldOffset** node. Add comment for proper description as shown below.

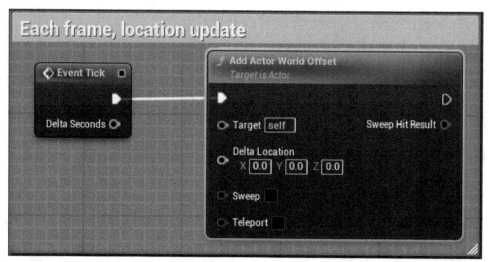

6) Join the output pin of the **Vector x Float** node to the "**Delta Location**" input pin of the **AddActorWorldOffset** node. The Event Tick should resemble this:

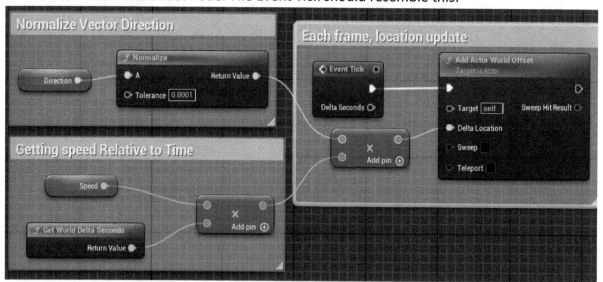

By following these steps, we've set up the Blueprint to continuously update the location of the Cylinder target based on the normalized direction vector and the relative speed calculated using delta time. This approach ensures smooth and consistent movement across different frame rates in our game. Remember to **compile** and **save** your Blueprint changes before testing them in the game environment. Remember that the Cylinder target moves based on the defined speed and direction immediately after the game begins. Nevertheless, since we don't make any instructions that cause the target to stop moving, it will continue in the same direction for as long as the game runs, even moving in and out of the Level we created. To prevent this problem, Next, we will cause the Cylinder target to change its direction occasionally.

IMPLEMENTING DIRECTION CHANGE LOGIC

Now we'll configure the Blueprint to change the direction of our moving Cylinder target sporadically. This will make the target move back and forth between two points, similar to a shooting gallery target.

1) Right-click any empty space of the "**Event Graph**" to open the **Context** menu. Search for "**custom event**" and choose "**Add Custom Event**". Change the event to "**ChangeDirection**".

2) Next, you will invert the Direction vector by using -1 to multiply it. Drag the "**Direction**" variable from the "**My Blueprint**" panel into the **EventGraph**. Select "**Get Direction**" to create a node.

3) Drag from the output pin of the "**Direction**" node and drop it to an empty space. Enter an asterisk (*****) in the search field and choose the "**Multiply**" node.

4) The earlier step generated a **Vector** x **Vector** node. Next, we will multiply the vector with a float. Right-click on the second input pin of the "**Multiply**" node, choose "**To Float (single-precision)**" and enter "**-1**" in the "**Float**" parameter.

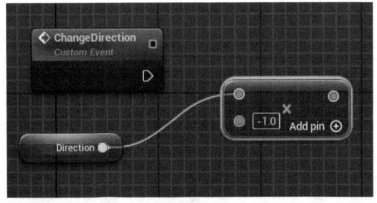

5) Drag the "**Direction**" variable from the "**My Blueprint**" panel again into the "**EventGraph**. Choose "**Set Direction**" to create a node that sets the direction. Join the output pin of the "**Multiply**" node (which now contains the inverted direction vector) to the input pin of the "**Set Direction**" node. Join the "**ChangeDirection**" event to the execution pin of the "**Set Direction**" node to complete the logic for changing the direction.

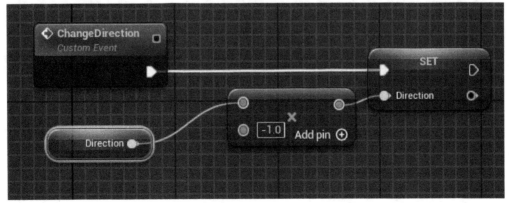

6) Next, you will use a **Timer** to Run **ChangeDirection** Periodically. Right-click in an empty space of the "**EventGraph**" to open the context menu. Search for "**timer event**" and choose "**Set Timer by Event**". Tick the "**Looping**" feature to ensure that the timer repeats.

7) Right-click to access the **Context Menu** and select "**Event BeginPlay**". Drag the "**ChangeTime**" variable from the "**My Blueprint**" panel and choose "**Get ChangeTime**" to retrieve its value. Join the nodes as shown in the diagram below. Once all nodes are connected properly, "**Compile**" and "**Save**" your Blueprint to apply the changes

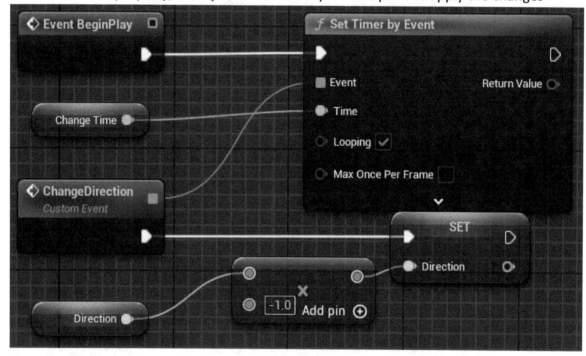

TESTING MOVEMENT OF BP_CYLINDERTARGET

Since we've updated our Blueprint to include movement logic for BP_CylinderTarget, it's time to test and verify that the instance moves correctly. Follow these steps to ensure everything functions as expected:

1) Position the **BP_CylinderTarget** instance in your Level where it can move along the Y-axis without colliding with other objects.

94

2) Example coordinates used: **230** on the X-axis, **-700** on the Y-axis, and **230** on the Z-axis.

Note: These values are relative to the default of the **First Person** template map layout. If you have changed these coordinates according to your Level layout, then you can change the location of the **Cylinder** in your Level or adjust the values of the instance editable variables like speed, direction, or change time as illustrated in the diagram below.

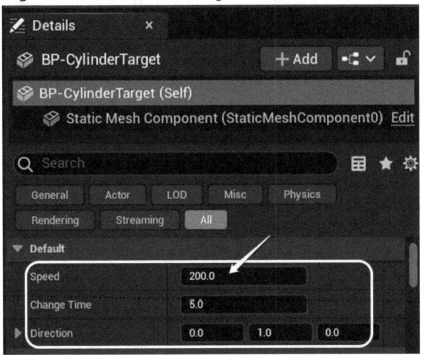

3) Click on the **Play** button to start testing your game. Observe the movement of BP_CylinderTarget. It should move smoothly back and forth between two points based on the configured variables.

4) You can experiment more by adding multiple instances of BP_CylinderTarget and try different directions for movement, such as along the X-axis or the Z-axis, to see how the Blueprint behaves with varied setups.

CHAPTER FIVE
IMPROVING PLAYER ABILITIES

Next, we shall be building on the primary shooting interaction we developed in Chapter 4 by making changes to the player character Blueprint. At first glance, the player character Blueprint provided with the First-Person template might seem complex, particularly when compared to the simple Cylinder target Blueprint we created from scratch. We'll break down this Blueprint to understand how its different sections contribute to the player's experience which enables them to shoot a gun and control their character.

While it might be tempting to use an existing asset that works right out of the box, bypassing the effort to learn its functionality, it's crucial to understand how these assets operate. This knowledge not only helps us troubleshoot issues as they arise but also allows us to extend and customize player controls to better fit our needs. Therefore, it's always a good idea to spend some time exploring and learning about any external assets you incorporate into your project.

Before concluding this chapter, you should be able to improve your player character by adding the ability to sprint, zoom the view, and destroy objects with exciting explosions and sound effects.

ADDING THE SPRINT FUNCTIONALITY

We'll start by modifying the **FirstPersonCharacter** Blueprint to include a sprinting feature, giving players more tactical options for movement within the level. Currently, the player moves at a single speed. We will update the Blueprint to increase the movement speed of the **Character Movement** Component when the player presses the **Left Shift** key. Before diving into this modification, let's explore the **Actions** that are available in the Event Graph of **FirstPersonCharacter.**

BREAKING DOWN CHARACTER MOVEMENT

Let's start by opening the **FirstPersonCharacter** Blueprint. In the **Content Browser**, go to the **Content > FirstPerson > Blueprints** folder and double-click on the **FirstPersonCharacter** Blueprint. This opens the **Event Graph**.

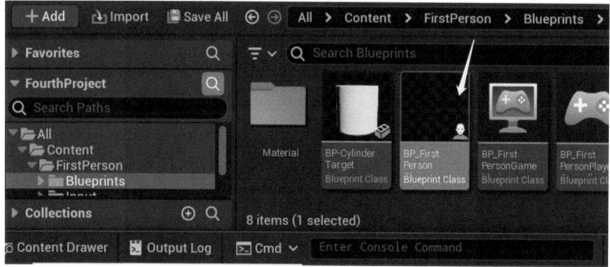

To navigate around the **Event Graph**, right-click and drag to explore the different sections. The input axis and actions you will be seeing in the subsequent diagrams can be accessed by right-clicking on **Context Menu** in the **Event Graph** but you must have added the **axis** or **action** in the **Level** Editor via (**Settings** > **Project Settings** > **Engine** > **Input**) before they can become available in the **Context Menu** on the Event Graph.

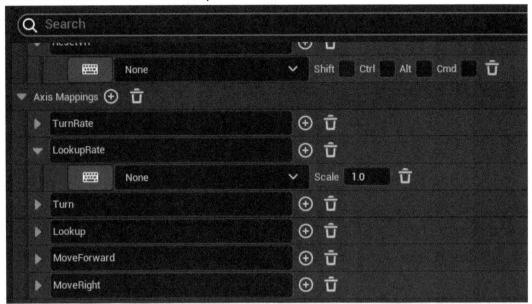

You can learn them in detail in the subsequent section labeled (**Customizing Control Inputs**).

First, let's focus on the group of nodes labeled "**Input (Stick)**" in the Event Graph:

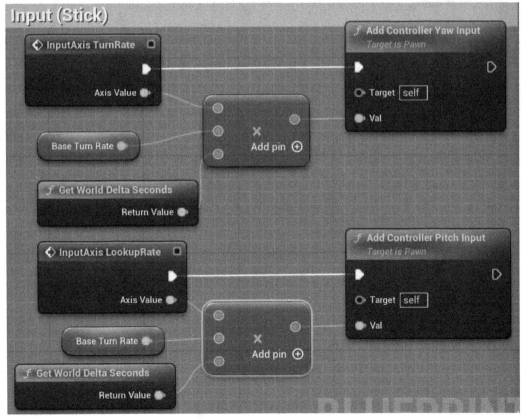

The red Event nodes are triggered on every frame and receive the **Axis Values** for **TurnRate** and **LookUpRate** from the controller input. These values are typically mapped to the **left/right** and **up/down** axis triggers of an analog stick. Observe that there are only two axis triggers. Detecting movements like looking down or turning left event is handled by these nodes and is symbolized as a negative value in the **Axis Value** that passed.

These **Axis** Values are each multiplied by a variable that represents the base rate upon which the player can turn or look up and down. The values are also multiplied by the world delta seconds to ensure consistent behavior across varying frame rates. The resulting values from these calculations are then passed to the **Add Controller Pitch Input and Add Controller Yaw Input** functions. These functions translate the controller inputs into corresponding movements of the player camera.

Under the "**Stick input**" group of Blueprint nodes, another section labeled "**Input (Mouse)**" which looks quite similar to the "**Stick input**" group has been added:

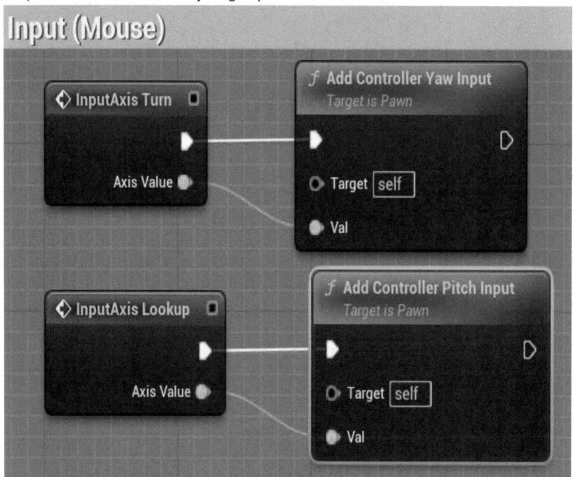

Mouse input turns input from mouse movement into data and passes these values directly to the camera yaw and pitch input functions. This process doesn't require the same calculations necessary for analog stick input.

Next, let's examine the group of nodes "**Input (Movement)**" that control player movement as described in the diagram below:

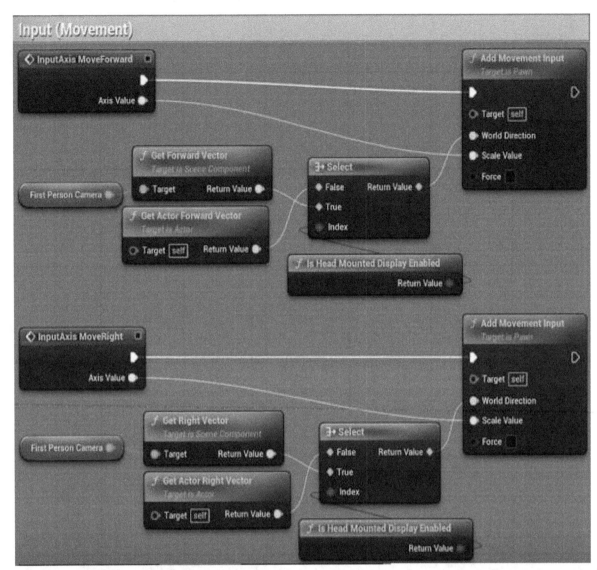

The **Select** nodes check if the player is using a **virtual reality head-mounted display (VR HMD)**. If a VR HMD is activated, the vectors used are from the **FirstPerson Camera**; if not, the vectors come from the Actor root Component.

In Practice, these nodes are similar to the "**Stick input**" and "**Mouse input**" groups. The axis value is taken from the right and forward movement axis inputs on a controller or keyboard. Once more, these nodes signify left and backward movement also, appearing in negative values for the Axis Values output.

The key difference in translating movement is that we need the direction in which the Actor is moving so that the movement can be applied correctly. This direction is obtained from the **Get Actor Vector** nodes (both forward and right) and connected to the **World Direction** input of the **Add Movement Input nodes.**

Another movement-related group of nodes we will be checking is within the comment block labeled "Jump". This group consists of a trigger node that detects when the key mapped to jumping is pressed and released. When the button is pressed, the Jump function is activated, and it remains active until the button is released.

99

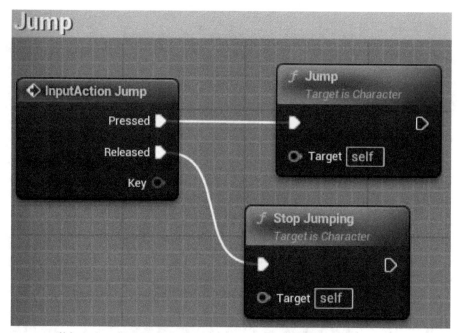

The last group we will be checking is labeled **Spawn Projectile** group as shown in the screenshot below: We will be developing this group as we move further, simply add it now, and we will pick it up later in the subsequent section.

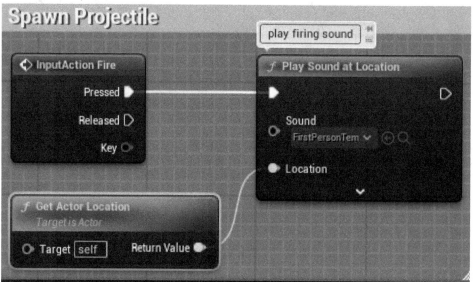

We've examined the Actions of the FirstPersonCharacter Blueprint that control character movement. Now, we'll check how to map a keypress to an Action.

CUSTOMIZING CONTROL INPUTS

We have checked how the FirstPerson template maps specific player input actions, like moving forward or jumping, to Blueprint nodes to produce specific behaviors. To create new behaviors, we need to map new physical control inputs to additional player actions. Follow these steps to customize control inputs:

1) To change the input settings for your game, click on the **Settings** button on the extreme right of the toolbar, and select the **Project Settings** option.

2) From the left side of the opened Window, find the **Engine** category and choose the **Input** option.

3) Go to the **Input Settings** menu, under the **Bindings** class, there are two sections: **Action Mappings** and **Axis Mappings**. Click on the disclosure triangle (**>)** symbol next to each section to expand and view the existing mappings.

  ✓ **Action Mappings**: These are keypress and mouse click events that trigger player actions.

  ✓ **Axis Mappings**: These map player movements and events that have a range, like the **W** and **S** keys affecting the **Move Forward action** from different ends of the range.

Both **Sprint** and **Zoom** functions are simple actions that are either active or inactive, so you will add them as **Action Mappings**.

4) Click on the + sign next to **Action Mappings** two times to add two new **Action Mappings** with the ones that have been added earlier.

5) Name the first **Action Sprint** and choose the **Left Shift** key from the drop-down menu to map that key to your **Sprint** event. Title the second action "**Zoom**" and map it to the **Right Mouse** Button. The changes are automatically saved as you close the window.

Note: Jump and **Fire** action inputs have already been added, you can add this from your end as well.

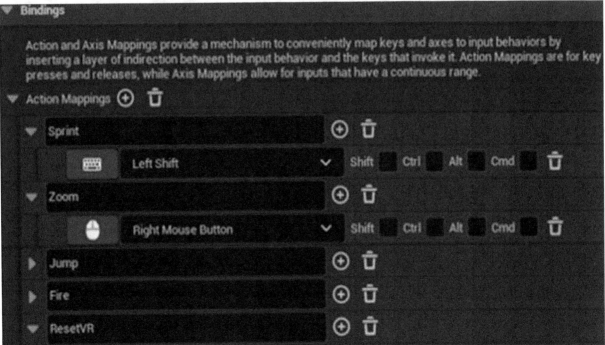

101

ADDING A SPRINT ABILITY

Since you've understood how the movement input nodes translate controller input to our in-game character, we'll extend that functionality with a Sprint ability. We'll configure a new series of nodes within the FirstPersonCharacter Blueprint, as shown in the figure below:

We have to add the Event that will activate our Sprint Action first. Remember that we previously mapped the **Sprint** Action to the **Left Shift key**. To add the Event, follow these steps:

1) Right-click in the empty grid space to the left of the other movement functions and search for "**Sprint**". Choose the **Sprint** Event to place the node.

2) Go to the **Components** panel of the Blueprint Editor, and select **Character Movement (CharMoveComp).** The **Details** panel displays a long list of variables related to movement, as shown in the diagram below:

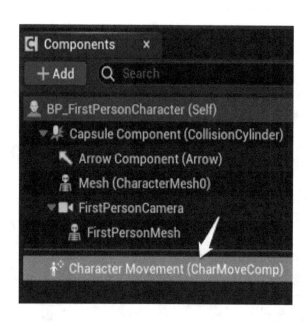
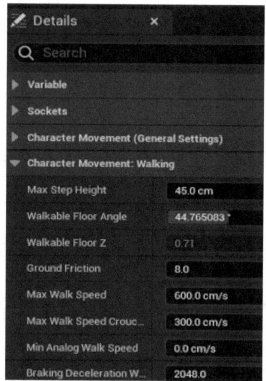

In this list, look for **Max Walk Speed** in the **Walking** category. This value controls the maximum speed at which the player can move. We need this to be the target of our **Sprint** function. Nevertheless, altering this value directly in the **Details** panel from the default of **600** would consistently modify the player's movement speed, irrespective of whether the **Left Shift** key is pressed. rather, we will drag this value out of the **Character Movement** Component and place it in Blueprint's **Event Graph.**

3) Click on the **Character Movement** Component in the Components panel and drag it onto the **Event Graph** near our **InputAction Sprint** Event. This will create a **Character Movement** node as illustrated below.

4) Click and drag the output pin from the Character Movement node to an empty grid space, then type "**Walk Speed**". Choose the "**Set Max Walk Speed**" option. This connects the **Character Movement** node to the new node, allowing you to set the maximum walk speed value.

5) Join the **Pressed** output execution pin from the **InputAction Sprint** trigger to the input execution pin of the **Set Max Walk Speed** node. This enables the **Left Shift** key to modify the maximum movement speed.

6) Change the **Max Walk Speed** value within the node from **0.0** to **2000** to provide a significant speed boost.

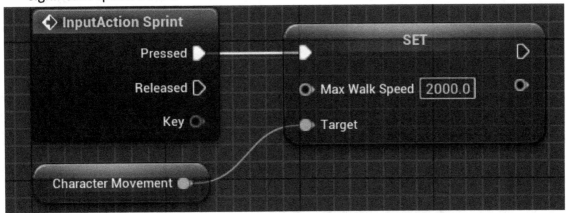

You should ensure the player slows down again once the **Shift** key is released. To do this:

7) Drag the output pin from the **Character Movement** node again, search for and select another "**Set Max Walk Speed**" node, and put it on the **Event Graph**. Join the **Released** output execution pin of the **InputAction Sprint** node with the input execution pin of the new node. Change the **Max Walk Speed** value back to the default of **600**.

To comply with good commenting practice, click and make a selection box across all four nodes, right-click on one of the selected nodes, select "**Create Comment from Selection**" and name the group of nodes **Sprint**.

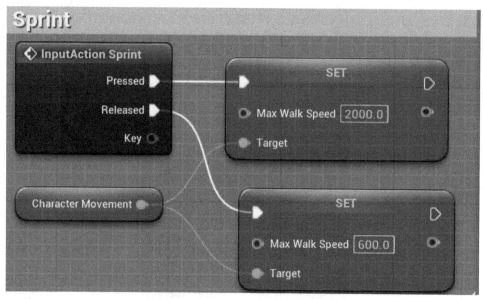

8) **Compile**, **save**, and press the **Play** button to test your work. You should observe a great boost in speed when you press the **Left Shift** key.

We have learned how to map a keypress to an **Action** and adjust the max speed of the character to simulate a sprint ability. Your next step is to add a feature that allows the player to have a closer view of a target.

ANIMATING A ZOOMED VIEW

A major element of recent first-person shooters is a variable field of view (FOV) that allows players to look down the scope of a gun for a clearer view of a target. This functionality significantly enhances the feeling of correctness and control. Next, we will add a basic version of this feature to our prototype by following these steps:

1) In an empty section of the grid beside the **Mouse input** nodes, right-click, and search for "**zoom**," to add a **Zoom** Event node.

2) To modify the **FOV** value within the First-Person Camera Component, go to the **Components** panel and drag the **First Person Camera** to the **Event Graph**.

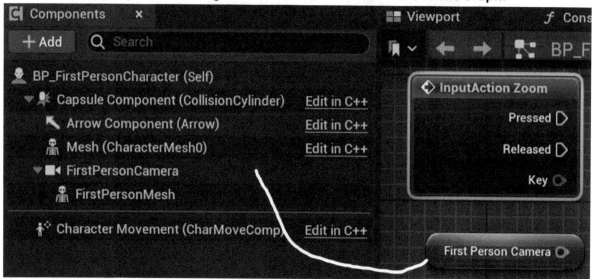

3) Drag the output pin of the **First Person Camera** node to an empty grid space, search for the "**Set Field of View**" node, and select it. Reducing the **FOV** gives the effect of zooming in to the thinner area in the middle of the screen. Because the default **FOV** value is **90**, set the **FOV** in the **Set Field Of View** node to **45** as shown here.

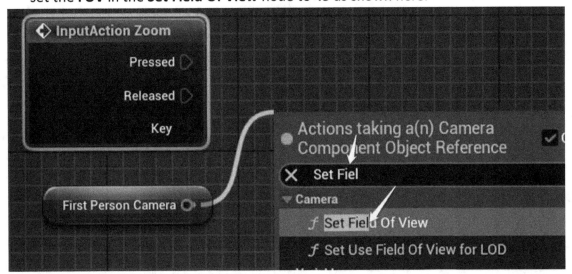

4) Click and drag the output execution pin from the **InputAction Zoom** node to the input execution pin of the **Set Field Of View** node.

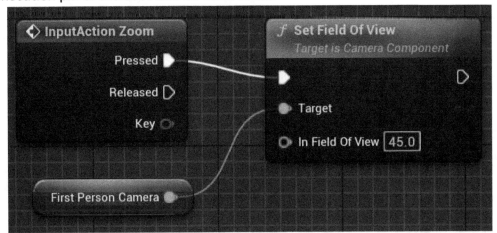

5) **Compile, save,** and click **Play.**

You will observe that when playing the game and pressing the right mouse button, the **FOV** snaps to a narrow, zoomed-in view.

However, the sudden snap from one position to another can be jarring for players, and the FOV does not revert when the key is released. We'll address both issues using a timeline in the next steps.

SMOOTHING TRANSITIONS WITH A TIMELINE

To alter the FOV smoothly, we'll create an animation that gradually changes the Actor's FOV in the long run. Follow these steps in the Event Graph of the **FirstPersonCharacter** Blueprint to achieve this:

1) Press **Alt** and click on the **Pressed** output execution pin of the **InputAction Zoom** node to break the connection.
2) Pull a new wire from the **Pressed** output execution pin to an empty grid space. Search for **"Add Timeline",** to add a timeline node.

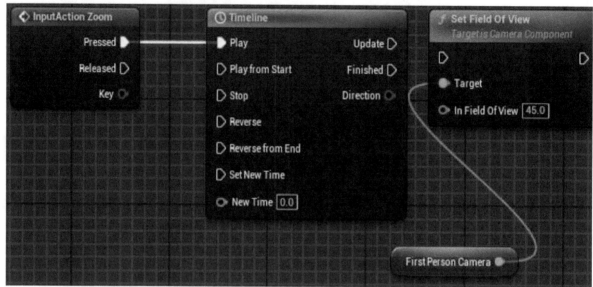

Hint: There are various ways to handle animations in Unreal Engine 5. Timelines are ideal for simple value changes, like the rotation of a door. For more intricate, character-based, or cinematic animations, consider using **Sequencer**, Unreal Engine's built-in animation system. While Sequencer and complex animations are beyond the scope of this book, there are many dedicated learning resources available. Start with the Unreal documentation at **https://docs.unrealengine.com/en-us/Engine/Sequencer).**

3) A timeline enables us to change a value (such as the FOV of a camera) over a chosen period. To edit the timeline, double-click on the **Timeline** node.

This opens the Timeline Editor. There are key buttons at the top right corner of the Timeline Editor.

4) Click on the **(+ Track)** button and choose **"Add Float Track"**. This adds a track to the timeline and prompts you to name this track.

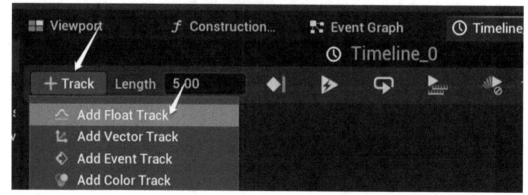

5) Name this track **"Field of View"**. This track will control the FOV value over time.
6) To adjust the values, hold down **Shift** and click near the **0.0** point on the graph. This displays the **Time** and **Value** fields in the upper-left area of the graph.

7) Confirm that the **Time** is set accurately to **0.0** and set the **Value** to **90**, which is the default FOV. Use the two tiny zoom buttons at the top-left of the graph to adjust the view if needed, ensuring the point is visible.

8) For a quick zoom animation, locate the field beside **Length** at the top of the **Timeline Editor**. Change the value to **0.3** seconds to limit the duration of the animation.

9) Press **Shift** and click at the end of the light gray part on the right side of the graph. Set the Time to **0.3** seconds and the Value to **45.**

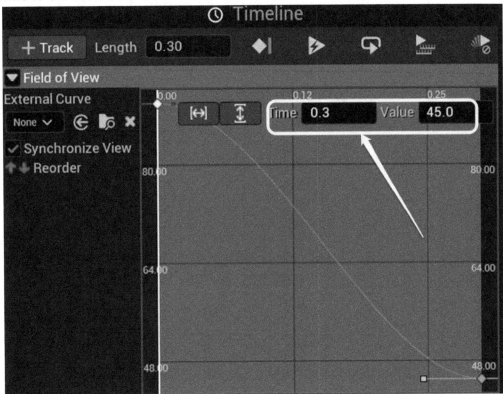

Notice how the line gradually slopes down from 90^0 to 45^0 degrees on the graph. This ensures that when the animation is triggered, the player's FOV smoothly transitions from zoomed out to zoomed in, avoiding a sudden switch between values. This is a key advantage of using timelines over direct value changes with Blueprints.

10) Return to the **Event Graph**. Join the output pin labeled "**Field Of View**" from the **Timeline node** to the In **Field Of View** input pin of the **Set Field of View** node. Additionally, join the **Update** output execution pin from the **Timeline** node to the **Set Field of View** node.

This setup ensures that every time the FOV value updates, it passes the new value to the **Set Field Of View** function. Due to the timeline setup, values between **90** and **45** will smoothly transition over the defined **0.3**-second duration.

11) To end the zoom effect when the right mouse button is released, drag the **Released** pin from the **InputAction Zoom** node to the **Reverse** pin of the **Timeline** node. This causes the timeline animation to play in reverse when the right mouse button is released, smoothly transitioning back to the normal camera view. To maintain clarity in your Blueprint, apply a comment to the node group describing this functionality. This helps in understanding the purpose of the nodes when revisiting them later.

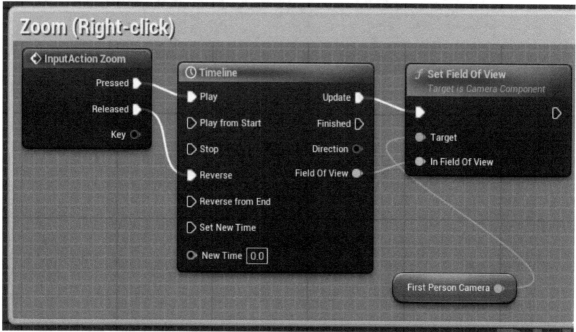

12) Lastly, **compile** and **save** your Blueprint. Press **Play** to test the transition in and out of the zoomed view by holding down the right mouse button.

You have successfully implemented a smooth animation for zooming in and out using Unreal Engine's timeline functionality. Next, you can proceed to make adjustments to the **FirstPersonProjectile** Blueprint to further enhance your project.

RAISING PROJECTILE SPEED

Since you've added a new gameplay option for player movement, let's refine the shooting mechanics by improving the projectile speed. Currently, the shots fired from the gun arc slowly through the air, resembling spheres. To achieve a more realistic representation of fast-moving bullets found in traditional shooters, follow these steps:

1) Open the Blueprint named **FirstPersonProjectile** located in the **Content** > **FirstPerson** > **Blueprints** folder. Go to the Blueprint Editor, in the **Components** panel and select **Projectile**. This is a projectile movement **Component** added in the **FirstPersonProjectile** Blueprint to control how the sphere will travel immediately after it is created.

2) Go to the Details panel, there is a Projectile with a long list of variables to define its movement. We will only be checking a few of them:

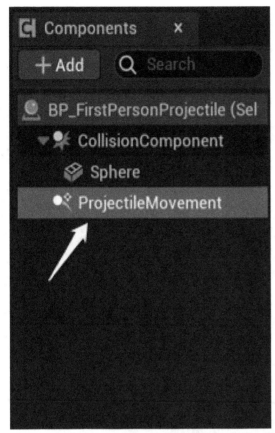 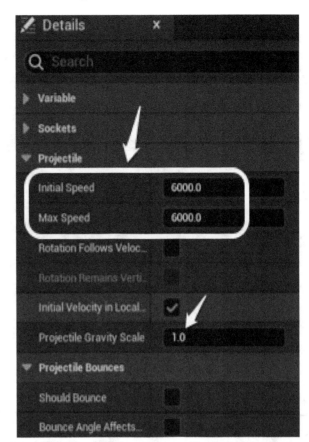

✓ **Initial Speed and Max Speed:** These fields are presently set to **3000**. **Initial Speed** controls the projectile's velocity when it's first spawned at the gun's tip, while **Max Speed** defines its potential maximum velocity if further acceleration is applied after creation. For a bullet fired from a gun, it's logical to set both values to their maximum potential speed. Increase both **Initial Speed** and **Max Speed** to **6000**.

✓ **Projectile Gravity Scale:** Currently set to 1.0, this value dictates how much gravity affects the projectile. To simulate a light bullet that isn't significantly affected by gravity, lower the Projectile Gravity Scale to 0.1.

By adjusting these parameters, the projectile fired from the gun will move faster and be less influenced by gravity, creating a more realistic and dynamic shooting experience in your game.

In addition to enhancing the projectile speed, you may have noticed that the current projectile behaves like a rubber ball, bouncing off walls and objects. To simulate a more impactful and realistic projectile, follow these steps:

3) In the **FirstPersonProjectile** Blueprint, locate the **Projectile Bounces** section in the **Details** panel. **Uncheck** the box beside the **Should Bounce**. This prevents the projectile from bouncing off surfaces.

The other settings within the Projectile Bounces section are relevant only when Should Bounce is checked, so no further adjustments are necessary.

4) Within the **Event Graph** of the **FirstPersonProjectile** Blueprint, Join the **False** pin of the **Branch** node to the **DestroyActor** function. This ensures that the projectile is destroyed upon collision with any object or surface.

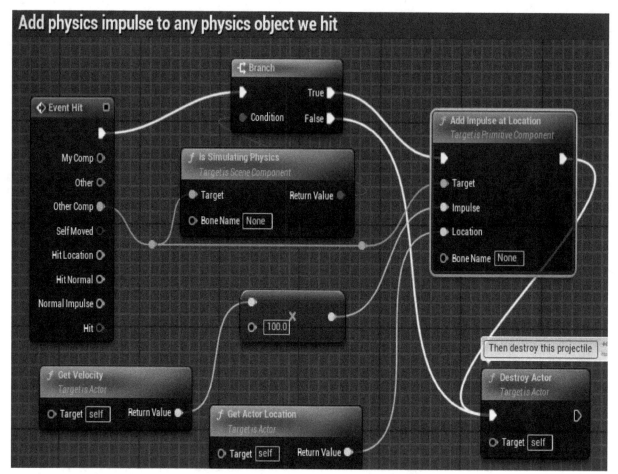

5) **Compile** and **save** your Blueprint changes. Click on **Play** to test the modifications. You will observe that firing the gun now results in a faster projectile that travels farther without bouncing off walls.

By adjusting the projectile speed and disabling bouncing, we have simulated a bullet-like behavior for the projectile. Next, we will adjust the **BP_CylinderTarget** Blueprint to incorporate an explosion effect upon its destruction.

ENHANCING ENEMY INTERACTION WITH SOUND AND PARTICLE EFFECTS

With the player's movement and shooting mechanics refined, let's enhance the interaction with enemy targets. Currently, shooting a target Cylinder changes its color to blue, but there's no mechanism to destroy it completely.

To add more dynamics to the enemy interaction:

Create Blueprint logic that enables the target to be destroyed when shot multiple times. This involves setting up conditions within the BP_CylinderTarget Blueprint to detect when it has been hit enough times to trigger destruction.

Upon destruction of the target, enhance the player's experience by incorporating:

✓ **Sound Effects**: Integrate satisfying sound effects that signify the destruction of the target. This can include explosion sounds or any other audio cue that complements the gameplay.

110

✓ **Particle Effects:** Implement visual effects such as explosions or particle bursts at the location of the destroyed target. These effects provide immediate visual feedback to the player, reinforcing the impact of their actions.

USING BRANCHES TO CHANGE TARGET STATES

To enhance the behavior of the target Cylinder in response to player actions, follow these steps within the BP_CylinderTarget Blueprint:

1) Go to the **Content > FirstPerson > Blueprints** folder and open the **BP_CylinderTarget** Blueprint. Locate the node group connected to **Event Hit,** which currently changes the Cylinder's material to blue upon hitting with the projectile

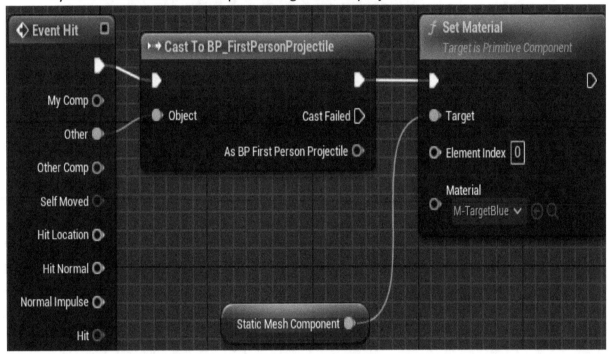

2) To introduce a mechanism where the Cylinder's behavior changes upon being hit multiple times, incorporate a Branch node:

The Branch node uses a Boolean variable as an input. It has two output execution pins: one for True and another for False.

3) Go to the **My Blueprint** panel, click the plus **(+)** sign to add a new **Boolean** variable, and title it **"Primed"**. This variable will indicate whether the target Cylinder has been hit and is primed for destruction with subsequent hits.

4) **Compile** and **Save** the Blueprint. Since we don't want our targets to be in a **Primed** state before when they will be hit for the first time. The default value is **False** (unchecked), indicating that the target is not primed initially.

5) Drag the **"Primed"** variable from the **My Blueprint** panel into the **Event Graph** and choose the **Get option** from the submenu option.

6) Pull a wire from the output pin of the **"Primed"** variable node to an empty space on the **Event Graph**. Search for a **Branch** node to add it to the **Event Graph**. This node will evaluate the value of the **"Primed"** variable to determine the subsequent actions.

7) Next, we can add **Branch** to our **Event Hit** Blueprint group. Break the connection between the **Set Material and Cast To BP-FirstPersonProjectile** nodes by pressing down the **Alt** key and clicking either of the execution pins.

8) Temporarily, drag the **Set Material** node out of the way and then join the execution pin of the **Cast To** node to the input execution pin of the Branch node. This Blueprint is now called Branch Evaluation whenever the projectile hits the target Cylinder.

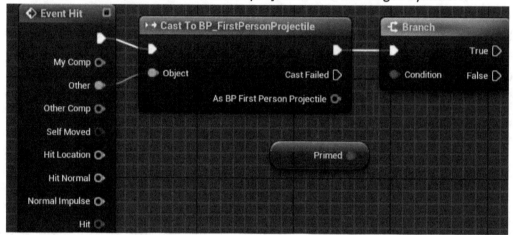

Since we have our **Branch** node configured now, we need to instruct the target Cylinder on what actions to take in each state. Specifically, we need to determine what happens when it is first hit (when the Primed variable is False) and what happens when it is hit a second time (when the Primed variable is True).

First, let's address the scenario when the target is hit for the first time. In this situation, we need to change the **Material** to **TargetBlue** and set the **Primed** Boolean variable to **True**. In this manner, when the target is hit again, the **Branch** node will direct the behavior to the **True** execution pin. The **False** execution sequence of nodes resembles this screenshot:

9) Move the **Set Material** node that you previously set aside to the right of the **Branch** node. Join the **False** output execution pin of the **Branch** node to the input execution pin of the **Set Material** node.

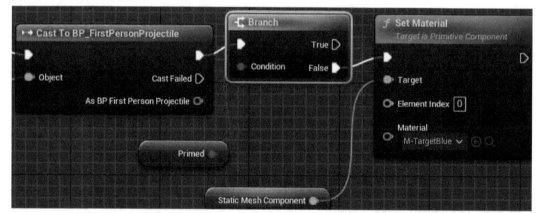

10) Drag the **Primed** variable from the **My Blueprint** panel to the **Event Graph**, and select the SET option. Join the **SET** node to the output execution pin of the **SET Material** node. Check the checkbox beside **Primed** within the **SET** node. This ensures that the next time the target is hit, the Branch will evaluate to True.

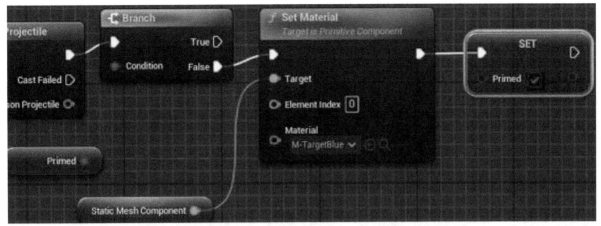

Having decided the actions for the False path of the Branch node, the next step is to outline the sequence of actions that will be triggered from the **True** path of the Branch node.

TRIGGERING SOUND EFFECTS, EXPLOSIONS, AND DESTRUCTION

When destroying a target in our game, we aim to achieve three things: hearing an explosion, seeing an explosion, and removing the target object from the game world. Let's start with a frequently underestimated but vital aspect of a satisfying game experience: sound.

To create a basic interaction with sound, we'll play a .wav sound file at a specific location in the game world. This simple approach works perfectly for our needs. Here's how to do it:

1) Pull a wire from the **True** execution node of the **Branch** node to an empty space in the grid. Search for and select the "**Play Sound at Location**" node.

The "**Play Sound at Location**" node receives a **Sound** file input and a **Location** input. As the name suggests, it plays the sound at the specified location. The Starter Content includes numerous sound files.

2) By clicking on the drop-down menu under the **Sound** input, you can see the available options. Select "**Explosion02**" to set the explosion sound effect.

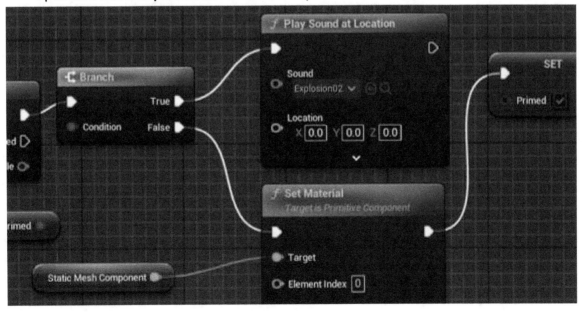

Next, we need to determine where the sound will play. You can do this by using the location of the Static Mesh Component of the Cylinder target. Extract its location value and link that location vector directly to our Sound node. Nevertheless, using the **Event Hit** trigger will simplify this process for us.

One of the several output pins on the **Event Hit** node is named **Hit Location**. This pin indicates the specific point in space where the two objects assessed by the **Event Hit** collide. It represents the exact spot where our projectile makes contact with its target, making it an ideal location to trigger an explosion effect. To connect this,

3) simply Pull a wire from the **Hit Location** pin of the **Event Hit** node to the **Location** input pin of the **Play Sound at Location** node.

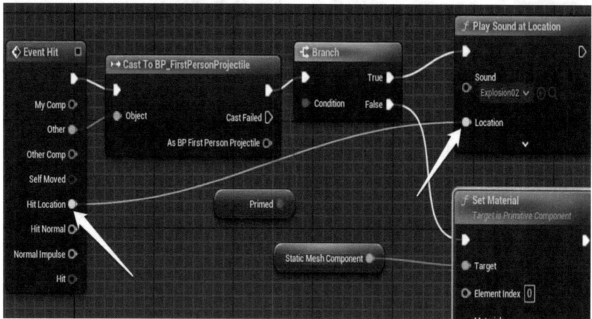

After making these connections, **compile** your Blueprint, **save** it, and test it by **playing**. Shooting one of the moving targets will turn it blue upon impact. Subsequent hits will trigger an explosion sound effect.

With the explosion sound set up, the next step involves adding the visual effect and destroying the Cylinder using the following steps:

4) Pull a wire from the output execution node of **Play Sound at Location** to an empty grid space. Search for and choose the **Spawn Emitter at Location** node.

Hint: An emitter is an object designed to create particle effects in a specific location. Particle effects consist of small elements that together produce visual effects of objects like fluid, gaseous, or intangible objects like waterfall splashes, explosions, or beams of light.

The Spawn **Emitter at Location** node resembles the **Sound** node we're linking it to, but it offers additional input parameters and an **Auto Destroy** switch.

5) From the dropdown menu under **Emitter Template**, locate and select the **P_Explosion** effect. This asset is part of the **Starter Content** included in our project and will generate a visually satisfying explosion wherever its emitter is placed.

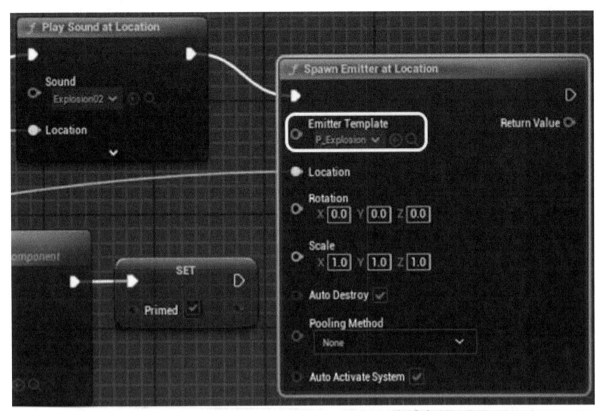

6) To ensure the explosion occurs exactly where the sound of the explosion originates, drag the **Hit Location** pin from the **Event Hit** node and drop it onto the **Location** pin of the **Spawn Emitter at Location.**

Since the explosion effect is 3D and looks the same from any angle, we can leave the **Rotation** input unchanged. The **Auto Destroy** switch decides if the emitter can be activated more than once. In our case, we'll destroy the Actor containing this emitter once the particle effect has been created, so we'll keep the **switch** checked.

7) Finally, after playing the sound and visual explosion effects, we want to remove the target Cylinder from the game world. Drag the output execution pin from the **Spawn Emitter at Location** node to an empty space on the grid. Search for and select the **DestroyActor** node. This node receives only a single **Target** input, which defaults to **'self'**, referencing the current instance.

8) Expand the **comment** box around the entire sequence of **Event Hit** nodes and update the description to reflect the actions of this new sequence. For example, I selected *"When hit, turn red and set to primed. If it is primed already, destroy self"*. Ensure the sequence of nodes matches the screenshot provided.

After you have dropped helpful comments around the Blueprint nodes, compile, save, and click the Play button to examine the new interactions. You should hear and see the Cylinders explode once they have been shot two times by the player's gun.

CHAPTER SIX
WORKING WITH SCREEN UI ELEMENTS

In any gaming experience, effectively communicating the game's goals and rules to the player is essential. One common method used by game designers to achieve this is through a Graphical User Interface (GUI). A GUI displays crucial information to the player, ensuring they understand and engage with the game.

In this chapter, we will design a GUI that tracks the player's health and stamina and displays counters for targets eliminated and ammo. You'll learn how to configure a basic User Interface (UI) using Unreal Engine GUI Editor and how to link that interface to gameplay values using Blueprints. We'll create UI elements with the **Unreal Motion Graphics (UMG)** UI Designer.

USING UMG TO CREATE SIMPLE UI METERS

We'll explore how to use the **UMG** Editor to create and position the UI elements for our game.

The UMG Editor is a visual tool for designing user interfaces. With it, we can create **menus** and a **Heads-Up Display (HUD)**. A HUD is a transparent display that offers information without asking the user to look away from the major view. This concept was originally developed for military aviation. In gaming, the term HUD has become commonplace because it displays information directly on the game screen. Our goal is to show meters on the HUD that reflect the player's current health and stamina. These meters are referred to as UI meters.

To create a HUD that displays the health and stamina UI meters, we'll first have to create variables within the player character to track these values. We'll also set up variables to count the targets eliminated and the player's ammo.

Create the necessary variables with the following steps:

1) In the Content Browser, go to the **Content > FirstPerson > Blueprints** folder. Double-click on the "**FirstPersonCharacter**" Blueprint.
2) In the Blueprint Editor, locate the **Variables** category in the **My Blueprint** panel. Click the plus (**+**) sign to add a variable, title it "**PlayerHealth**" and change the **Variable Type** to "**Float**".
3) Repeat the same steps to create another Float variable. Name this one "**PlayerStamina**".
4) Create a third variable, but this time select "**Integer**" as the **Variable Type** title it "**PlayerCurrentAmmo**". Lastly, create another **Integer** variable. Title it "**TargetsEliminated**". Your variables list should resemble this.

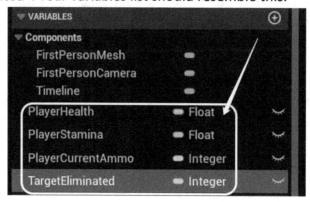

5) Compile the "**FirstPersonCharacter**" Blueprint. Choose the "**PlayerCurrentAmmo**" variable and set its **DEFAULT VALUE** to **30** in the Details panel:

6) Set the **DEFAULT VALUE** of "**PlayerStamina**" and "**PlayerHealth**" to **1.0**. These values will be used with the **UI** meters to display the fullness degree from **0.0** to **1.0**. The "**TargetsEliminated**" variable's **DEFAULT VALUE** should automatically be set to **0**, which is appropriate and doesn't need adjusting.

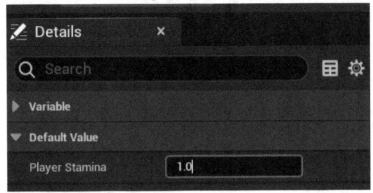

7) **Compile**, then **save**, and **close** the Blueprint Editor.

Next, we will check how to draw shapes that symbolize UI meters.

USING WIDGET BLUEPRINTS TO DRAW SHAPES

The UMG Editor uses a specialized type of Blueprint known as a **Widget Blueprint**. Because the **First Person** template doesn't have any User-Interface elements by default, we need to create a new folder to store our GUI work. Create a folder and a Widget Blueprint with the following steps:

1) In the Content Browser, go to the **Content** > **FirstPerson** folder. Right-click in an empty space beside the list of folders and select the "**New Folder**" option. Label the folder **User-Interface**

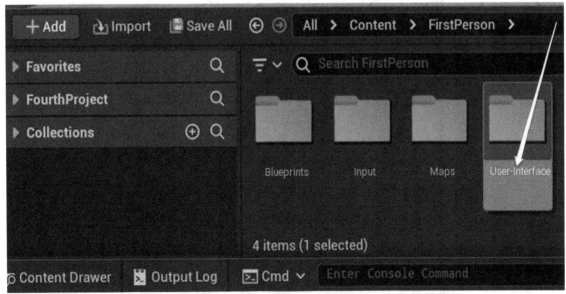

2) Open the "**User-Interface**" folder you just created. Right-click in the empty folder space, and navigate to **User Interface** > "**Widget Blueprint**". Title the resultant Blueprint "**HUD**".

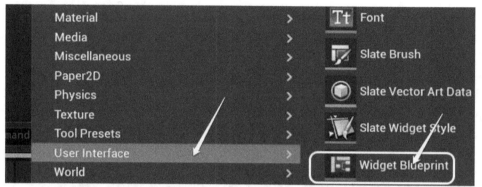

3) Double-click on the "**HUD**" Blueprint to open the UMG Editor. You will use this tool to decide how your **User-Interface** will appear on the screen.

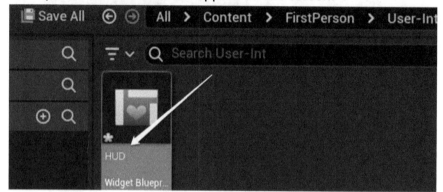

4) In the UMG Editor, locate the **Panel** named **Palette**. Open the grouping named "**PANEL**" inside the **Palette**. You will see several containers listed that can organize **User-Interface** information.

5) Select and drag the **Canvas Panel** object to the **Hierarchy** panel.

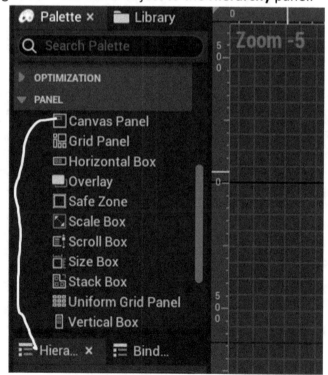

6) Select and drag "**Horizontal Box**" from the **Palette** panel to the **Hierarchy** panel, releasing it in the **Canvas Panel** object. Click on "**Horizontal Box**" below the **Canvas Panel** to select it. In the **Details** panel on the right side of the **Editor**, rename the "**Horizontal Box**" to "**Player Statics**".

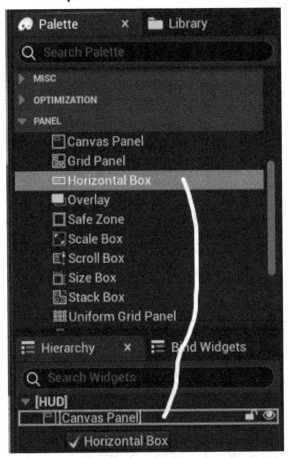
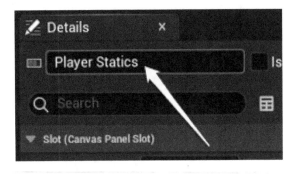

7) You will now see the "**Player Statics**" horizontal box fixed under the "**Canvas Panel**" object in the **Hierarchy** panel. Our objective is to create two labeled **Player Statics** bars using a combination of vertical boxes, text, and progress bars.

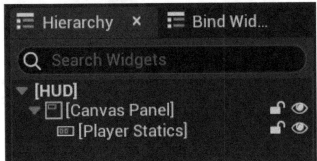

8) Look in the "**Panel**" category within the **Palette** panel. Drag a "**Vertical Box**" object into the "**Player Statics**" horizontal box in the **Hierarchy** panel and rename it "**Player Statics Texts**". Repeat this step to add another "**Vertical Box**" under "**Player Statics**" and rename it "**Player Statics Bars**".

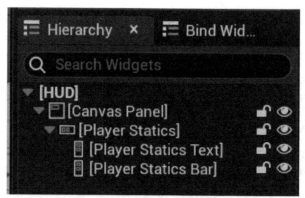

9) Go to the **Palette** panel, and switch to the "**Common**" category to find the **textboxes** and **progress bars** needed for the **User-Interface** creation. Drag two "**Text**" objects into "**Player Stats Texts**". Drag two "**Progress Bar**" objects onto "**Player Stats Bars**".

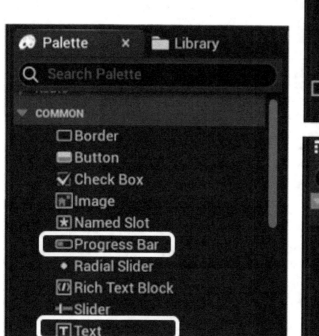

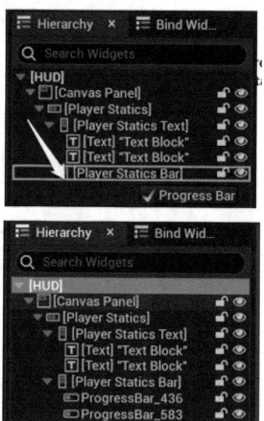

Now, we have the User-Interface elements necessary to display Player Stats in our HUD. Next, we will adjust their appearance and positions on the screen.

CUSTOMIZING THE METER'S APPEARANCE

Currently, we need to adjust the UI elements and arrange them on the screen. The large rectangular outline in the **Graph** view represents the borders of the screen that the player will see, known as the **canvas**. This is the "**Canvas Panel**" object at the upper level of the Hierarchy. Elements placed toward the upper-left corner of the canvas will appear in the upper-left corner of the in-game screen.

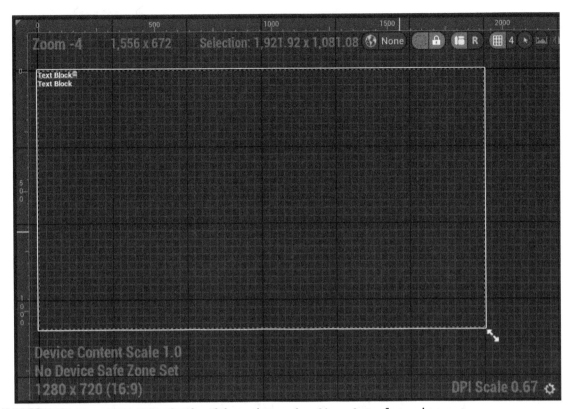

Follow these steps to set up the **health** and **stamina User-Interface** elements:

1) Choose the "**Player Statics**" from the **Hierarchy** and study the central graph panel. You'll notice size controls that allow you to adjust the size of the selected objects with the mouse. Go to the **Details** panel, and specify the position and size of the "**Player Statics**" horizontal box as follows:
   - ✓ **Position X:** 60.0
   - ✓ **Position Y:** 35.0
   - ✓ **Size X:** 500.0
   - ✓ **Size Y:** 80.0

2) In the **Hierarchy** panel, choose the first **progress bar** below "**Player Statics Bars**". Go to the **Details** panel, and rename it to "**Health Bar**". Below the **SLOT** category, click the "**Fill**" button in the **Size** field to alter the vertical height of the bar.

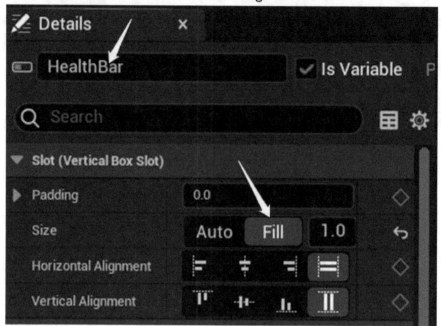

3) Go to the **Details** panel, and find the "**Fill Color and Opacity**" option under the **APPEARANCE** category. Click on the colored rectangle to access the **Color Picker** and choose any **blue** color.

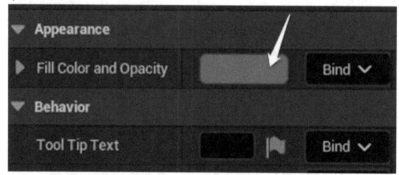

4) Go to the **Hierarchy** panel, and click on the **second progress** bar. Go to the **Details** panel, and rename it to "**Stamina Bar**". Click on the "**Fill**" button to adjust the size. Under "**Fill Color and Opacity**", choose any **magenta** color.

5) Go to the **Hierarchy** panel, and select the "**Player Statics Bars**" vertical box. Go to the **Details** panel, and click the "**Fill**" button to scale the horizontal size of both bars.

6) Next, we will modify the text labels. Go to the **Hierarchy** panel, and click on the first text object under "**Player Statics Texts**". Go to the **Details** panel, and rename it to "**Health Tag**".

7) Click the "**Right Align Horizontally**" button beside **Horizontal Alignment** to position the text against the bar. Change the "**Text**" field below the **CONTENT** category to "Health". If you desire to adjust the font size or style, adjust it from the **Font** drop-down menu and fields under the **APPEARANCE** category.

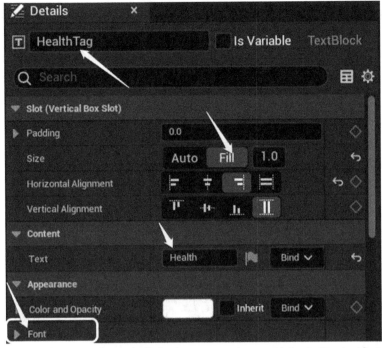

8) Go to the **Hierarchy** panel, and click the second text object. Go to the **Details** panel, and rename it to "**Stamina Tag**."

9) Click the "**Right Align Horizontally**" button beside the **Horizontal Alignment** to position the text against the bar. Change the "**Text**" field to "**Stamina**" and modify the font size and style if desired.

To ensure the UI elements remain in the same relative position on the screen, we need to anchor them. **Anchors** keep widgets in place regardless of screen size or ratio.

10) Choose the "**Player Statics**" top-level object. In the **Details** panel, click the "**Anchors**" dropdown and choose the **first** option, which shows a gray rectangle at the upper-left corner of the screen.

This will anchor the meters to the upper-left corner, ensuring they always appear in that position irrespective of the resolution or aspect ratio.

You can experiment with the progress bars by adjusting the "**Percent**" property in the **PROGRESS** category. The range of "**Percent**" values is from **0.0** (empty) to **1.0** (full). Do this for both the **Health Bar** and **Stamina Bar**.

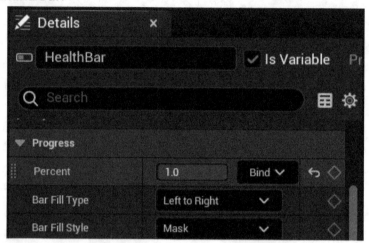

The following screenshot shows the progress bars with the Percent set to 1.0:

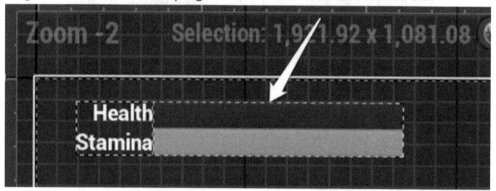

When the customization of health and stamina User-Interface elements is completed. The configuration should look like this:

Next, you will create text elements for displaying the ammo and target eliminated counters.

CONSTRUCTING AMMO AND TARGETS ELIMINATED COUNTERS

The ammo and targets eliminated counters display will function similarly to our player statistics meters, but instead of using continuous meters, we will display these values as text.

To focus on the **Weapon Statics and Goal Tracker** elements, **Player Statics** is minimized. Create the next User-Interface elements with the following steps:

1) Select and drag "**Horizontal Box**" from the **Palette** panel to the **Hierarchy** panel, releasing it at the top of the **Canvas Panel** object. Go to the **Details** panel, and rename the **Horizontal Box** to "**Weapon Statics**".

2) We will position the "**Weapon Statics**" horizontal box at the upper-right side of the screen. Go to the **Details** panel, click the "**Anchors**" dropdown, choose the **third** option, and set the following properties:
   - ✓ **Position X**: -200.0
   - ✓ **Position Y**: 30.0
   - ✓ **Size X**: 165.0
   - ✓ **Size Y**: 40.0

3) Drag a "**Text**" object to "**Weapon Statics**". Go to the **Details** panel, and rename it to "**Ammo Tag**". Adjust the "**Text**" field under the **CONTENT** category to "**Ammo:**" (add it along with the colon).

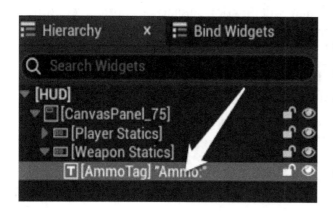

4) Drag another "**Text**" object to "**Weapon Statics**". Go to the **Details** panel, and rename it to "**Ammo Left**". The value of this element will be altered as ammo is utilized though we can attach a default value to it to visualize on the UMG Editor. Because we have specified **30** as the default ammo variable on the player Blueprint, you can move on to alter the **Text** value of **Ammo left** to **30** also.

5) Choose "**Weapon Statics**" in the **Hierarchy** panel. The icon that resembles a **flower** is the **Anchor Decoration**, indicating the anchor position of the selected element on the canvas panel.

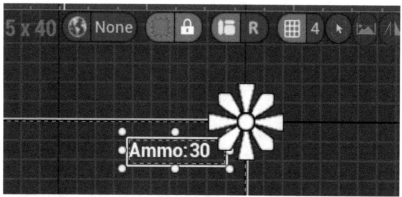

6) You will use similar steps for the goal tracker. Drag a "**Horizontal Box**" from the **Palette** panel to the **Hierarchy** panel, releasing it at the top of the **Canvas Panel** object. Go to the **Details** panel, and rename the "**Horizontal Box**" to "**Goal Tracker**".

7) To position the "**Goal Tracker**" horizontal box at the upper-center of the screen. Go to the **Details** panel, click on the **Anchors** dropdown, and choose the **second** option. Then set the following properties:
   ✓ **Position X**: -100.0, Size X: 100
   ✓ **Position Y**: 60.0, Size Y: 30

8) Tick the "**Size To Content**" checkbox so that the size of this horizontal box automatically adjusts based on its child elements.

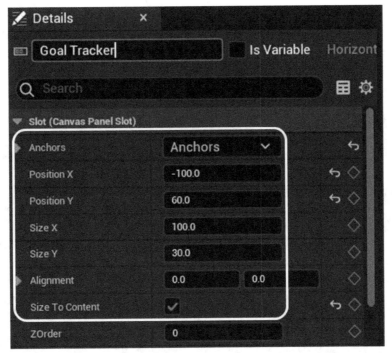

9) Drag a "**Text**" object to the "**Goal Tracker**". Go to the **Details** panel, and rename it to "**Targets Tag**". Change the "**Text**" field in the **CONTENT** category to "**Targets Eliminated**:" (add it along with the colon).

10) To make the text stand out, increase the font size of the **Text** objects in "**Goal Tracker**". In the **APPEARANCE** category of the **Details** panel, alter the **Font size** to **3**.

11) Drag another "**Text**" object to the "**Goal Tracker**". Rename it to "**Target Count**" in the Details panel. Set the "**Text**" field under the **CONTENT** category to "**0**" and adjust the **Font size** to **34** to match the style. Your Goal Tracker should resemble this:

12) Compile and save the HUD Widget Blueprint. Close the HUD Widget Blueprint editor. Your Goal Tracker should resemble the screenshot below:

With the User-Interface elements now aligned and styled as desired, the next step is to ensure that the game knows how to display this HUD. This involves revisiting the Character Blueprint.

HOW TO DISPLAY HUD

The following steps show how to display the HUD in your game:

1) Go to the **Content > FirstPerson > Blueprints** folder in the Content Browser and double-click the "**FirstPersonCharacter**" Blueprint to open it.
2) To locate and modify the "**Event BeginPlay**" function in the EventGraph. I will teach you another simple method to add an "**Event BeginPlay**". In the **My Blueprint** panel, under the **Graphs** category, double-click the "**Event BeginPlay**". The Editor will shift to the location in the **Event Graph** where the Event BeginPlay is already positioned.

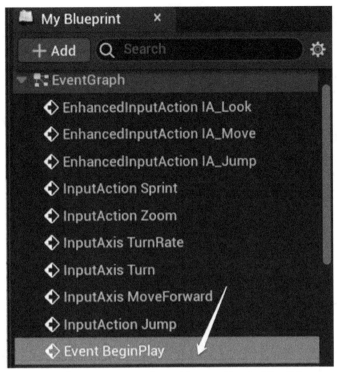

3) Delete any previous nodes connected to "**Event BeginPlay**" because they are related to the VR gameplay setup. These nodes are unnecessary for our example game and won't be used.

Hint: Event BeginPlay triggers actions as soon as the game starts or when the Blueprint instance spawns. Because the "**FirstPersonCharacter**" player instance is present immediately after the game starts, attaching the display logic to this event will promptly create the HUD.

4) Go to the **EventGraph** of the "**FirstPersonCharacter**" Blueprint, and pull a wire from the output execution pin of "**Event BeginPlay**" to add a "**Create Widget**" node. Within this node, locate the **Class** dropdown menu and choose the "**HUD**" option from the dropdown menu. This refers to the Widget Blueprint named **HUD** that we previously created. When you select it, the player Character Blueprint will generate the User-Interface elements you created. The diagram below shows the **Create HUD Widget** node connected with our HUD Widget Blueprint:

5) After configuring the "**Create Widget**" node, pull a wire from the "**Return Value**" output pin to an empty space in the graph to add an "**Add to Viewport**" node.

129

6) Surround these three nodes (**Create Widget, Event BeginPlay,** and **Add to Viewport**) with a comment box. Title the comment "**Sketch HUD on Screen**".

7) After organizing the nodes, **compile** and **save** your changes. Click on **Play** to test the game.

During gameplay, you should now see the two meters signifying the health and stamina meters, along with numerical counters for ammo and eliminated targets on the screen. However, you may notice that these values do not update as you shoot. We will address this issue in the next section.

CONNECTING USER-INTERFACE VALUES TO PLAYER VARIABLES

To ensure our User-Interface elements reflect player data dynamically, we'll create bindings between our player variables and the HUD Widget Blueprint. Rather than manually updating both the player's health stats and our Widget whenever the player takes damage (to let the health meter display changes), we may bind the meter to the PlayerHealth player variable. Afterward, only the value will need to be updated.

CREATING BINDINGS FOR HEALTH AND STAMINA

Follow these steps to establish bindings for the "**PlayerHealth**" and "**PlayerStamina**" variables with the **User-Interface** progress bars:

1) Go to the **Content > FirstPerson > User-Interface** folder in the Content Browser. Double-click the "**HUD**" Widget Blueprint to open it in the UMG Editor.
2) In the **HUD UMG** Editor, locate the "**Hierarchy**" panel and select the "**Health Bar**" object nested under "**Player Statics Bars**".

3) In the **Details** panel, find the "**Percent**" field under the **Progress** category. Click the "**Bind**" button beside **Percent** and choose "**Create Binding**".

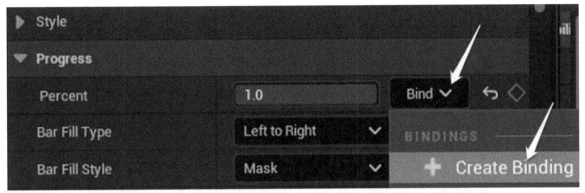

4) The **UMG Editor** will switch from **Designer View** to **Graph View** where a new function is created for the binding.

5) Right-click in the empty area in the graph view to add a "**Get Player Character**" node. Pull a wire from the "**Return Value**" output of the "**Get Player Character**" node to an empty space to add a "**Cast To BP_FirstPersonCharacter**" node.

6) Break the execution pin link between the "**Get Health Bar Percent**" and **Return Node** nodes and then connect **Get Health Bar Percent** to our casting nodes illustrated below.

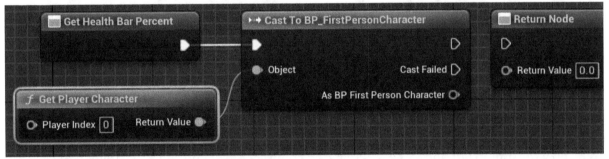

7) Pull a wire from the "**As BP_First Person Character**" output pin to an empty space to add a "**Get Player Health**" node. Then connect the "**Cast To BP_FirstPersonCharacter**" node's execution pin to the "**Return Value**" node.

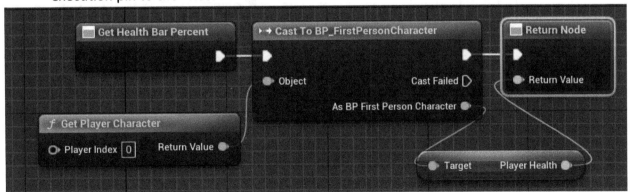

8) These are the steps we need to take to join **Player Health** to the **Health Bar** User Interface. You have to follow similar steps as above to join the "**Player Stamina**" to the "**Stamina Bar**" User-Interface element. Return to the **Canvas** view by clicking the "**Designer**" button at the upper-right of the screen.

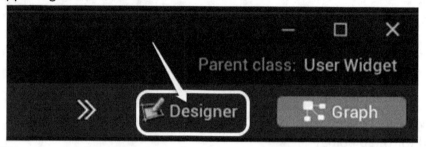

9) Select "**Stamina Bar**" in the **Hierarchy** panel. Repeat the steps outlined for the "**Health Bar**" to create a binding that uses the "**Player Stamina**" variable to the meter.

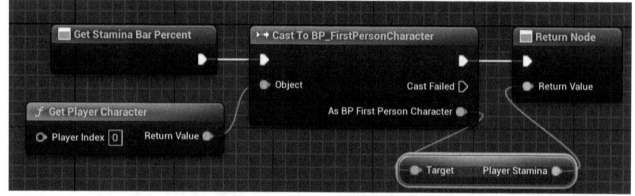

10) Once both bindings are set up, **compile** and **save** your work to ensure the changes are applied correctly.

Next, we'll proceed to connect the User-Interface elements for ammo and goal counters to complete the HUD functionality.

CREATING TEXT BINDINGS FOR AMMO AND TARGETS ELIMINATED COUNTERS

To display the ammo left and targets eliminated counters as text on the HUD, follow these steps:

1) Click on the "**Designer**" button to switch back to the canvas interface. Locate the "**Ammo left**" text object under "**Weapon Stats**" in the **Hierarchy** panel.

2) Go to the **Details** panel of the "**Ammo left**" text object, and locate the "**Bind**" button beside the "**Text**" field. Click on "**Bind**" and select "**Create Binding**".

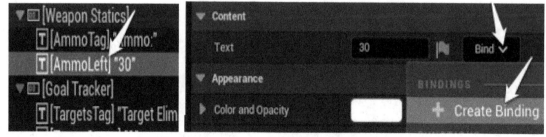

3) We will use the same method we adopted for health and stamina. Go to the **Graph** view that appears after creating the binding, and add a "**Get Player Character**" node. Cast the

output of "**Get Player Character**" using "**Cast To BP_FirstPersonCharacter**". Pull a wire from the "**As BP_First Person Character**" pin to add a "**Get Player Current Ammo**" node.

4) Lastly, Connect the output of a cast node and "**Player Current Ammo**" to the "**Return Node**". When you connect the output pin of "**Get Player Current Ammo**" to the "**Return Value**" input pin, Unreal Engine automatically creates a **ToText (integer)** node and links. This node converts the integer value of ammo into a text format that can be displayed on the HUD.

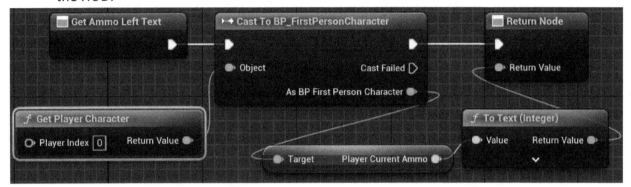

Note: Unreal Engine handles the conversion from integer **To Text** to ensure the numerical value is displayed correctly.

5) Next, we will create the last binding for the target count. Click on the "**Designer**" button to switch to the Canvas interface. Locate the "**Target Count**" text object under "**Goal Tracker**" in the **Hierarchy** panel. Go to the **Details** panel of the "**Target Count**" text object, and find the "**Bind**" button beside the "**Text**" field.

6) Click on "**Bind**" and select "**Create Binding**". Go to the **Graph** view that appears after creating the binding: Add a "**Get Player Character**" node and cast the output of "**Get Player Character**" using "**Cast To BP_FirstPersonCharacter**". Pull a wire from the "**As BP_First Person Character**" pin to add a "**Get Targets Eliminated**" node. Connect the output of "**Get Targets Eliminated**" to the "**Return Node**".

When you connect the output pin of "**Get Targets Eliminated**" to the "**Return Value**" input pin, Unreal Engine automatically creates a "**ToText (integer)**" node.

This node converts the integer value of targets eliminated into a text format that can be displayed on the HUD.

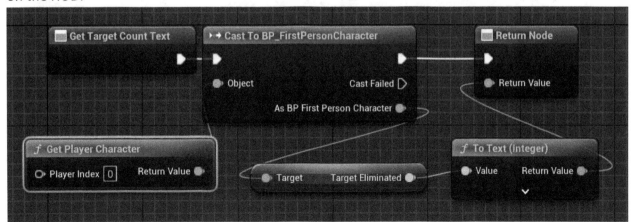

Note: Unreal Engine handles the conversion from integer **To Text** to ensure the numerical value is displayed correctly.

Compile and save your work to ensure all bindings are set up correctly. These bindings allow the HUD to respond appropriately to in-game events that affect the player's stats. In the next section, we will focus on implementing events that will update these variables based on player actions.

TRACKING AMMO AND TARGETS ELIMINATED

To enable our UI to reflect player interactions with the game world, we'll adjust the player and target Blueprints. Let's first focus on decreasing the ammo counter when the player fires their gun.

REDUCING THE AMMO COUNTER

To ensure the ammo counter decreases each time the player fires a shot, follow these steps:

1) Go to **Content > FirstPerson > Blueprints** folder in the **Content Browser**. Double-click the "**FirstPersonCharacter**" Blueprint to open it in the Blueprint Editor.

2) Inside the Blueprint, find the section of nodes related to **firing** projectiles. This is typically within a **comment block** labeled "**Spawn projectile**". Add nodes to decrease the player's current ammo count by one each time they fire a shot. The required Blueprints script should resemble this.

3) Locate the last node in the chain, **Play Sound at Location.** Pull a wire from the output execution pin of this node to the empty area and select a **SET Player Current Ammo** node.

4) Pull a wire from the **Play Current Ammo** input pin to the empty grid space and then create a **Subtract** node.

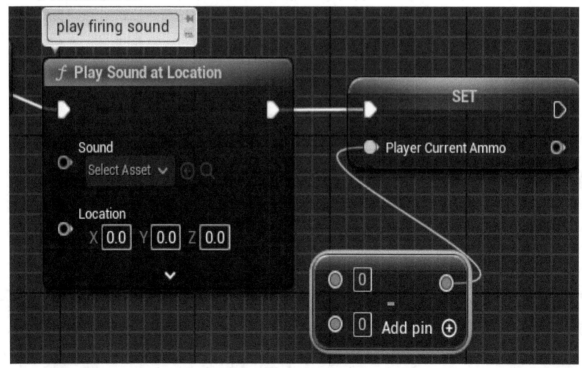

5) Pull a wire from the upper input pin of the "**Subtract**" node and select a "**Get Player Current Ammo**" node.

6) In the bottom field of the "**Subtract**" node, type "**1**". This ensures that each time the player fires, their current ammo count decreases by one.

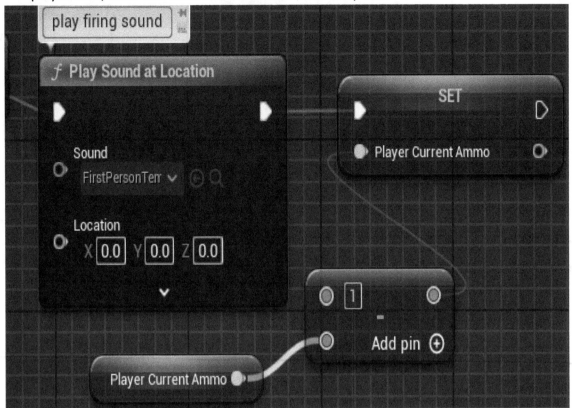

7) Once you've set up the nodes, compile the **Blueprint** and **save** your changes. Press the **Play** button to test your game. You should observe the ammo counter decreasing every time the player fires a shot. Note that the current setup allows the ammo counter to register negative numbers when the player continues to shoot after running out of ammo. This behavior will be addressed in Chapter 7, where constraints and gameplay objectives will be introduced.

Note: The Set Player Current Ammo node and the subtract node of the previous screenshot can be substituted by the Decrement Int node, which subtracts **1** from the input variable and specifies a new value in it. in the same way, there is an **Increment Int** node, which adds 1 to the input variable.

INCREASING THE TARGETS ELIMINATED COUNTER

To increase the targets eliminated counter by 1 each time a target Cylinder is destroyed, follow these steps carefully:

1) Go to **Content** > **FirstPerson** > **Blueprints** folder in the Content Browser and double-click on the "**BP_CylinderTarget**" Blueprint to open it in the Blueprint Editor.
2) You will add new nodes near the end of **Event Hit.** Inside the Blueprint, find the **Event Hit** node. Ensure that the nodes are added after all existing nodes except for "**DestroyActor**". "**DestroyActor**" must be the last node because it removes the current instance of the cylinder from the game world.

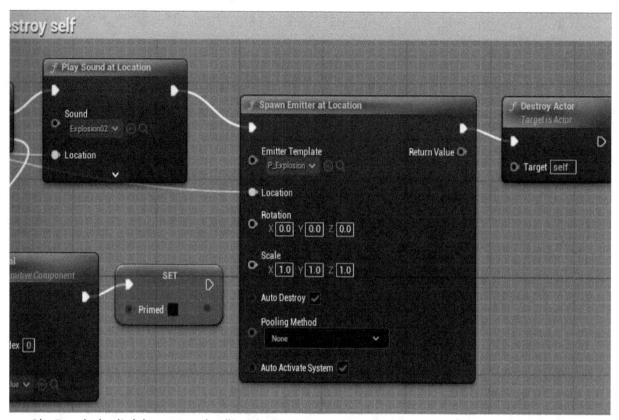

3) Break the link between the "**Spawn Emitter at Location**" and "**DestroyActor**" nodes. Then move the "**DestroyActor**" node to the right to create space for the new nodes.

4) You need to create a series of nodes that will open the **Targets Eliminated** variable from the player character and increase it by **1**, before moving to destroy the Actor. Right-click on an empty graph space to add a "**Get Player Character**" node.

5) Pull a wire from the "**Return Value**" output pin of the "**Get Player Character**" node to add a "**Cast To BP_FirstPersonCharacter**" node.

6) Pull a wire from the "**As BP_First Person Character**" pin to add a "**GET Targets Eliminated**" node.

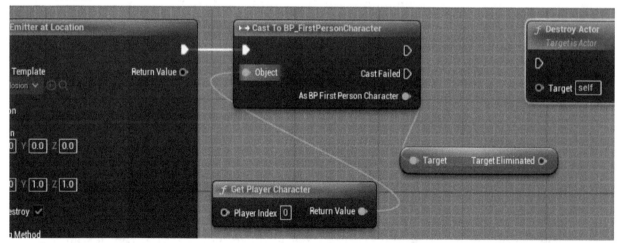

7) Pull a wire from the output pin of the "**GET Targets Eliminated**" node. Add an "**Increment Int**" node. This adds **1** to the **"Targets Eliminated"** variable.

8) Join the execution pins of the "Cast To BP_ FirstPersonCharacter", Increment Int, and DestroyActor nodes, certifying that **DestroyActor** is the last node in the chain. Your outcome should look like this.

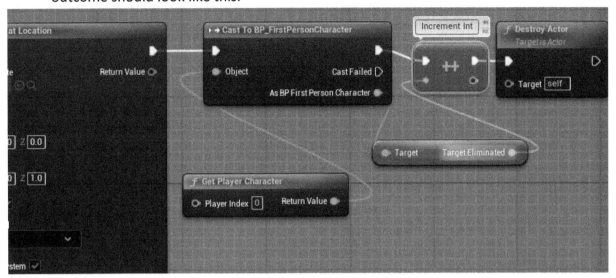

9) **Compile** your Blueprint, **save,** and **play** the game to see how the **Target Eliminated** counter increases each time you destroy a Cylinder target on the screen.

137

CHAPTER SEVEN
HANDLING CONSTRAINTS AND GAMEPLAY OBJECTIVES

Next, we'll establish the rules for our game, which will guide the player's journey through the gameplay experience. Our goal is to enable players to start the game and immediately understand what they need to do to win. At its core, a game is defined by its win condition and the steps players must take to achieve it. We aim to make each of those steps enjoyable and engaging.

To start, we'll introduce some constraints to raise the difficulty level. A game without challenges quickly loses its appeal, so we want every game mechanic to offer an interesting choice or challenge for the player. Next, we'll set a clear goal for the player to accomplish and adjust the enemy targets accordingly to ensure that reaching this goal is both challenging and rewarding.

By the end of this chapter, you'll have a game with well-defined constraints and goals that enhance the gameplay, making it more engaging. We'll dive into creating collectible objects and designing a menu system.

CONSTRAINING PLAYER ACTIONS

When adding new capabilities for the player, it's crucial to consider how these changes affect both the challenge and overall feel of the game. For instance, in Chapter 5, we introduced the sprint function, allowing the player to move faster by holding down the **Shift** key. However, without any constraints, the player could sprint continuously, which undermines our goal of providing meaningful choices.

Our intention with the sprint functionality was to offer more options, but if sprinting is too advantageous, it becomes the default choice, reducing the diversity of player decisions. It would be similar to simply increasing the player's base speed to match the sprint speed, eliminating the need for strategic use of sprinting.

To address this and other similar issues in our game prototype, we need to implement constraints that limit player abilities. This will enhance decision-making and ensure that every action has a meaningful impact on gameplay.

DRAINING AND RESTORING STAMINA

To add a stamina constraint to the player's sprinting ability, we'll return to the player character blueprint where we initially defined this ability. We'll create several variables to track whether the player is sprinting, the stamina cost of sprinting, and the stamina recharge rate.

Next, we'll set up a custom event that drains the player's stamina at a steady rate while they are sprinting and recharges it when they are not. Additionally, we'll create other variables and macros to keep the script organized.

CREATING THE VARIABLE

Create the necessary variables for the new stamina system as listed below:

1) Go to **Content** > **FirstPerson** > **Blueprints** folder in the Content Browser and double-click the **FirstPersonCharacter** Blueprint.

2) In the **Variables** category of the My **Blueprint** panel, click the plus (**+**) button to add a new variable. Go to the **Details** panel, label the variable "**IsSprinting**" and alter its **Variable Type** to **Boolean**.

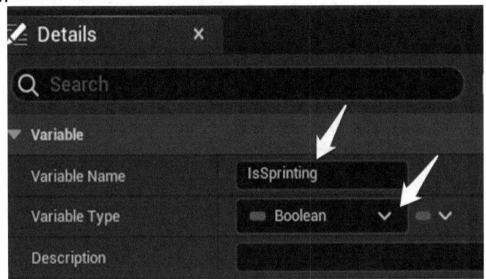

3) Create another **variable** in the **My Blueprint** panel, variable. In the **Details** panel, label the variable "**StaminaManagerName**" and alter its **Variable Type** to **String**. Compile the Blueprint and set the **Default Value** to **ManageStamina**.

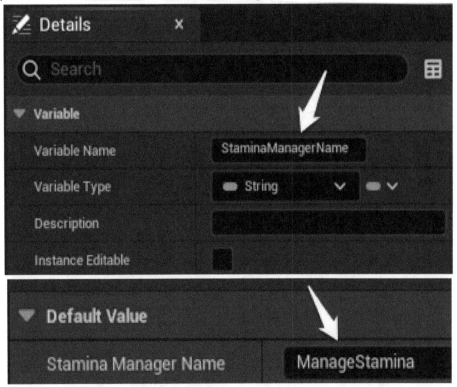

4) Now we'll create the necessary **Float** Variables. Go to the **Variables** category of the **My Blueprint** panel, and click the plus (**+**) button to add a new variable. Go to the **Details** panel, label the variable "**SprintCost**" and alter its **Variable Type** to **Float**. Compile the Blueprint and set the **DEFAULT VALUE** to **0.05.**

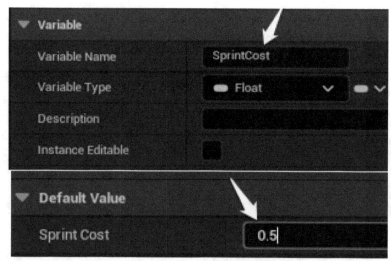

5) Use the same steps to create another **Float** variable titled "**StaminaRechargeRate**". Compile the Blueprint and set the **DEFAULT VALUE** to "**0.01**".

6) Next, create a **Float** variable titled "**StaminaDrainAndRechargeTime**". Compile the Blueprint and set the DEFAULT VALUE to **0.2**.

7) Then, create a Float variable titled "**WalkSpeed**". Compile the Blueprint and set the DEFAULT VALUE to **600**.

8) Finally, create a Float variable titled "**SprintSpeed**". Compile the Blueprint and set the DEFAULT VALUE to **2200**.

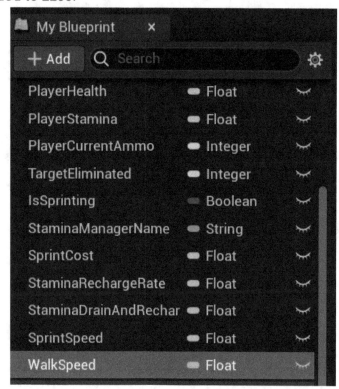

Creating the "**WalkSpeed**" and "**SprintSpeed**" variables allows us to easily adjust the speed values in one place, rather than searching through the script for the several instances where these values are used.

CREATING MACRO (STOPSPRINTING)

Next, we shall create our first **macro "StopSprinting"**. Follow these steps to create the macro:

1) Go to the **My Blueprint** panel, and click the plus (**+**) button in the **MACROS** category to create a new macro. Name this macro **StopSprinting**.

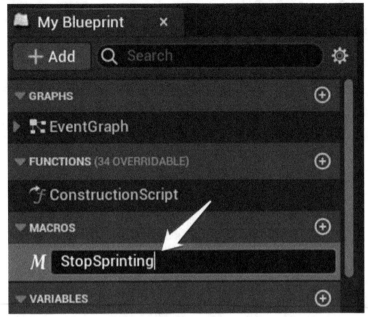

2) By default, the **macro** doesn't have execution pins, so we need to add them as parameters. In the **Details** panel of the macro, create an input parameter titled "**In**" of the **Exec** type and an output parameter named "**Out**" of the **Exec** type.

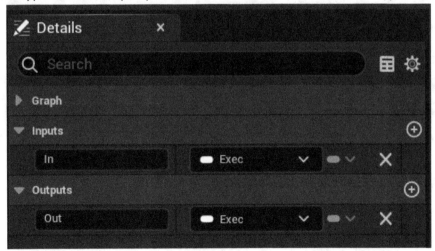

3) On the **StopSprinting** macro tab, you will add the necessary nodes to set "**IsSprinting**" to false and reset the **Max Walk Speed** to the value stored in the **WalkSpeed** variable as we will unveil in the subsequent steps.

4) Pull a wire from the "**In**" pin of the Inputs node to add a **SET** "**IsSprinting**" node. Ensure the "**Is Sprinting**" input parameter is unchecked.

5) Click the **Character Movement** component in the **Components** panel and drag it to the **Event Graph**.

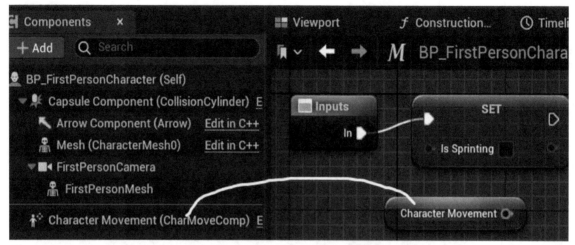

6) Pull a wire from the output pin of the **Character Movement** node to add the **SET Max Walk Speed** node.

7) Pull a wire from the input pin of the **SET Max Walk Speed** node to add a **GET Walk Speed** node.

8) Join the white execution pins of the **SET Is Sprinting,** SET **Max Walk Speed**, and **Outputs** nodes.

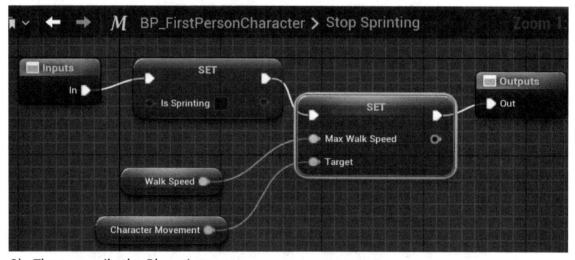

9) Then compile the Blueprint.

CREATING MACRO (STARTSPRINTING)

Next, we shall create another macro **"StartSprinting"** for configuring the sprinting. Follow these steps to create the macro:

1) Click the plus **(+)** button in the **MACROS** category. Rename the new macro to "**StartSprinting**".

2) In the **Details** panel, create an input parameter titled "**In**" of the "**Exec**" type and an output parameter titled **Out** of the **Exec** type as illustrated below.

3) On the **StartSprinting** macro tab, we will be adding the necessary nodes just like the stop printing. The initial part of the StartSprinting macro is similar to StopSprinting but with the appropriate values. The Branch node checks if the **Stamina Manager** timer is active. If it is, the macro completes and you can exit. If the timer is not active, you will set it.

4) Pull a wire from the "**In**" pin of the Inputs node to add a **SET** "**IsSprinting**" node. Ensure the "**IsSprinting**" input parameter is checked.

5) Click the **Character Movement** component in the **Components** panel and drag it to the **Event Graph**.

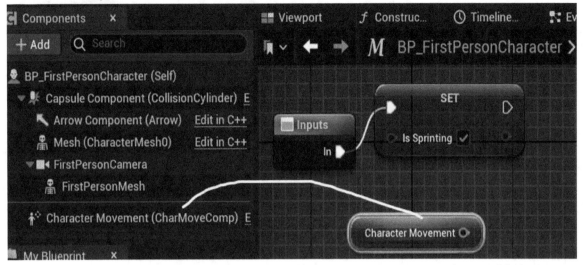

6) Pull a wire from the output pin of the **Character Movement** node to add the **SET Max Walk Speed** node.

7) Pull a wire from the input pin of the **SET Max Walk Speed** node to add a **GET Sprint Speed** node.

8) Join the white execution pins of the **SET Is Sprinting** and **SET Max Walk Speed** nodes.

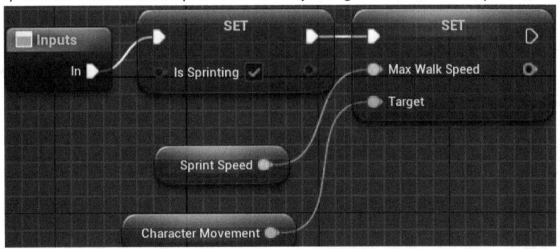

9) Pull a wire from the white output pin of the **SET Max Walk Speed** node to add a **Branch** node.

10) Pull a wire from the **True** output pin of the **Branch** node and join it to the **Out** pin of the **Outputs** node

11) Pull a wire from the **Condition** inputs pin of the **Branch** node to add a **Does Timer Exist by Function Name** node.

12) Pull a wire from the **Function Name** pin of the **Does Timer Exist by Function Name** node to add a **GET Stamina Manager Name** node.

13) Pull a wire from the **False** output pin of the **Branch** node to add a **Set Timer by Function Name** node. Join the white output pin of the **Set Timer by Function Name** node to the **Out** pin of the **Outputs** node.

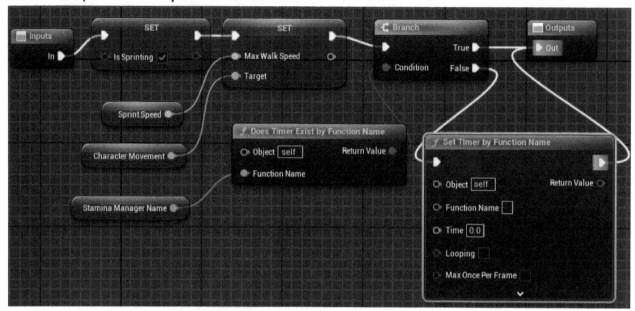

14) Pull a wire from the **Get Stamina Manager Name** and join it to the **Function Name** pin of the **Set Timer by Function Name** node.

15) Pull a wire from the **Time** pin of the **Set Timer by Function Name** node to add a **Get Stamina Drain and Recharge Time** node.

16) Tick the **Looping** input checkbox of the **Set Timer by Function Name** node. Because the value of the **Stamina Drain and Recharge Time** variable is **0.2,** this timer will trigger the function/event five times a second. Compile your Blueprint.

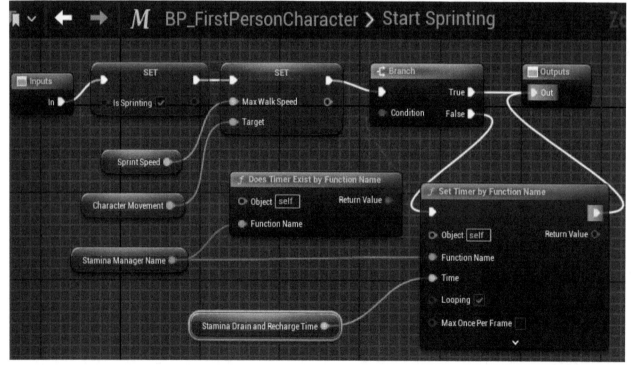

CREATING MACRO (MANAGESTAMINADRAIN MACRO)

The **ManageStaminaDrain** macro exhausts the **Player's Stamina** and examines conditions that stop sprinting. Follow these steps to create the macro:

1) Go to the **My Blueprint** panel, and click the plus (**+**) button in the **MACROS** category to create a new macro. Rename the new macro to **ManageStaminaDrain**.

2) In the macro's **Details** panel, create an input parameter titled "**In**" of the **Exec** type. Create an output parameter titled "**Out**" of the **Exec** type.

3) On the **ManageStaminaDrain** macro tab, you will add the necessary nodes. The player can keep sprinting and drain stamina if two conditions are met: the player must be moving, and their stamina must be greater than zero.

4) Pull a wire from the **In** pin of the **Inputs** node to add a **Branch** node. Pull a wire from the **Condition** input pin of the **Branch** node to add an **AND** Boolean node.

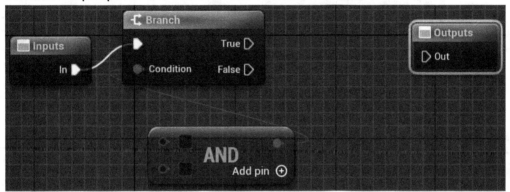

5) Pull a wire from the upper input pin of the **AND** node to add a **Greater** node.

6) Right-click any empty space in the Event Graph to add a **Get Velocity node**.

7) Pull a wire from the **Return Value** pin of the **Get Velocity** node to add a **VectorLengthSquared** node. If the return value of the **VectorLengthSquared** node is greater than zero, then the player is moving. Using **VectorLengthSquared** instead of **VectorLength** avoids calculating the square root, which is sufficient for checking if the velocity is greater than zero.

8) Pull a wire from the **Return Value** pin of the **VectorLengthSquared** node and join it to the upper input pin of the **Greater** node.

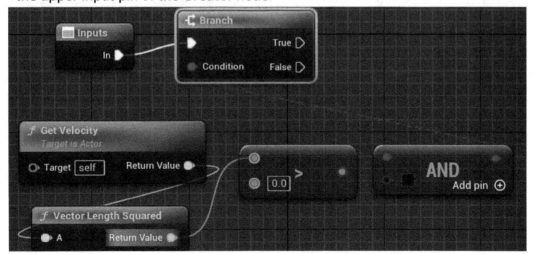

145

9) Pull a wire from the lower input pin of the **AND** node to add another **Greater** node.
10) Pull a wire from the upper input pin of this **Greater** node to add a **GET Player Stamina** node.
11) Pull a wire from the **True** output pin of the **Branch** node to add a **SET Player Stamina** node. Join the white output pin of the **SET Player Stamina** node to the **Out** pin of the **Outputs** node.

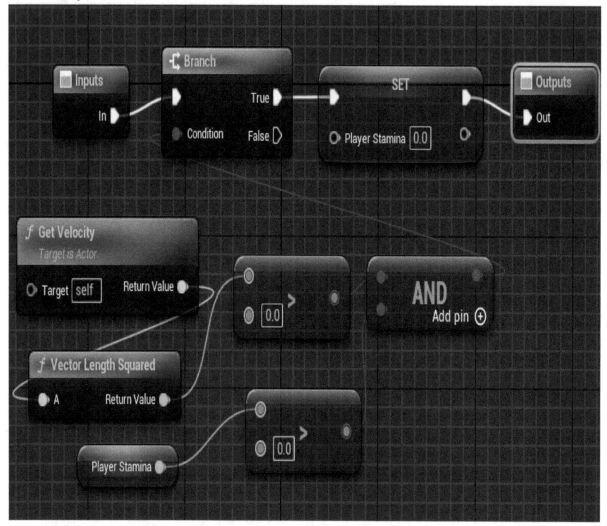

12) Pull a wire from the input pin of **SET Player Stamina** to add a **Max (float)** node. This node ensures that **Player Stamina** never drops below 0.0.
13) Pull a wire from the upper input pin of the **Max (float)** node to create a **Subtract** node.
14) Pull a wire from the upper input pin of the **Subtract** node to add a **GET Player Stamina** node.
15) Pull a wire from the lower input pin of the **Subtract** node to add a **GET Sprint Cost** node.
16) Pull a wire from the **False** output pin of the **Branch** node to add the **Stop Sprinting** macro node. Join the white output pin of the **Stop Sprinting** node to the **Out** pin of the **Outputs** node.

146

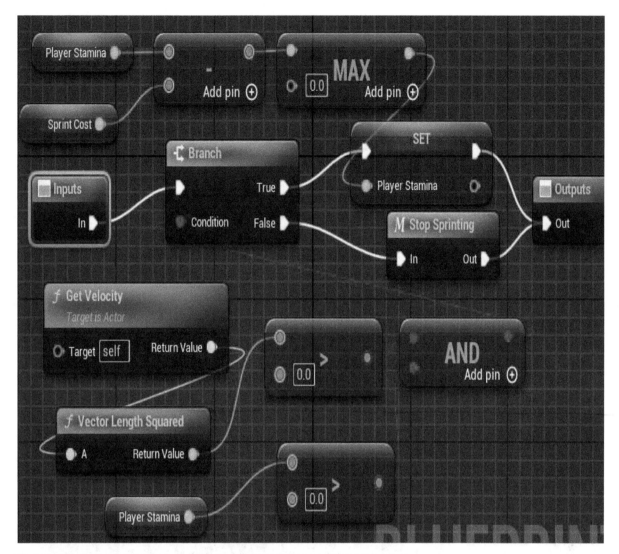

CREATING THE MANAGESTAMINARECHARGE MACRO

The **ManageStaminaRecharge** macro ensures Player Stamina is recharged until it is full. Create the macro using the following steps:

1) Go to the **My Blueprint** panel, and click the plus **(+)** button in the **MACROS** category to create a new macro. Rename the macro to **ManageStaminaRecharge**.

2) In the macro's **Details** panel, create an input parameter titled **In** of the **Exec** type. Create an output parameter titled **Out** of the **Exec** type, as shown below.

3) On the **ManageStaminaRecharge** macro tab, you will add the necessary nodes. if **Player Stamina** is full (almost equal to **1.0**) you will either clear it for **Stamina Manager** or increase it, if the timer of the Player Stamina is not full.

4) Pull a wire from the **In** pin of the **Inputs** node to add a **Branch** node.

5) Pull a wire from the **Condition** input pin of the **Branch** node to add a **Nearly Equal (float)** node. Enter **1.0** value in the **B** input feature of the **Nearly Equal (float)** node. This node is used because it has an **Error Tolerance** property required for comparing floating-point values.

147

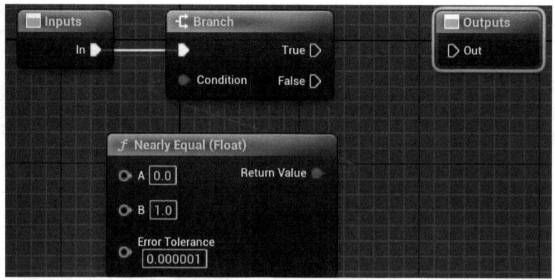

6) Pull a wire from the **A** input feature of the **Nearly Equal (float)** node to add a **GET Player Stamina** node.

7) Pull a wire from the **True** output pin of the **Branch** node to add a **Clear Timer by Function Name** node.

8) Pull a wire from the **Function Name** feature of the **Clear Timer by Function Name** node to add a **GET Stamina Manager Name** node.

9) Join the white output pin of the "**Clear Timer by Function Name**" node to the **Out** pin of the **Outputs** node.

10) Pull a wire from the **False** output pin of the **Branch** node to add a **SET Player Stamina** node. Join the white output pin of the **SET Player Stamina** node to the **Out** pin of the **Outputs** node.

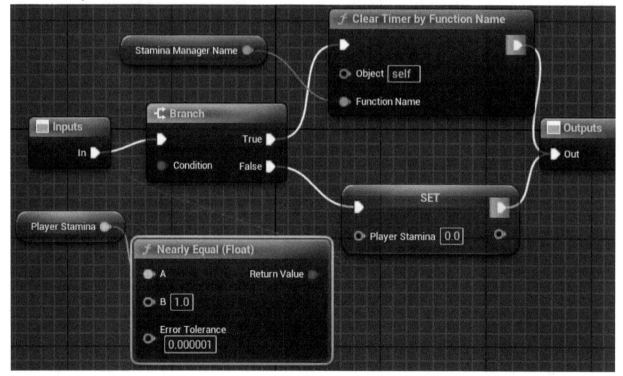

11) Pull a wire from the input pin of the **SET Player Stamina** node to add a **Min (float)** node. Enter **1.0** value in the second input feature of the **Min (float)** node. This node ensures **Player Stamina** does not exceed **1.0.**
12) Pull a wire from the upper input pin of the **Min (float)** node to create an **Add** node.
13) Pull a wire from the upper input pin of the **Add** node to add a **GET Player Stamina** node.
14) Pull a wire from the lower input pin of the Add node to add a **GET Stamina Recharge Rate** node.

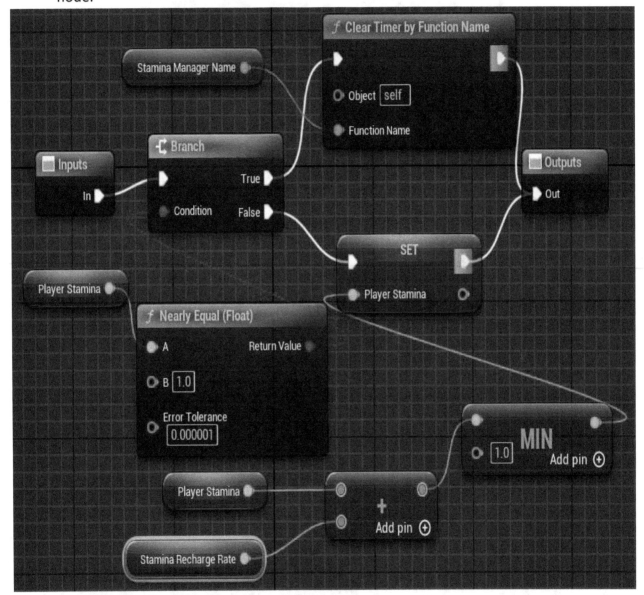

UPDATING THE INPUT ACTION SPRINT EVENT

You have to update the **InputAction Sprint** event, so you can use the new stamina system. These steps show you how to do that:

1) Go to the **GRAPHS** category in the **My Blueprint** panel and double-click on **InputAction Sprint**. This action takes you to the current position in the **Event Graph** where **InputAction Sprint** is located.

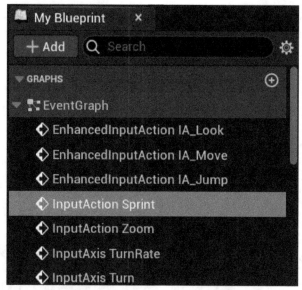

2) Delete the existing nodes connected to **InputAction Sprint**. Replace them with the nodes that will be added in this section. when you press the **Shift** key, the game inspects if there is adequate stamina to start sprinting e.g., if **PlayerStamina** is greater than or equal to **SprintCost**. If there is enough stamina, the **Start Sprinting** macro will be called. When the **Shift** key is released, the Stop Sprinting macro will be called.

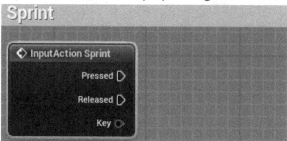

3) Pull a wire from the "**Pressed**" output pin of the "**InputAction Sprint**" node to add a **Branch** node.
4) Pull a wire from the **Condition** input pin of the "**Branch**" node to add an **OR Boolean** node.
5) Pull a wire from the upper input pin of the **OR** node to add a **Greater** node. We use the **Greater** node instead of **Greater Equal** to ensure precise comparison with the **Nearly Equal (float)** node.

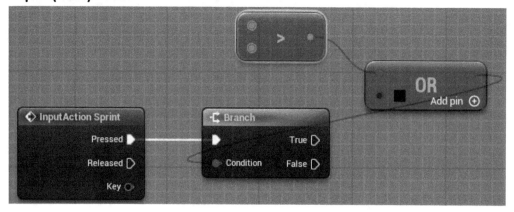

150

6) Pull a wire from the upper input pin of the **Greater** node to add a **GET Player Stamina** node.
7) Pull a wire from the lower input pin of the **Greater** node to add a **GET Sprint Cost** node.
8) Pull a wire from the lower input pin of the **OR** node to add a "**Nearly Equal (float)**" node.
9) Pull a wire from the "**A**" input pin of the "**Nearly Equal (float)**" node to add a "**GET Player Stamina**" node.
10) Pull a wire from the **B** input pin of the **Nearly Equal (float)** node to add a "**GET Sprint Cost**" node.

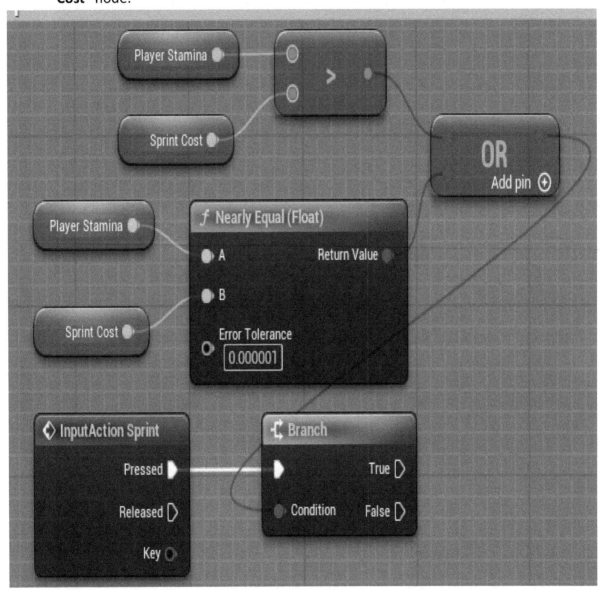

11) Pull a wire from the "**True**" output pin of the "**Branch**" node to add the **Start Sprinting** macro node.
12) Pull a wire from the **Released** output pin of the **InputAction Sprint** node to add the **Stop Sprinting** macro node.
13) Alter the label of the comment box to **start and stop sprinting (Inputs)**.

151

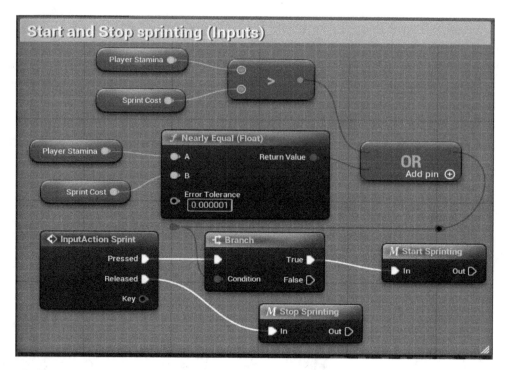

CREATING THE MANAGESTAMINA CUSTOM EVENT

Let's proceed by creating the ManageStamina custom event, designed to monitor the player's sprinting status and call the right macro to drain or recharge. Follow these steps to build the custom event:

1) Right-click any empty space in the **Event Graph**. Select "**Add Custom Event**" on the **Context menu** and rename it to "**ManageStamina**".

2) Add the nodes illustrated in the diagram below. These nodes assess whether the player is currently sprinting and call the suitable macro.

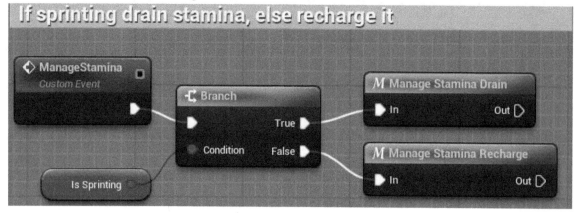

3) Ensure to compile, save, and then test the game.

As you sprint through the level, you should observe the stamina meter draining when holding down the **left Shift** key for sprinting. It should recharge when the key is released or when the player is walking or stationary.

You are done implementing the functionality to manage stamina and sprinting in your game. Next, you can proceed to set up constraints related to player ammunition.

AVERTING FIRING ACTIONS WHEN OUT OF AMMO

To enforce a constraint on the player's ability to fire their gun when they have zero ammo, follow these steps:

1) Double-click on the **InputActionFire** in the **Graphs** section to move to its position in **Event Graph**. Drag from the **Pressed** pin of **InputAction Fire** and drop on any empty space to open the **Context Menu**. Select **Add Branch** node from the **Context Menu**. The Branch node automatically connects to **InputAction Fire** to the subsequent node in the sequence.
2) Pull a wire from the **Condition** input pin of the **Branch** node to any empty space. Then add a **Greater** node to perform the comparison.
3) Pull a wire from the upper input pin of the "**Greater**" node to add a "**GET Player Current Ammo**" node. Let the lower input field of the Greater node stay untouched (at **0** which is the default value).

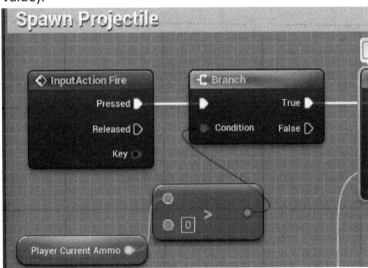

Compile the Blueprint to apply the changes made. **Save** the Blueprint to retain the modifications. Test the game to verify the functionality. You should observe that the gun stops firing when the ammo counter reaches 0, preventing the player from shooting without available ammunition.

CREATING COLLECTIBLE OBJECTS

Limiting the player from firing their gun when they exhaust ammo causes the player to be thoughtful of the accuracy of the shots they try within the game. Nevertheless, limiting ammo would be unreasonably punishing without a way of obtaining more. we won't configure ammo to normally recharge like the stamina meter. Rather, you will create a collectible ammo recovery to enable the player to recover ammo by crossing and using the level.

To build a **BP_AmmoRecovery** Blueprint in your game, follow these steps:

1) Open the **Content Browser** and go to **Content > FirstPerson > Blueprints**. Click on the "**Add**" button and select **"Blueprint Class"** from the dropdown menu.
2) Select "**Actor**" as the parent class for your new Blueprint.
3) Title your Blueprint "**BP-AmmoRecovery**". Double-click on "**BP-AmmoRecovery**" to open it in the Blueprint Editor.

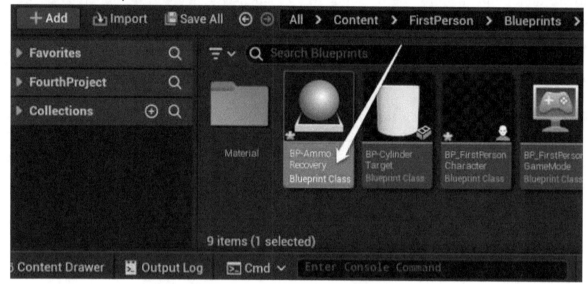

4) Within the Blueprint Editor, locate the "**Components**" panel. Click the "**Add**" button within the **Components** panel and choose "**Static Mesh**". In the **Details** panel, select the "**Shape_Pipe**" **Static Mesh** from the dropdown. Go to the "**Materials**" and select "**M_Door**" on the Element 0 field. Adjust the **Scale** feature values to **0.5** for the **X, Y,** and **Z** dimensions.
5) Alter **Collision Presets** of **Static Mesh** to **Overlap AllDynamic.**

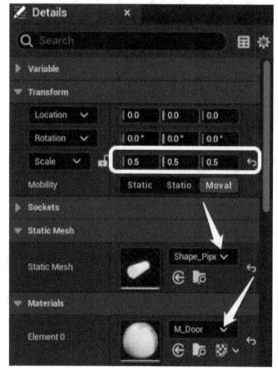
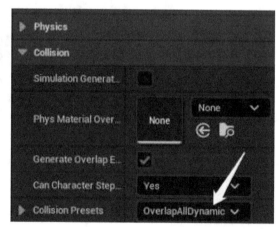

Hint: While modeling a game. It is usually helpful to explore the readily available assets instead of taking the time to create every asset from scratch. This enables you to target your effort and time on defining what approaches will result in the best play experience instead of spending time building art assets that might later be dismissed if the approach is removed from the design.

6) Next, you will create the **AmmoRecoveryCount** variable that will store the amount of ammo the player will get when receiving the ammo picking. Click the plus **(+)** button in the **My Blueprint** under the **VARIABLES** category to create a new variable. Go to the **Details** panel, Title it "**AmmoRecoveryCount**", set the **Variable Type** to **Integer,** and tick the **Instance Editable** checkbox.

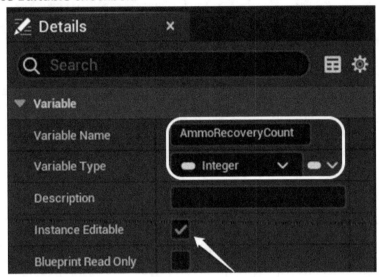

7) Compile the **Blueprint** and enter **15** into the **AmmoRecoveryCount Default Value.**
8) The **Event ActorBeginOverlap** of BP-AmmoRecovery will be used to inspect whether the player (**FirstPersonCharacter**) is intersecting the instance of BP-AmmoRecovery and to raise the Player Current Ammo value. We will be using the following nodes:
9) Right-click on any empty space on the Event Graph and select Event ActorBeginOverlap to add it.
10) Pull a wire from the Other Actor output pin of the Event ActorBeginOverlap node to add the Cast to BP_FirstPersonCharacter node.
11) Pull a wire from the **As BP First Person Character** pin to add a **SET Player Current Ammo** node.

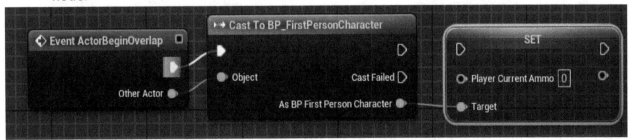

12) Pull a wire once again from the **As BP First Person Character** pin to add a **GET Player Current Ammo** node.
13) Pull a wire from the **GET Player Current Ammo** output pin to an empty space to create an **Add** node.

14) Pull a wire from the lower input pin of the **Add** node to add a **Get Ammo Recovery Count node.**

15) Join the output pin of the **Add** node to the input pin of the **SET Player Current Ammo** node.

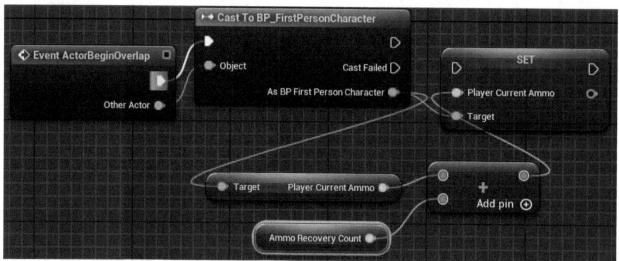

16) Next, you will play a sound and destroy the instance once the collectible is recovered

17) Pull a wire from the white output pin of the **SET Player Current Ammo** node to an empty space and select a **Player Sound at Location** node to add it.

18) For this modeling, you will use a sound wave from **Engine Content**. Click the **Sound** dropdown, and click on the **Settings** icon to open the **VIEW** options. Activate the **Show Engine Content** option and choose the **CompileSucess** sound wave from the list.

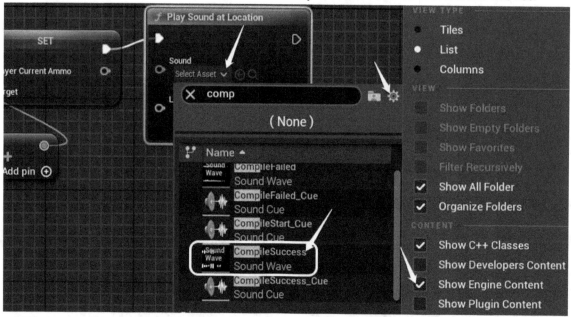

19) Pull a wire from the **Location** input pin to an empty space to add a **GetActorLocation** node

20) Pull a wire from the white output pin of the **Play Sound at Location** node to an empty space to add a **D**estroy**A**ctor. This ensures that every collectible can only be grabbed once. Compile and save your **BP-AmmoRecovery** Blueprint.

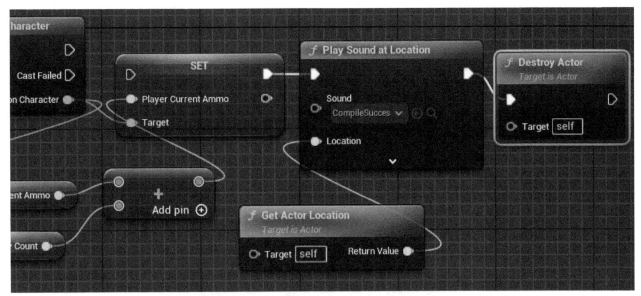

21) Next, return to the level editor and then drag the **BP-AmmoRecovery** Blueprint from the **Content Browser** to the level to create an instance. Add several instances in various locations across the Level to seed the area with ammo pickups. Save Level and click **Play** to check the game. You will notice your ammo counter increase each time you step into one of the ammo pickups.

You have mastered how to create a Blueprint for pickup that adjusts the player's status when it is collected. To establish a complete game loop, you will build a condition for the player to will. We examine that in the next section.

CONFIGURING A GAMEPLAY WIN CONDITION

You will adjust the **HUD** Blueprint and player character Blueprint to cater to a target goal that the player must seek to attain. You have to display the target goal in the HUD beside the target count, so the player can effortlessly see how many targets need to be destroyed to achieve their goal.

157

You will also create another **Widget Blueprint** symbolizing a win menu screen that will be displayed to the player when they reach their goal. Lastly, you will execute the logic needed to examine whether the player has won and to display the win menu screen.

DISPLAYING A TARGET GOAL IN THE HUD

You have to create a variable in the **FirstPersonCharacter** Blueprint that will configure how many targets we are asking the player to destroy to win the game. After that, you will display this information to the player in the HUD Blueprint.

1) In the **Content Browser,** go to **Content > FirstPerson > Blueprints** folder. Double-click on the **FirstPersonCharacter** Blueprint to open it.

2) In the **Variables** category of the **My Blueprint** panel, click on the plus (+) sign to add a new variable. Title the variable "**TargetGoal**" and set its **Variable Type** to **Integer**.

3) Compile the Blueprint and set the Default Value of "**TargetGoal**" to **2** (or any initial value you desire).

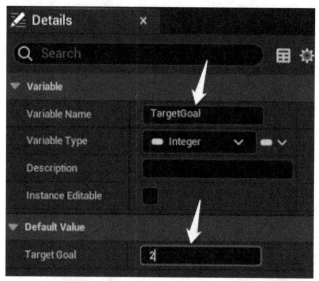

4) In the Content Browser, go to **Content > FirstPerson > User-Interface** folder Double-click the **HUD** Blueprint to open the UMG Editor. Inside the **UMG** Editor, locate the **Goal Tracker** section in the Hierarchy panel where you want to display the target goal.

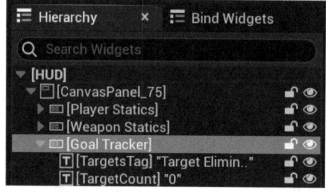

5) Drag a **Text** object from the **Palette** panel onto the **Goal Tracker** object. Go to the **Details** panel, Rename the newly added Text object to "**Slash**". Set the **Text** field under the **Content** category to " **/** " (including the spaces). Adjust the **font** size to **34**.

158

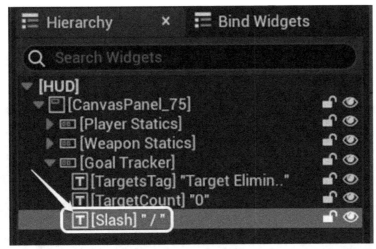

6) Drag another **Text** object to the **Goal Tracker** object. Go to the **Details** panel for this new Text object, and rename it to "**Target goal**". Set the **Text** field under the **Content category to** "0". Adjust the font size to **32** to match the other text.

Your Goal Tracker should now look like this.

7) Next, you will bind the **Target** goal of the HUD to the **TargetGoal** variable of the **FirstPersonCharacter** Blueprint. Locate the **Bind** button beside the **Text** field in the **Details** panel to create a binding as illustrated below:

8) You will use the same method for this binding just as the one we did to other HUD bindings we made in Chapter 6. Add a **Get Player Character** node, then cast it using the **Cast To BP_FirstPersonCharacter** node. Drag from the **As BP First Person Character** pin to add a **Get Target Goal** node. Lastly, connect both the **Cast To** node and the **Target Goal** node to the **Return** Node.

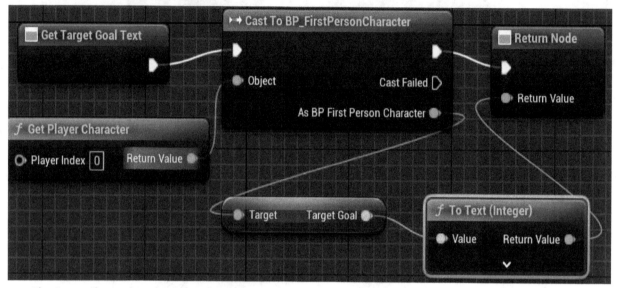

9) Compile and save your Blueprint.

You should observe that the target counter increases as targets are destroyed. The Target Goal displayed on the right of the target counter does not change. Next, we want to confirm that the player receives feedback when they attain their target goal.

CREATING A WIN MENU SCREEN

To give the player feedback when they have won the game, you need to create a **WinMenu** screen that will show after destroying the required number of targets. To create the **WinMenu.** You will need to get another Blueprint widget.

To create the **WinMenu** screen in your game, follow these steps:

1) Go to the **Content** > **FirstPerson** > **User-Interface** folder in the **Content Browser**. Right-click in the empty space and go to **User Interface** > **Widget Blueprint**.

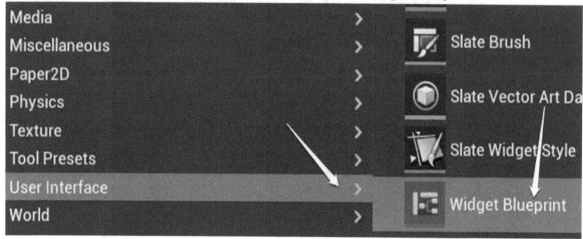

2) Title the Blueprint "**WinMenu**" and double-click it to open the UMG Editor. Next, you will create three elements for this menu screen. The first element is going to be a simple text object that transmits **You Won**! To the player. The remaining two elements are going to be the buttons that will let the player **restart** or **quit** the game.

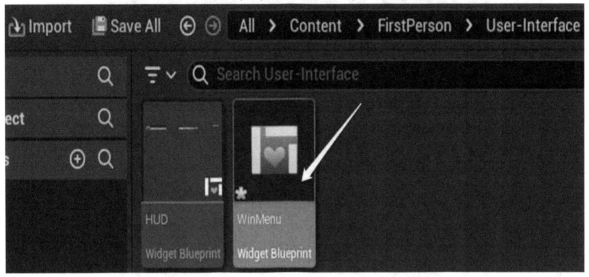

3) Select and drag the **Canvas Panel** object to the **Hierarchy** panel.
4) Drag a **Text** widget from the **Palette** panel to the **canvas panel**. In the **Details** panel, change the name to **Win msg**, click the **Anchors** dropdown, and choose the option that anchors in the center of the screen.

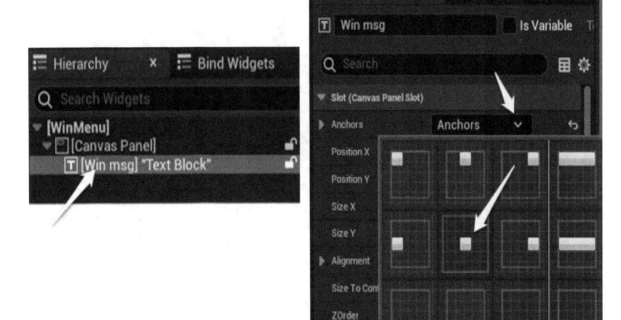

5) Adjust Position **X** to -**185.0** and Position **Y** to -**240**.0. Tick the **Size To Content** checkbox, so you won't adjust the values of Size **X** and Size **Y**.

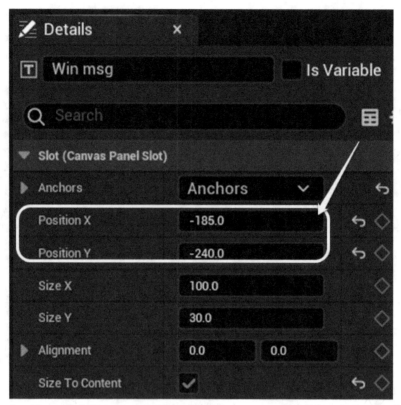

6) Rename the **Text** field in the **CONTENT** category to **You Won**! Go to the **APPEARANCE** category, Adjust **Font Size** to **68** and **Color and Opacity** to any **Magenta** color.

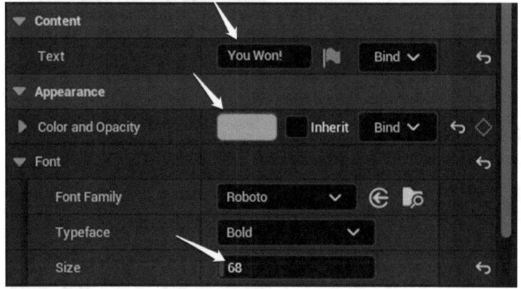

7) Drag a **Button** widget from the **Palette** panel to the **Canvas Panel** object in the **Hierarchy** panel. In the **Details** panel, change the name of the **Button** widget to "**Button restart**". click on the **Anchors** dropdown and choose the option that anchors the button in the center of the screen.

8) Set Position X to -**185**.0 and Position Y to -**60**.0. Set Size **X** to **360**.0 and Size **Y** to **110**.0 to define the dimensions of the button.

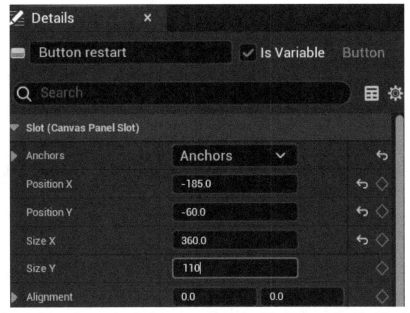

9) Drag a **Text** widget from the **Palette** panel to the "**Button restart**" object in the **Hierarchy** panel. Go to the **Details** panel and change the name of the **Text** widget to **Txt restart**. In the **CONTENT** category, change the **Text** field to "**Restart**" and change the Font Size to **46**.

10) Drag another **Button** widget from the **Palette** panel to the **Canvas Panel** object in the **Hierarchy** panel. Go to the **Details** panel, and rename the button widget to "**Button quit**". Click the **Anchors** dropdown and choose the option that anchors the button in the center of the screen.

11) Set **Position X** to -**190**.0 and Position Y to **140**.0. Set Size **X** to **360**.0 and Size **Y** to **110**.0.

12) Drag a **Text** widget from the **Palette** panel onto the "**Button quit**" object in the **Hierarchy** panel. Go to the **Details** panel, and change the name of the **Text** widget to "**Text quit**". Under the "**CONTENT**" category, change the **Text** field to "**Quit**" and change the **Font** Size to **50**.

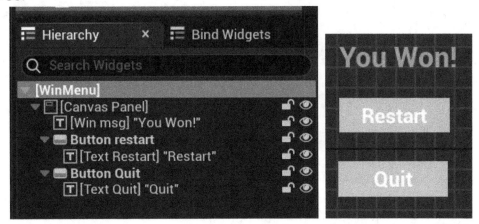

13) Next, you will add actions to execute when the **Restart** button is pressed. Click the **Button restart**" object, and scroll down to the lower area of the **Details** panel. Click on the plus "**+**" button beside the **On Clicked** event. This adds an event that will trigger when the **Restart** button is clicked

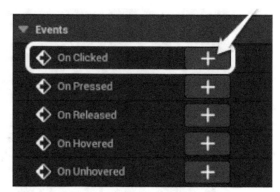

14) The **Graph** panel opens and shows the **On Clicked** (**Button restart**) node. In the **Graph** mode, you can now add nodes to define what happens when the Restart button is clicked. Drag from the output pin of **On Clicked (Button restart)** to the **Graph** to add an **Open Level (by Object Reference)** node to the Graph. In the "**Level**" feature choose the level you want to reload. In this case, it should be "**FirstPersonExampleMap**". This node ensures that clicking the **Restart** button reloads the level, resetting all game aspects such as targets, ammo collectibles, and player statics.

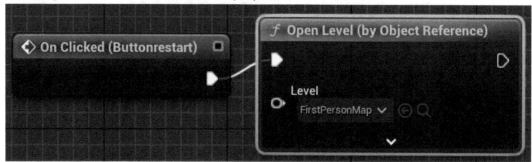

15) After adding the "**Open Level**" node, drag from its output pin to add a **Remove from Parent** node to the Graph. This node removes the **WinMenu** widget from the view once the level is reset, ensuring the menu disappears after the player clicks **Restart**.

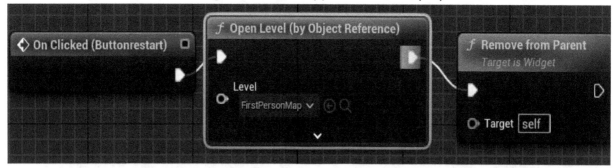

16) Next, you will use the same methods to set up the **Quit** button. Return to the **Designer** view of the UMG Editor. Click the **Button quit** object in the **Hierarchy** panel. Scroll down to the lower area of the **Details** panel, and click the plus (**+**) button beside **On Clicked** Events to create an event for the **Quit** button.

17) You will also be taken to the **Graph** view with the **On Clicked (Button quit)** node display on the graph. Drag from the output pin of **On Clicked (Button quit)** onto the **Graph** to add a **Quit Game** node to the Graph. This node allows the player to shut down the game entirely by clicking the **Quit** button.

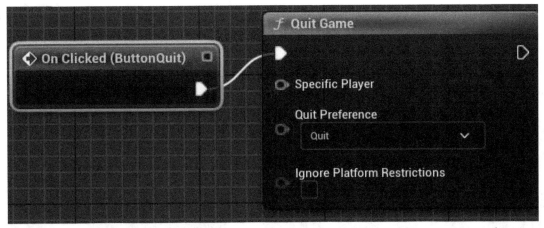

18) **Compile** and **save** the **WinMenu** Blueprint. Close the UMG Editor once you have verified everything works as intended.

Since the WinMenu has been created, you need to direct the game when to display it to the player.

SHOWING THE WINMENU

To set up the display of the WinMenu in response to game completion, follow these steps within the **FirstPersonCharacter** Blueprint:

1) Go to **Content > FirstPerson > Blueprints** folder in the **Content Browser and** double-click on the **FirstPersonCharacter** Blueprint to open it in the Blueprint Editor.

2) Right-click the **Event Graph** and select "**Add Custom Event**" from the context menu. Rename the custom event to "**End Game**". This event will be triggered when the game reaches its end condition.

3) Pull a wire from the output execution pin of "**End Game**" to add a "**Set Game Paused**" node to the **Event Graph**. Tick the "**Paused**" checkbox in the "**Set Game Paused**" node. This pauses the game, allowing the player to interact with the **WinMenu** without interference from ongoing gameplay.

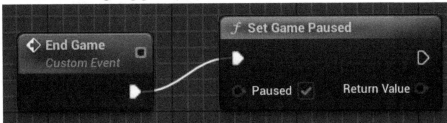

4) Right-click the **Event Graph** to add a "**Get Player Controller**" node from the **Context Menu**. Pull a wire from the "**Return Value**" output pin of the "**Get Player Controller**" node

165

to add a "**SET Show Mouse Cursor**" node to the **Event Graph**. Tick the checkbox beside "**Show Mouse Cursor**" in the **SET Show Mouse Cursor** node. Join the output execution pin of "**Set Game Paused**" to the input execution pin of "**SET Show Mouse Curso**r". This allows the player to recover control over the mouse cursor once the game is paused

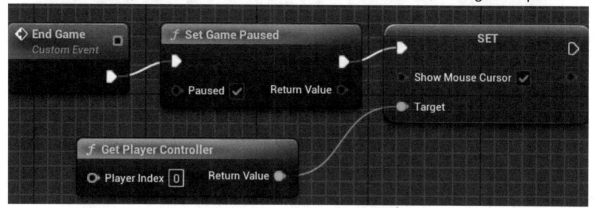

5) Pull a wire from the output execution pin of the "**SET Show Mouse Cursor** to add a "**Create Widget**" node to the Event Graph. In the **Class** feature of the "**Create Widget**" node, choose **Win Menu**.

6) Drag the "**Return Value**" output pin of the "**Create Widget**" node to an "**Add to Viewport**" node.

7) Select all the nodes related to the "**End Game**" event. Right-click and choose **Comment** from the context menu. Label the comment as "**End Game: Shows Win Menu**" to document the purpose of these nodes.

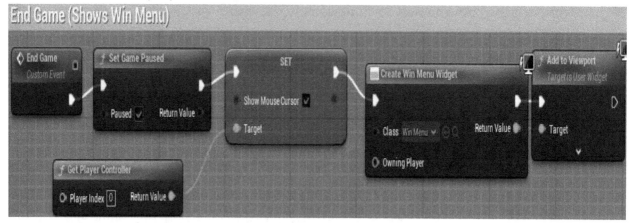

ACTIVATING A WIN

We need the **End Game** event to occur as soon as the player destroys adequate cylinder targets to meet the target goal. Next, you will create a custom event titled **CheckGoal** in the **FirstPersonCharacter** Blueprint that will be called by BP-CylinderTarget every time a target is destroyed.

Use the following steps to create a CheckGoal custom event:

1) Right-click the **Event Graph** of the **FirstPersonCharacter** Blueprint to add a "**Custom Event**" from the context menu. Rename the custom event to "**CheckGoal**".

2) Pull a wire from the white output pin of the "**CheckGoal**" node to an empty space on the graph to add a "**Branch**" node from the context menu that appears.

3) Pull a wire from the **Condition** input pin of the **Branch** node to an empty space to add a **Greater Equal** node from the context menu.

4) Pull a wire from the upper input pin of the "**Greater Equal**" node to add a "**GET Targets Eliminated**" node.

5) Pull a wire from the lower input pin of the **Greater Equal** node to add a "**GET Target Goal**" node.

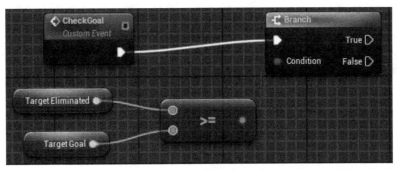

6) Pull a wire from the **True** output pin of the **Branch** node to add a **Delay** node. Type **1.0** into the **Duration** feature. This node is used to wait for **1** second before displaying the **WinMenu**.

7) Pull a wire from the **Completed** output pin of the **Delay** node to add the **End Game** node. This specific node calls the **End Game** custom event which we created to display the **WinMenu**.

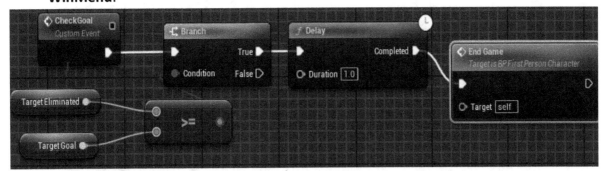

8) Compile and save the "**FirstPersonCharacter**" Blueprint to apply the changes. Close the Blueprint Editor.

Next, you will alter the BP_CylinderTarget Blueprint to call the **CheckGoal** event every time a target is destroyed:

1) Go to the **Content > FirstPerson > Blueprints** folder in the Content Browser. Double-click on the **BP_CylinderTarget** Blueprint to open it in the Blueprint Editor.

2) Move to **Event Graph** along the end of the **Event Hit** actions; Move the "**DestroyActor**" node if needed to make space for other nodes.

3) Pull a wire from the "**As BP_First Person Character**" output pin of the "**Cast To**" node to add the **Check Goal** node. Join the white output pin of the **++** node to the white input pin of the **Check Goal** and join the output pin of the **Check Goal** node to the white input pin of the **DestroyActor** node.

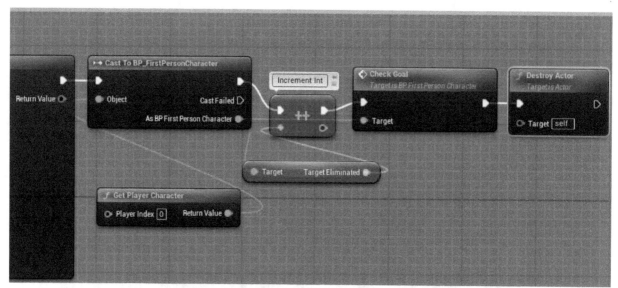

4) Compile and save the "**BP-CylinderTarget**" Blueprint to apply the changes. If the whole Blueprints are configured correctly, you should observe the game pause and the **WinMenu** displays immediately when you destroy a second target. When you click the **Restart** button, it will reload the level, while clicking the **Quit** button closes the session.

CHAPTER EIGHT
USING ARTIFICIAL INTELLIGENCE TO BUILD SMART ENEMIES

Next, we'll introduce a new challenge to our gameplay by creating enemies that can truly threaten our players. we'll design enemies with sophisticated AI behavior. These enemies will be able to analyze their surroundings and make decisions, significantly increasing the game's difficulty.

To achieve this, we'll explore Unreal Engine's built-in tools for managing AI behavior and learn how these tools work with our Blueprint scripting. By the end of the chapter, you will be able to create a Behavior Tree that guides enemy movement across the level and enables them to chase the player whenever they come into view.

CONFIGURING THE ENEMY ACTOR TO NAVIGATE

Up to this moment, our targets have been characterized by basic cylinder geometry. This was effective for prototyping a non-responsive target that served as a simple aiming challenge for the player. Nevertheless, for an enemy that moves around and poses a threat, we need a familiar appearance that specifies its direction of travel to the player. Luckily, Epic provides an easily accessible asset package for Unreal Engine that includes a humanoid model, perfect for our new enemy type.

Next, we'll cover how to import an asset package from the Marketplace, extend the play area, use a navigation mesh, and then create the AI assets used by the enemies.

IMPORT ASSET FROM THE MARKETPLACE

You have to move out from the Unreal Engine to concentrate on the Epic Games Launcher. The following steps show you how to import some free asset packages from the Marketplace:

1) Access **Epic Games Launcher** and click the **Unreal Engine** section from the left side of the window.
2) Click the **Marketplace** tab at the top and enter **Animation Starter Pack** in the Search bar.
3) Click the "**Add to Cart**" button for the **Animation Starter Pack**.

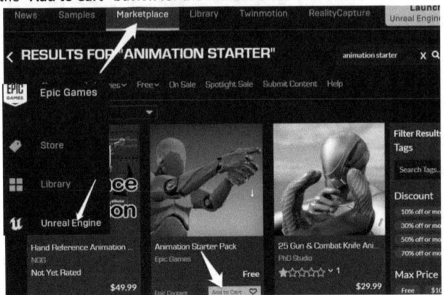

4) Click the **Shopping Cart** icon at the top right and click on the **Checkout** button in the **Shopping Cart** panel.

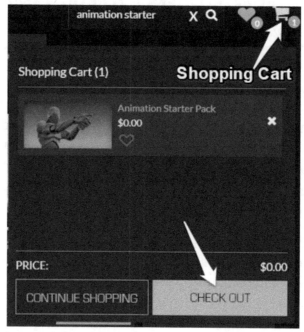

5) Once the panel closes, click on the image of the **Animation Starter Pack** to see its asset page.

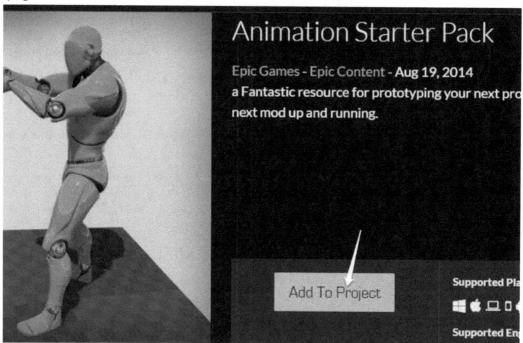

6) Click the "**Add to Project**" button and choose the project you have been using to construct your game. A folder named **AnimStarterPack** will be added to the **Content** folder of your project.

The Animation Starter Pack includes the assets we need to act out the enemy. currently, we need extra space in the play area for both the player and the enemies.

EXPANDING THE PLAY AREA

To create an engaging environment for our intelligent enemies to chase the player, you have to modify the default first-person example map layout. The existing layout, while adequate for shooting targets, is too narrow for a player to effectively avoid a chasing enemy.

To hurriedly enhance gameplay variety, we'll expand the play area to be double as wide as before. Additionally, we'll create an elevated area accessible by ramps for both the player and the enemies. The following screenshot illustrates the new level layout:

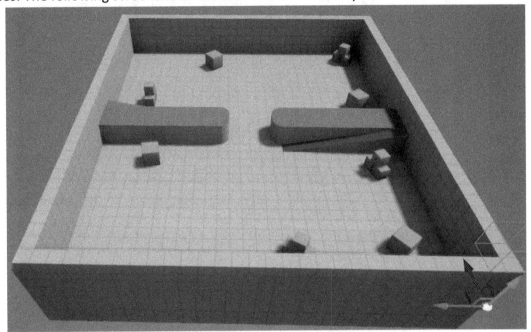

To modify the level layout, use the following steps:

1) Open your project in the Unreal Editor.
2) Remove the "**First Person Template**" label. Also, delete all instances of **BP-CylinderTarget** from the level. You can select them either by clicking the instances in the Viewport or by locating them in the Outliner.
3) Select the **Floor**. Hold the **Alt** key, then click and drag the **Y**-axis arrow to create a copy of the **Floor**. Move the copied **Floor** along the Y-axis until the play area is double as wide.

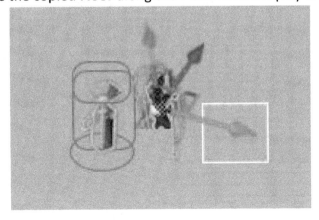

4) You need to scale up **PostProcessVolume** and **LightmassImportanceVolume** to cover the new play area. These volumes are utilized for lighting and effects.

5) Go to the **Outliner** panel, and select "**PostProcessVolume**". Go to the **Details** panel, and specify a **45.0** value to the **Y**-axis (green) scale. Then, in the **Level** Editor, move "**PostProcessVolume**" along the **Y**-axis until it covers the play area.

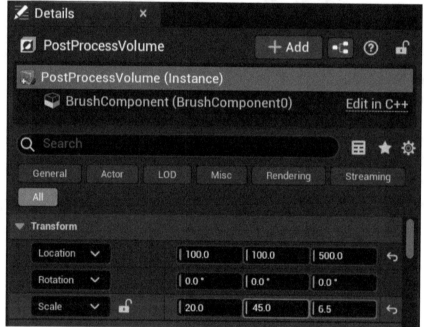

6) Go to the **Outliner** panel, and select " **LightmassImportanceVolume** ". Go to the **Details** panel, click the **Lock** icon beside the **Scale** property to unlock it, and then set the Y-axis (green) scale value to 2.0.

7) Now, in the **Level** Editor, move "LightmassImportanceVolume" along the **Y**-axis until it covers the play area.

8) In the **Level** Editor, select the wall named "**Wall3**" located in the middle of the play area. In the **Details** panel, specify the **5945.0** value for the **Y-axis (green)** location.

9) Next, click on the wall named "**Wall1**". Hold the **Alt** key and then click and drag the Y-axis arrow to create a copy of the wall. In the Details panel, specify a **4000.0** value for the Y-axis (green) location.

10) Now, click on the wall named "**Wall2**". Hold the **Alt** key and click and drag the **Y-axis** arrow to create a copy of this wall. Go to the **Details** panel, and specify a **4000.0** value for the Y-axis (green) location. The screenshot below displays the current updated play area:

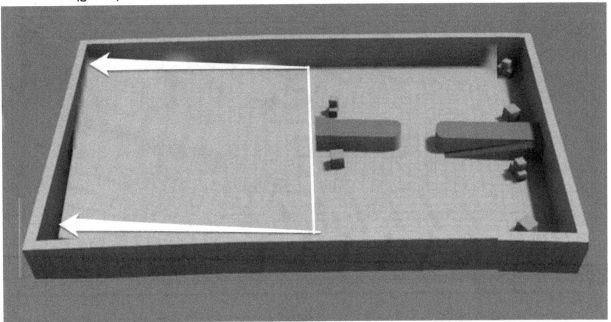

11) Click on the piece of wall named "**BigWall2**." Hold the **Alt** key and then click and drag the Y-axis arrow to create a copy of the wall. Go to the Details panel, and specify the 5295.0 value for the Y-axis (green) location.

12) We will convert "**BigWall2**" to make a larger wall in the middle of the play area. Click on "**BigWall2**" to select it. Go to the **Details** panel, set the location values to X = -280, Y = 2000, and Z = **322**, and the scale values to X = **30**, Y = **4**, and Z = **3**.

13) Next, let's add a ramp to access an elevated area. In the Content Browser, go to **Content > StarterContent > Shapes**" folder. Drag the "**Shape_Wedge_B**" asset to the level. Go to the Details panel, set the Location values to X = -1630, Y = 2500, and Z = 170, the Rotation values to X = 0, Y = 0, and Z = 90, and the Scale values to X = 6, Y = 3, and Z = 3.

14) Go to the **MATERIALS** section, and alter Element 0 from "**Shape_Wedge_B**" to the gray "**CubeMaterial**" material:

15) Next, we'll create another ramp to access the elevated area. Select the "Shape_Wedge_B" instance already in the level. Hold the Alt key and click and drag the X-axis arrow to make a copy of the ramp. Go to the Details panel, set the Location values to X = 1070, Y = 1500, and Z = 170, and the Rotation values to X = 0, Y = 0, and Z = -90.

16) Move some of the white boxes from one side of the level and distribute them on the other side.

17) Add several instances of "**BP_AmmoPickup**" throughout the level.

We have now created a level layout with a bigger space for action between the player and enemies. Next, we will create a NavMesh to enable enemy movement through the level.

USING A NAVMESH ASSET TO MAKE THE LEVEL TRAVERSIBLE

To make AI behavior that allows our enemies to navigate the level, we need to construct a map of the environment that the AI can read and use. This map is created with an asset called **NavMesh** (Navigation Mesh). These steps guide you on how to create a **NavMesh** for our play area:

1) Go to the **Level** Editor, and click the "**Create**" button positioned on the toolbar. mouse over "**Volumes**" to show a submenu, and then click on "**Nav Mesh Bounds Volume**":

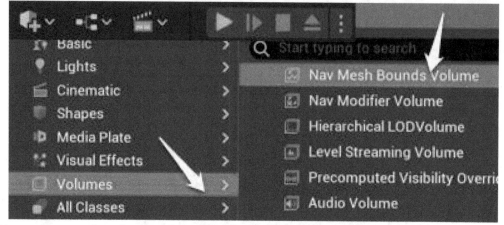

2) Next, move and scale the "**Nav Mesh Bounds Volume**" object so that it covers the entire walkable space of our level. Go to the **Details** panel, set the **Location** values to X = -**316**, Y = 2118, and Z = **460**, and the **Scale** values to X = **20**, Y = **46**, and Z = **7**.

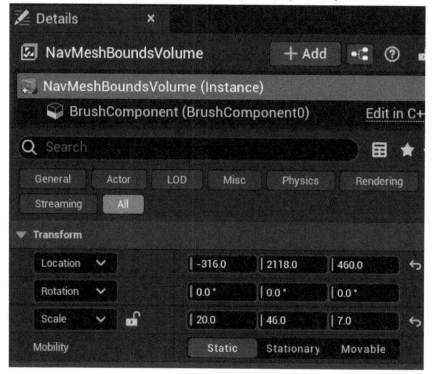

3) Press the "**P**" key on your keyboard to check if the **NavMesh** is placed correctly. If done right, you'll see a green mesh overlaying your floors.

With our play area and **NavMesh** set up, we can now focus on creating the enemy and its **AI**.

CREATING THE AI ASSETS

To manage the behavior of our enemy, we need to create four types of assets that will work together:

- ✓ **Character**: A blueprint class representing the enemy character in the level.
- ✓ **AI Controller**: A blueprint class that acts as a connection between the character and the Behavior Tree, routing information and actions from the Behavior Tree to the character.
- ✓ **Behavior Tree:** This is a decision-making logic that instructs our enemy on what actions to perform based on specific conditions.
- ✓ **Blackboard**: This is a data container shared between the AI Controller and the Behavior Tree, holding all the information used in decision-making.

Follow these steps to create the required assets:

1) In the Content Browser, go to the **Content** folder. Right-click on the empty space beside the list of folders and choose "**New Folder**". Title the new folder "**Enemy**".
2) Open the "**Enemy**" folder you just created. Right-click on the empty folder space and choose "**Blueprint Class**".
3) At the bottom of the popup, open the "**ALL CLASSES**" group and type "**ASP**" into the search bar. Select the "**Ue4ASP_Character**" class to create a new character blueprint. This class is from the **Animation Starter Pack** that we added to the project at the beginning of the chapter.

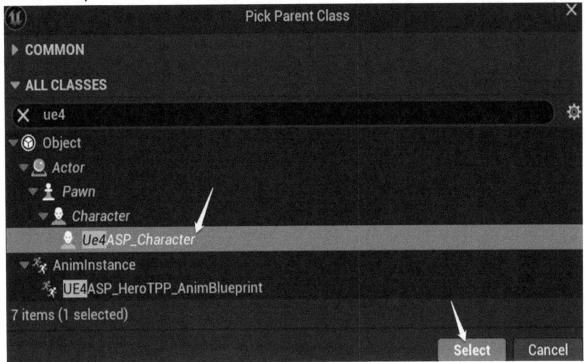

4) Change the new blueprint to "**BP-EnemyCharacter**".

5) Next, you will create the **AIController** child class. Right-click on the empty space of the "**Enemy**" folder and choose "**Blueprint Class**".

6) At the bottom of the popup, open the "**ALL CLASSES**" group and type "**AIController**" into the search box. Choose the "**AIController**" class and name the resultant blueprint "**BP-EnemyController**".

7) Next, you will create the **Behavior Tree** asset. Right-click on the empty space of the "**Enemy**" folder. Mouse over "**Artificial Intelligence**" to show a submenu, and then choose "**Behavior Tree**". Title the Behavior Tree asset as "**BT-EnemyBehavior**".

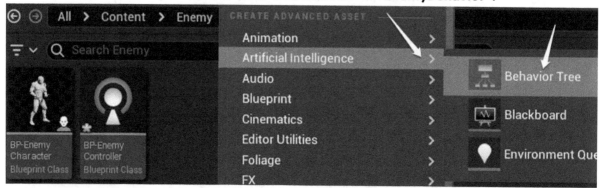

8) Lastly, you will create the **Blackboard** asset. Right-click on the empty space of the "**Enemy**" folder. Mouse over "**Artificial Intelligence**" to show a submenu, and then choose "**Blackboard**". Title it "**B-EnemyBlackboard**".

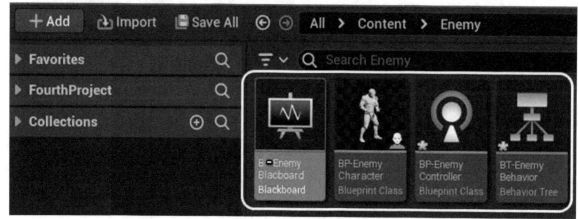

These assets are essential for implementing the AI behavior of the enemy character. Next, you will proceed with making necessary modifications to the "**BP-EnemyCharacter**" Blueprint.

SETTING UP THE BP-ENEMYCHARACTER BLUEPRINT

The **BP-EnemyCharacter** Blueprint, created as a child class of Ue4ASP_Character, inherits various properties such as the mesh, animations, and texture from the character we set up for the animation pack we imported. While we want to retain the mesh and animations, we need to make some adjustments to ensure **BP-EnemyCharacter** is controlled by the appropriate **AI Controller**. Additionally, we'll change the material of **BP-EnemyCharacter** and hide the capsule component that is visible in the game.

Note: When you open a Blueprint that lacks scripts, a simplified editor is displayed for editing default values only. To access the full layout, click on the "**Open Full Blueprint Editor**" link at the top.

NOTE: This is a data only blueprint, so only the default values are shown. It does not have any script
Open Full Blueprint Editor

Use the following steps to adjust BP-EnemyCharacter:

1) Open the **BP-EnemyCharacter** Blueprint and click the "**Class Defaults**" button on the toolbar.

2) In the **Details** panel, go to the "**PAWN**" category. At the end of this category, you'll find a drop-down list for "**AI Controller Class**". Alter the selection in this drop-down list to our new "**BP-EnemyController**" class.

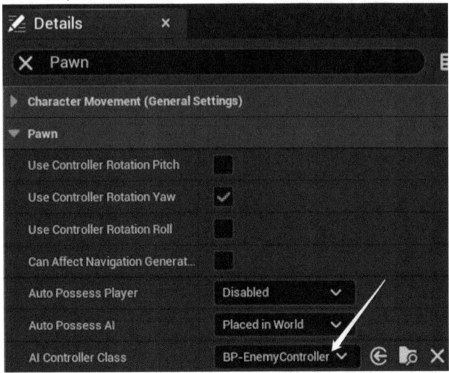

3) Go to the **Components** panel, and select **Mesh (CharacterMesh0) (Inherited)**. Next, go to the **Details** panel, locate the **MATERIALS** category, and alter **Element 0** to the **M_TargetBlue** material we created.

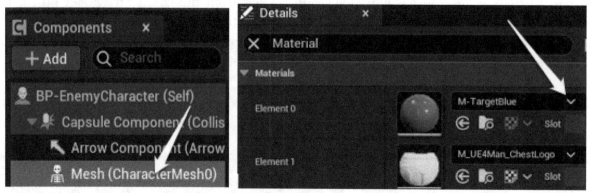

4) Go to the **Components** panel, and select **CapsuleComponent (CollisionCylinder) (Inherited)**. Then, in the **Details** panel, alter **Collision Presets** to **BlockAllDynamic**. Under the **RENDERING** category, Tick the **Hidden in Game** property.

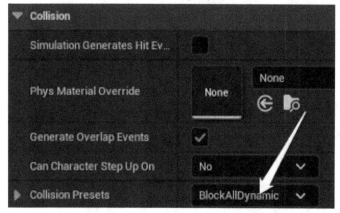

5) Compile the blueprint and drag the **BP-EnemyCharacter** blueprint into the level to create an instance of the enemy in our play area.

Thus far, you've learned how to import assets from the Marketplace, expanded the level to make it traversable using a **NavMesh**, and created the AI assets. Next, we are ready to implement the enemy's navigation behavior.

CREATING NAVIGATION BEHAVIOR FOR ENEMIES

The first step is to enable our enemy character to navigate between specified points on the map. This involves placing navigation points on the map and setting up behavior that directs the enemy to move from point to point in a loop.

CONFIGURING PATROL POINTS

We'll start by building the patrol path for the AI. You will use a **Trigger Sphere** to symbolize each patrol point, as it generates overlap events and remains invisible during gameplay. Each enemy character, represented by an instance of BP-EnemyCharacter, requires at least two patrol points to navigate between.

Use the following steps to create Patrol Points:

1) Open the **Level** Editor, and click the "**Create**" button on the toolbar. Select "**Trigger Sphere**" and place it on the floor.

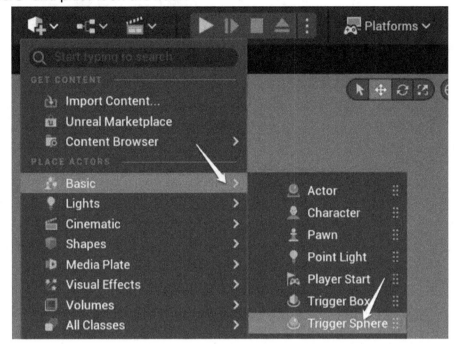

2) Go to the **Details** panel, and change the **Trigger Sphere** to "**PatrolPoint1**".

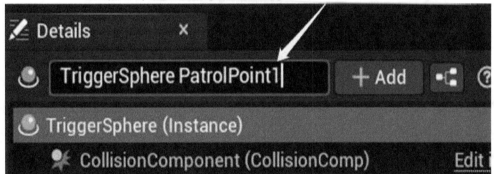

3) Repeat the process to create another **Trigger Sphere**. Rename it to "**PatrolPoint2**" and place it far from the first point to ensure noticeable movement.

With these patrol points set up, we can proceed to develop the enemy's AI to navigate these points effectively.

CREATING THE BLACKBOARD KEYS

A Blackboard stores information using keys and values. In our **BB-EnemyBlackboard**, we will set up two keys: one for the current patrol point and another for a reference to the player character. This information will be used by the Behavior Tree. Follow these steps to create the keys:

1) "Open **B-EnemyBlackboard**" in the content browser. "Click the "**New Key**" and choose "**Object**" as the Key Type.
2) Title this new key "**CurrentPatrolPoint**".
3) Click on the expansion arrow beside **Key Type** and change **Base Class** to **Actor** using the dropdown menu.

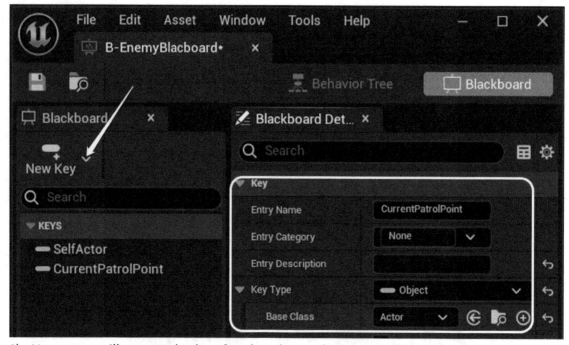

4) Next, you will create the key for the player character. click on "**New Key**" and choose "**Object**" as the **Key Type**.

5) Title this new key "**PlayerCharacter**". Click the expansion arrow beside **Key Type** and change **Base Class** to **Character**.

Next, we have to set the value of the "**CurrentPatrolPoint**" key in the **Blackboard** to the actual patrol point in the level. This can be done from the "**BP-EnemyCharacter**" Blueprint.

CREATING VARIABLES IN BP-ENEMYCHARACTER

In this section, we will create variables in the **BP-EnemyCharacter** to store patrol points and the Blackboard key names.

Use the following steps to create the variable:

1) Open **BP-EnemyCharacter** Blueprint. In the **Variables** category of the **My Blueprint** panel, click the plus **(+)** button to add a new variable. Title it "**PatrolPoint1**".

2) Go to the **Details** panel, click the **Variable Type** drop-down menu, search for "**Actor**" select it to display a submenu, and then select "**Object Reference**". Check the **Instance Editable** feature.

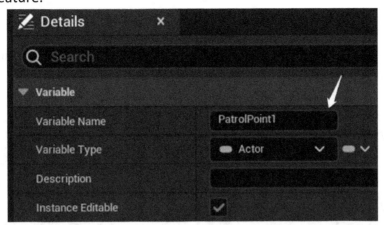

3) Follow the same steps as above to create a second **Actor** variable titled "**PatrolPoint2**".
4) Create another **Actor** variable called "**CurrentPatrolPoint**", but leave the **Instance Editable** feature unchecked.

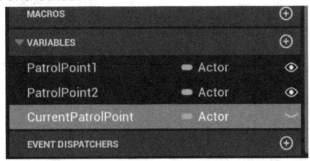

Now we have created three variables: **PatrolPoint1, PatrolPoint2, and CurrentPatrolPoint.** The open eye icon next to PatrolPoint1 and PatrolPoint2 indicates that these variables are instance editable, meaning their references can be set in the **Level** Editor.

5) Create another variable in the **My Blueprint** panel. In the **Details** panel, title the variable **PatrolPointKeyName** and alter **Variable Type** to **Name. Compile** the Blueprint and specify **DEFAULT VALUE** to **CurrentPatrolPoint**.

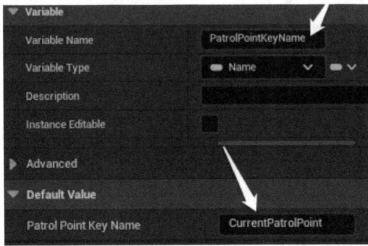

These variables will allow us to update the values on **B-EnemyBlackboard** efficiently.

UPDATING THE CURRENT PATROL POINT KEY

To update the "**CurrentPatrolPoint**" key in "**B-EnemyBlackboard**", we will create a macro that can be reused in multiple places. Follow these steps to create the macro:

1) Go to the "**My Blueprint**" panel, and click the plus "**+**" button in the "**MACROS**" category to create a new macro. Rename this macro to "**UpdatePatrolPoint**".
2) Go to the "**Details**" panel of the macro, and add an input parameter named "**In**" and an output parameter named "**Out**", both of the "**Exec**" types.

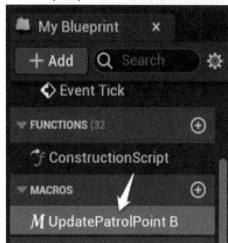
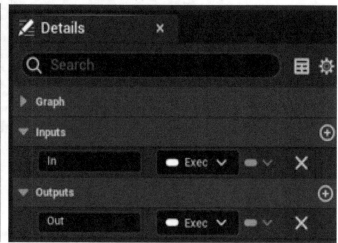

3) On the "**UpdatePatrolPointBB**" macro tab, you will add some nodes:
4) Right-click the graph to add a "**Get Blackboard**" node. This represents a utility function that hunts for the Blackboard being used by the AI controller.
5) Pull a wire from the "**Return Value**" pin of the "**Get Blackboard**" node to add a "**Set Value as Object**" node.

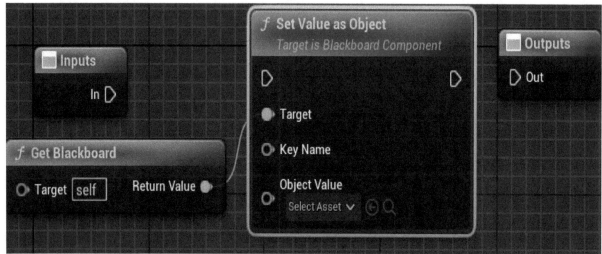

6) Pull a wire from the "**Key Name**" pin of the "**Set Value as Object**" node to add a "**GET Patrol Point Key Name**" node.
7) Pull a wire from the "**Object Value**" pin of the "**Set Value as Object**" node to add a "**GET Current Patrol Point**" node.

8) Join the white execution pins of the "**Inputs**", "**Set Value as Object**", and "**Outputs**" nodes. **Compile** the Blueprint.

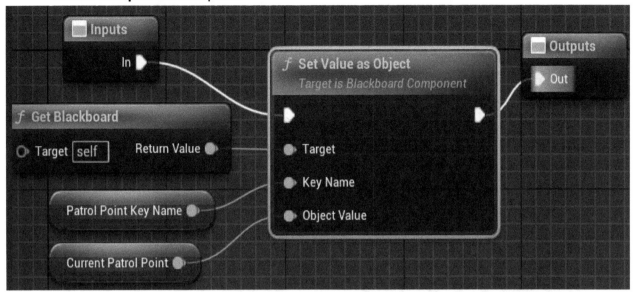

Finally, we need to ensure that the "**CurrentPatrolPoint**" key in "**BB-EnemyBlackboard**" is updated when an instance of "BP-EnemyCharacter" overlaps with a patrol point.

OVERLAPPING A PATROL POINT

To set up a patrol point system for our enemy character, we'll use the "**Event ActorBeginOverlap**" to detect when a "**BP-EnemyCharacter**" reaches one of its two patrol points and then switch to the target patrol point. Whenever we update the **CurrentPatrolPoint** variable, we have to call the **UpdatePatrolPointB** macro.

Use the following steps to create the events:

1) In the **"EventGraph"** of **"BP-EnemyCharacter"**, Pull a wire from the white execution pin of "**Event BeginPlay**" to add a "**SET Current Patrol Point**" node.

2) Pull a wire from the input pin of "**SET Current Patrol Point**" to add a "**GET Patrol Point 1**" node. Pull a wire from the white output pin of the "**SET Current Patrol Point**" node to add the "**UpdatePatrolPointB**" macro node.

3) Next, you will create the "**Event ActorBeginOverlap**" event to handle swapping patrol points. This event checks if the enemy overlaps with "**Patrol Point 1**". If true, it sets

"**Patrol Point 2**" as the "**Current Patrol Point**". If false, it checks if the enemy overlaps with "**Patrol Point 2**" and sets "**Patrol Point 1**" as the "**Current Patrol Point**".

4) Steps 4-7 will enable you to verify if the enemy overlaps with Patrol Point 1. Pull a wire from the white execution pin of the **Event ActorBeginOverlap** node to add a **Branch** node.
5) Pull a wire from the **Condition** input pin of the **Branch** node to add an **Equal** node.
6) Pull a wire from the upper pin of the **Equal** node to add a **GET Patrol Point 1** node.
7) Join the bottom input pin of the **Equal** node to the **Other Actor** output pin of the **Event ActorBeginOverlap** node.

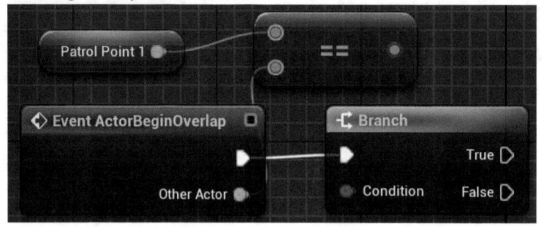

8) Steps 8-10 will help you to set **Patrol Point 2** as the **Current Patrol Point**. Pull a wire from the input pin of the **Branch** node to add a **SET Current Patrol Point** node.
9) Pull a wire from the input pin of the **SET Current Patrol Point** node to add a **GET Patrol Point 2** node.
10) pull a wire from the white output pin of the **SET Current Patrol Point** node to add the **UpdatePatrolPointB** macro node

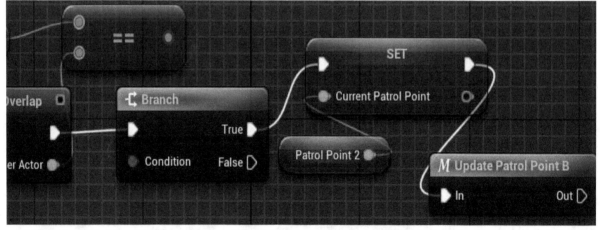

11) Steps 11-14 will enable you to verify if the enemy overlaps with **Patrol Point 2**. Pull a wire from the **False** output pin of the **Branch** node to add another **Branch** node.
12) Pull a wire from the **Condition** input pin of the second **Branch** node to add an **Equal** node.
13) Join the top input pin of the **Equal** node to the **Other Actor** output pin of the **Event ActorBeginOverlap** node.
14) Pull a wire from the bottom input pin of the **Equal** node to add a **GET Patrol Point 2** node.

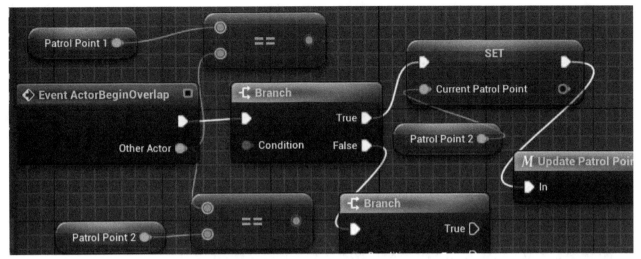

15) Steps 15-17 will enable you to set **Patrol Point 1** as the **Current Patrol Point**. Pull a wire from the **True** output pin of the second **Branch** node to add a **SET Current Patrol Point** node.

16) Pull a wire from the input pin of the new **SET Current Patrol Point** node to add a **GET Patrol Point 1** node.

17) Join the white output pin of the **SET Current Patrol Point** node to the input pin of the **UpdatePatrolPointB** macro node. **Compile** and **save** the Blueprint.

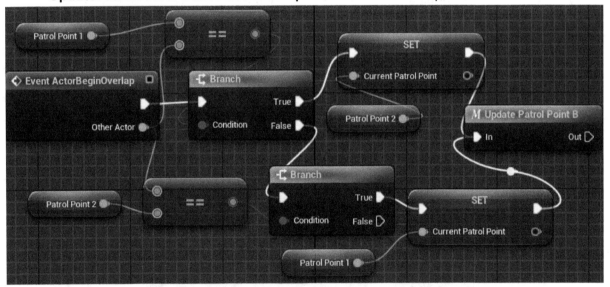

These steps configure the **BP-EnemyCharacter** Blueprint to handle patrol points correctly. The next step is to alter the **BP-EnemyController** Blueprint to run the Behavior Tree.

HOW TO RUN THE BEHAVIOR TREE IN THE AI CONTROLLER

Use the following steps to run the Behavior Tree:

1) Open the **BP-EnemyController** Blueprint. This Blueprint was created using the **AIController** class as its parent to execute the BT-EnemyBehavior Behavior Tree.

2) In the EventGraph, pull a wire from the white execution pin of the **Event BeginPlay** node to add a **Run Behavior Tree** node. Set the **BTAsset** input option to **BT-EnemyBehavior**.

185

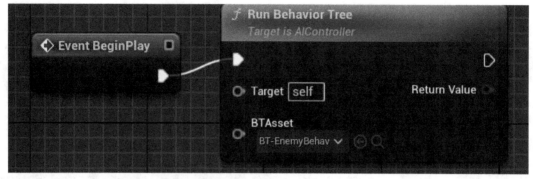

3) **Compile** and **Save** the Blueprint": This completes the necessary steps in the Blueprints to navigate the patrol points.

Now, the AI is ready to proceed to the core functionality—the Behavior Tree.

INSTRUCTING YOUR AI TO WALK WITH THE BEHAVIOR TREE

A Behavior Tree is a powerful tool used to model character behavior, consisting of control flow nodes and task nodes. The primary control flow nodes you'll use are **Selector** and **Sequence**:

✓ **Selector Node:** Runs its child nodes from left to right and stops as soon as one child successfully executes. If a Selector node has three children, the third will only run if the first two fail to execute because their conditions were not met.

✓ **Sequence Node:** Runs its child nodes in order from left to right and only succeeds if all the children succeed. If any child fails, the entire sequence fails, stopping execution.

Use the following steps to create your 1st Behavior Tree:

1) In the content browser, double-click the **BT-EnemyBehavior** asset. This opens the **Behavior Tree** Editor.

2) In the **Details** panel, under the **BEHAVIOR TREE** section, select **B-EnemyBlackboard** as the **Blackboard Asset**. The **KEYS** dropdown of **B-EnemyBlackboard** will show in the **Blackboard** panel at the bottom.

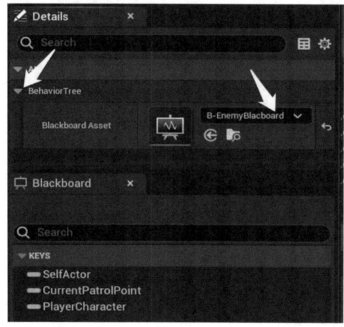

3) Examine the **Behavior Tree** graph. The "**ROOT**" Node is the starting point of the logic flow and the "**Node Connections**" is the darker line at the bottom of the **Behavior Tree** nodes representing the connection points between nodes.

4) Click and pull a wire from the dark area at the bottom of the **ROOT** node and drop it on the empty graph space. This opens a selection menu popup. Choose the **Sequence** option.

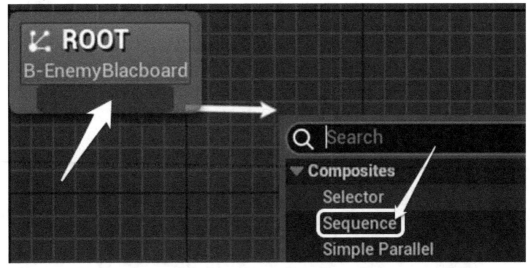

5) Go to the **Details** panel, and set the **Node Name** to "**Move to Patrol**".
6) Pull a wire from the **Move to Patrol** node to add a **Move To** node. This task node is **purple** and always appears at the bottom of the **Behavior Tree,** so it has no attachment points for additional nodes at the bottom.

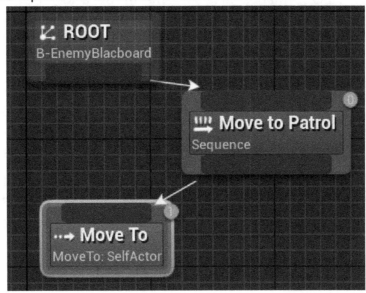

7) Go to the **Details** panel of the "**Move To**" task node, and change the **Blackboard Key** to "**CurrentPatrolPoint**". This key determines where the actor will move.

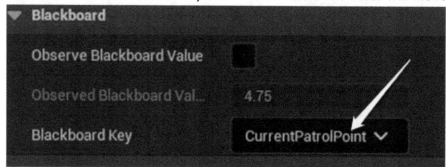

8) Pull a wire from the **Move** to **Patrol** sequence node to add a **Wait** node.
9) Go to the **Details** panel of the **Wait** node, and adjust the **Wait Time** to **4.0** to add a 4-second pause between patrols. Set the **Random Deviation** to **1.0,** which introduces a 1-second variation, resulting in a pause of random length between 2 and 4 seconds.

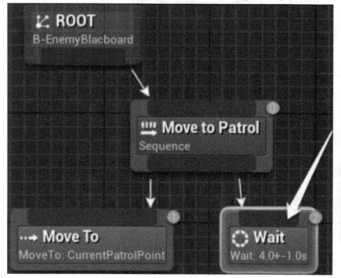
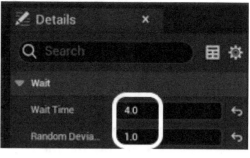

10) Save your changes. When running the game, the Behavior Tree will perform the **Move To** task node till the enemy reaches its destination. Once there, the **Wait** task node will execute, pausing the behavior briefly before resuming patrol.

Hint: observe the **small gray circles** with numbers in the upper-right corner of the nodes. These numbers indicate the execution order of the nodes, based on their left-to-right and top-to-down positions. The first node to be evaluated is labeled with a **0** badge.

Now, everything is configured to test the enemy patrol.

CHOOSING THE PATROL POINTS IN THE BP_ENEMYCHARACTER INSTANCE

We made the **PatrolPoint1** and **PatrolPoint2** variables **Instance Editable** in BP_EnemyCharacter, which allows us to set them in the Level Editor. Follow these steps to select the patrol points:

1) Go to the **Level** Editor, and click the instance of **BP-EnemyCharacter** that we placed in the level.
2) In the **Details** panel, go to the **Default** category. Set **Patrol Point 1** to the **PatrolPoint1** instance and **Patrol Point 2** to the **PatrolPoint2** instance.

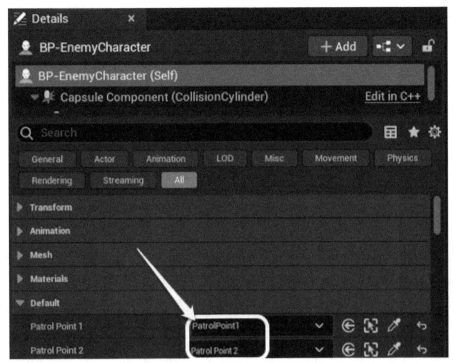

3) **Save** the level and click the **Play** button for assessment. You should see the enemy character start moving to the first patrol point. When it reaches the first point, it will briefly pause before moving to the second patrol point. This pattern will continue back and forth when the game is running.

With the patrol behavior determined, we can now give the enemy the ability to see the player and pursue them.

MAKE THE AI CHASE THE PLAYER

To make the enemy AI more threatening, we will use the PawnSensing component to add vision and hearing capabilities. We will then expand our Behavior Tree accordingly.

GIVE THE ENEMY SIGHT WITH PAWNSENSING

To enable the enemy to detect the player, we need to include the PawnSensing component in the **BP-EnemyController** and store the **PlayerCharacter** reference in **BB-EnemyBlackboard** when the enemy sees the player. You can use these steps to add a PawnSensing component:

1) Open the **BP-EnemyController** Blueprint in the editor.
2) In the **My Blueprint** panel, create a new variable. Name it "**PlayerKeyName**" in the **Details** panel and set its **Variable Type** to "**Name**". **Compile** the Blueprint and Set the **Default Value** to "**PlayerCharacter**".

3) Go to the **Components** panel, click the **Add** button, and search for "**pawn**". Choose the **Pawn Sensing** component.

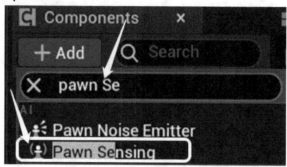

4) Go to the **Details** panel of the **PawnSensing** component, find the **Events** category, and click the plus **(+)** button beside the "**On See Pawn**" to add it to the **EventGraph**.

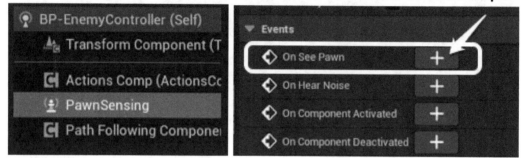

5) The **On See Pawn** event triggers when the enemy sees an instance of the **Pawn** class (or its child class, Character) within its line of sight. In the EventGraph, we have to check if the instance seen is the player (**FirstPersonCharacter** class). If it is the player, store the instance reference in the Blackboard.

6) Pull a wire from the **Pawn** output pin of the **On See Pawn** event to add a **Cast to BP_FirstPersonCharacter** node.

7) Right-click in the graph to add a **Get Blackboard** node.

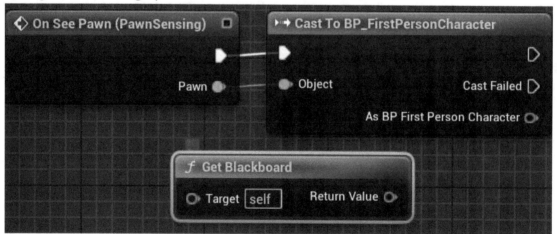

8) Pull a wire from the **Return Value** pin of **Get Blackboard** to add a **Set Value as Object** node.

9) Pull a wire from the **Key Name** pin of the **Set Value as Object** node to add a **GET Player Key Name** node.

10) Pull a wire from the **Object Value** pin of the **Set Value as Object** node and join it to the **As BP_FirstPersonCharacter** output pin.
11) Join the white execution pins of the **Cast to BP_FirstPersonCharacter** and **Set Value as Object** nodes. **Compile** the Blueprint.

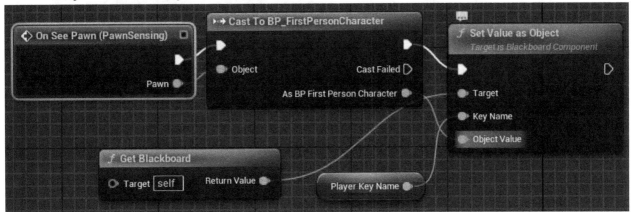

These changes in the **BP-EnemyController** Blueprint enable the enemy to detect the player. Next, let's work on the Behavior Tree.

CREATE A BEHAVIOR TREE TASK

Behavior Tree elements like Tasks, Decorators, and Services are dedicated types of Blueprints. We'll create a simple Task to clear a Blackboard key. Follow these steps:

1) In the content browser, double-click the **BT-EnemyBehavior** asset to open the Behavior Tree Editor.
2) Click the **New Task** button on the toolbar.

3) If you don't have existing **Tasks** in the project, the Blueprint Editor will open with a new Blueprint using **BTTask-BlueprintBase** as the parent class. If you have existing Tasks, select the **BTTask-BlueprintBase** class from the dropdown that displays.
4) Go to the **Details** panel, and set the **Node Name** field to "**Clear B Value**".

5) Go to the **Variables** section of the **My Blueprint** panel, and click the plus (**+**) button to add a variable. Name the variable "**Key**" in the Details panel and set its type to "**Blackboard KeySelector**", and ensure the Instance **Editable feature** is checked.

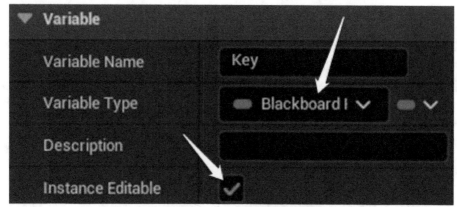

6) To add the **Event Receive Execute** event, navigate to the **My Blueprint** panel. Hover over the **FUNCTIONS** category, click the **Override** dropdown, and choose **Receive Execute** to add the event.

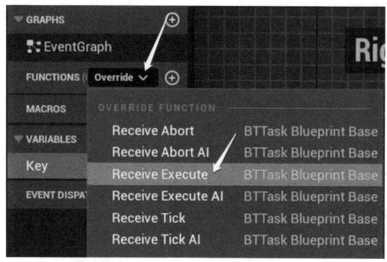

Next, you will clear the **Blackboard** value using the **Key** variable and use the **Finish** Execute to complete the task.

7) Pull a wire from the white output pin of **Event Receive Execute** to add a **Clear Blackboard Value** node.

8) Pull a wire from the "**Key**" input pin of **Clear Blackboard Value** to add a **Get Key** node.

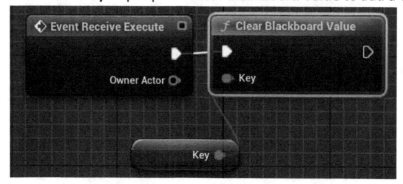

9) Pull a wire from the white output pin of **Clear Blackboard Value** to add a **Finish** Execute node. Ensure to check the **Success** parameter of the **Finish Execute** node.

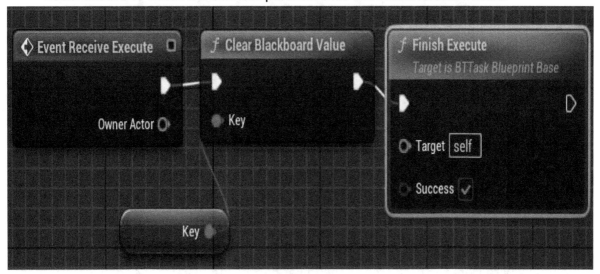

10) Compile, save, and close the Blueprint Editor. Rename the **BTTask** blueprint base to **BTTasks-ClearBValue** in the content browser,

This new Task, **BTTasks-ClearBBValue**, will be used to clear the "**PlayerCharacter**" reference in the Blackboard after an enemy attack to allow the player an opportunity to evade.

ADDING CONDITIONS TO THE BEHAVIOR TREE

To enhance our Behavior Tree, we'll introduce new Sequence and Selector nodes to direct the enemy to chase the player, controlled by conditions using a Decorator. A Decorator connects the top of a node and offers conditions that should be met before the Tasks can be executed.

Use the following steps to update the Behavior Tree:

1) Double-click the **BT-EnemyBehavior** asset in the content browser to open the **Behavior Tree** Editor.
2) Right-click on the center of the **ROOT** node and choose **Break Node Link(s)**.

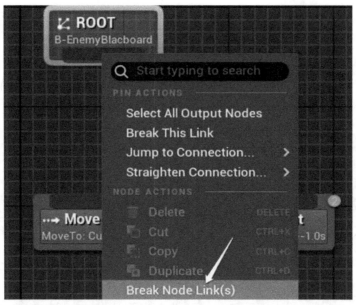

3) Pull a wire from the dark area at the lower part of the **ROOT** node to an empty space in the graph. Pick the **Selector** option from the popup menu.

4) Pull a wire down from the **Selector** node and join it to the existing **Move To Patrol** node.

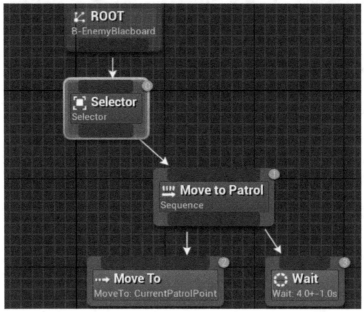

5) Pull another wire down from the **Selector** node to add a **Sequence** node. Position this node to the left of the **Move To Patrol** node to prioritize attacking over patrolling.

6) Go to the **Details** panel, and set the **Node Name** to "**Attack Player**".

7) Right-click on the **Attack Player** node, hover over **Add Decorator** to extend the menu, and choose **Blackboard** to add the **Decorator**. This is used to check if the enemy sees the player.

8) Click on the added "**Decorator**" node. Go to the **Details** panel, and configure it as follows:
   - ✓ **Observer aborts** to **Lower Priority**.
   - ✓ **Blackboard Key** to **PlayerCharacter**.
   - ✓ **Node Name** to "**Can see Player**?".

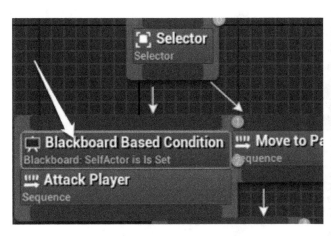 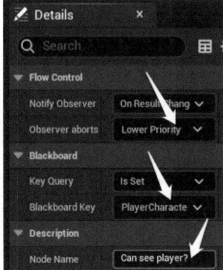

9) Save the changes. The **Decorator** ensures that the **Attack Player** sequence will only execute when the **PlayerCharacter** key has a valid reference in the Blackboard. It will also abort the **Move to Patrol** sequence to perform the **Attack Player** sequence.

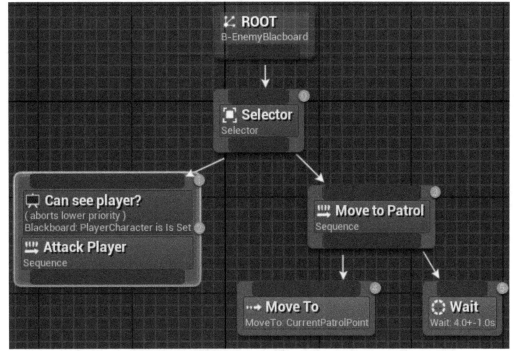

The next step involves adding Task nodes to complete the Attack Player sequence and fully implement the enemy's pursuit behavior.

CREATE A CHASING BEHAVIOR

To enable the enemy to chase the player, we'll utilize several **Task** nodes in the Behavior Tree. This setup includes using the "**Move To**" Task to pursue the **PlayerCharacter**, adding a pause between attacks with the **Wait** node, and clearing the **PlayerCharacter** reference using the **BTTask-ClearBValue** Task.

Add the Task nodes using the following steps:

1) Pull a wire from the **Attack Player** sequence node to add a **Move To** Task node. Go to the **Details** panel, and set the **Blackboard Key** to **PlayerCharacter**.

2) Pull a wire from the **Attack Player** sequence node to add a **Wait** Task node. Go to the **Details** panel, and adjust the **Wait Time** to **3.0** seconds.

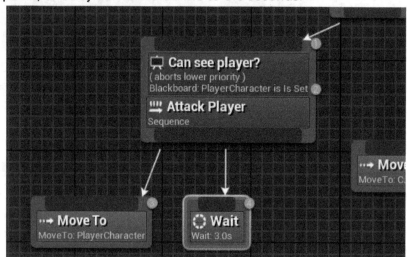

3) Pull another wire from the **Attack Player** sequence node to add a **BTTask-ClearBValue** task node. Go to the **Details** panel, change the **Key** to **PlayerCharacter,** and set the **Node Name** to "**Reset Player Seen**".

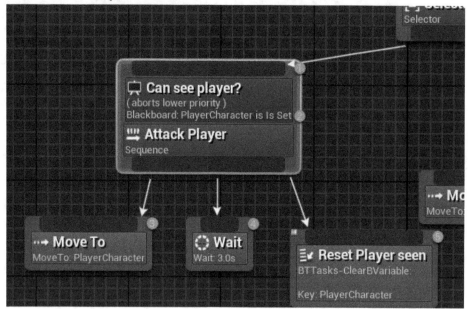

4) **Save** and **close** the Behavior Tree Editor. Click the **Play** button in the Level Editor to test the enemy's behavior.

As you move the player character in front of the patrolling enemy, the enemy will stop its patrol and chase the player. Once the enemy reaches the player, it will stop for 2 seconds before going to its patrol path. if it re-establishes a line of sight with the player, then it will intrude on its patrol and start chasing the player again.

CHAPTER NINE
DEVELOPING THE AI ENEMIES

Next, we will enhance the capabilities of our AI enemies, introducing a real risk of failure for the player and adding more variety to the gameplay. We aim to define the type of challenge we want to present. Our focus will be on creating zombie-like enemies that relentlessly chase the player, fostering an action-packed experience where survival against hordes of foes is key.

We'll begin by improving the AI's abilities, enabling it to deal with damage and utilize wandering patterns to make survival more difficult for the player. Next, we will empower the player with the means to combat these formidable enemies. Finally, we'll balance this increased difficulty by implementing a system to gradually spawn new enemies within the game world.

Chapter Summary and Enemy Spawner Setup

By the end of this chapter, you should have created an enemy spawner that generates AI enemies. These enemies will be able to attack the player, detect the player's footsteps and shots, and roam the level randomly.

CONSTRUCTING AN ENEMY ATTACK

To make our enemies a real challenge for the player, they need the ability to inflict damage on the player. In **Chapter 8**, we established the basic structure of an enemy attack pattern, triggered when the player enters the enemy's line of sight. Now, we will enhance this attack by adding a damage component, ensuring the player faces consequences if an enemy gets within melee range of a player.

CREATING AN ATTACK TASK

We'll create an attack task titled "BTTask-DoAttack" that deals with damage. This task will be part of the **"Attack Player"** sequence in the enemy Behavior Tree. The task will have two variables: one for the damage target and another for the damage amount. Create the attack task using the following steps:

1) In the Content Browser, go to the **Content > Enemy** folder and double-click on the **"BT-EnemyBehavior"** asset to open the Behavior Tree Editor.

2) Click on the **"New Task"** button on the toolbar and choose **"BTTask-BlueprintBase"** from the drop-down menu. The task will be created in the same folder as the Behavior Tree; **Content > Enemy**.

3) In the Content Browser, change the name of the newly created **"BTTask-BlueprintBase-New"** asset to **"BTTask-DoAttack"**. Double-click on **"BTTask-DoAttack"** to open it in the Blueprint Editor.

4) Go to the **Details** panel, and change the "**Node Name**" field to "**DoAttack**".

5) Go to the **My Blueprint** panel, and click the "**+**" button next to the **Variables** category. Go to the **Details** panel, title the variable "**TargetActorKey**", set its Variable type to "**BlackboardKeySelector**", and tick the "**Instance Editable**" feature.

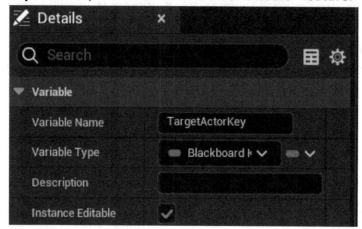

6) Go to the **My Blueprint** panel, and create a new variable. Go to the Details panel, title this variable "**Damage**", set its **Variable Type** to **Float**, and enable the **Instance Editable** feature. After compiling the blueprint, set the **Default Value** to **0.25**, meaning an attack will reduce the player's health by 25%.

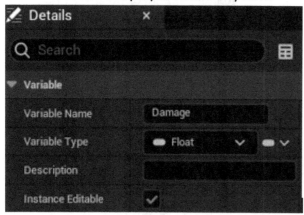

7) Go to the **My Blueprint** panel, hover over the **Functions** category, click the **Override** dropdown, and choose **Receive Execute** to add this event.

Within the **Event Receive Execute**, we want to ensure the **Target Actor** is valid before applying damage. The event uses the **Target Actor** reference from the blackboard to verify its validity, before calling the **Apply Damage** function.

Steps 8–11 involve retrieving the **Target Actor** reference from the blackboard and validating it:

8) Pull a wire from the white pin of the **Event Receive Execute** node to add an **Is Valid** macro node.

9) Drag the **Target Actor Key** variable from the **My Blueprint** panel, drop it in the **EventGraph**, and choose **Get Target Actor Key**.

10) Pull a wire from the **Target Actor Key** node to add a **Get Blackboard Value as Actor** node.

11) Pull a wire from the **Return Value** of the **Get Blackboard Value as Actor** node and join it to the **Input Object** pin of the **Is Valid** node.

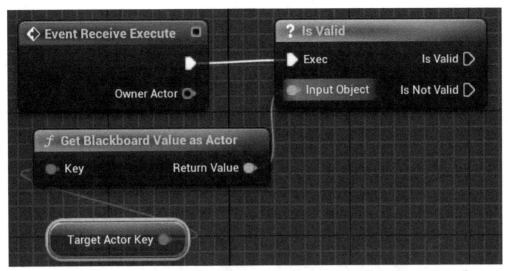

Steps 12–14 involve calling the **Apply Damage** function using the **Target Actor** reference:

12) Pull another wire from the **Return Value** of the **Get Blackboard Value as Actor** node to add an **Apply Damage** node. Join the **Is Valid** output pin to the white input pin of the **Apply Damage** node.

13) Pull a wire from the **Base Damage** input pin of the **Apply Damage** node to add a **Get Damage** node.

14) Pull a wire from the white output pin of the **Apply Damage** node to add a **Finish Execute** node. Tick the **Success** parameter of the **Finish Execute** node.

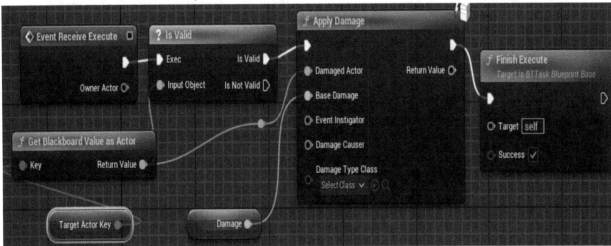

Finally, compile, save, and close the Blueprint Editor.

USE THE ATTACK TASK IN THE BEHAVIOR TREE

Next, you will add the attack task to the attack sequence in **BT-EnemyBehavior**. The enemy's attack is a melee attack, so it will only perform the attack after reaching the player. Follow these steps to utilize the DoAttack task:

1) In the Behavior Tree Editor, pull a wire down from the **Attack Player** sequence node to add a **BTTask-DoAttack** task node between the **Move To** and **Wait** task nodes.

2) In the **Details** panel, alter the **Target Actor Key** selection to **PlayerCharacter**. Set the **Node Name** to **Damage Player** to describe how we are using the **BTTask-DoAttack**.

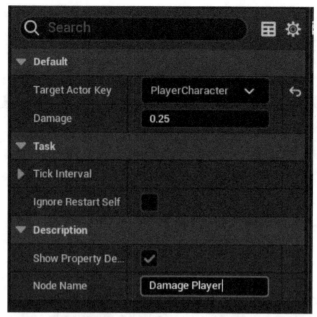

3) Save the Behavior Tree. The "**Attack Player**" sequence should resemble the screen below:

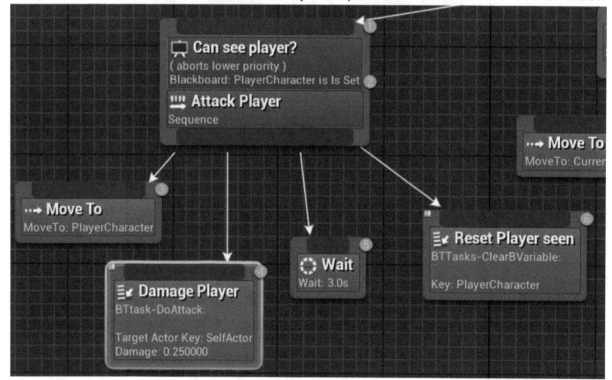

With the "Attack Player" sequence complete, the next step is to update the **FirstPersonCharacter** blueprint to reduce the health meter when damage is assigned.

UPDATE THE HEALTH METER

The health meter bar is connected to the Player Health variable in the **FirstPersonCharacter** blueprint. We will use the **Event AnyDamage** to decrease the Player Health variable accordingly. To create the **Event AnyDamage**, follow these steps:

1) Open the **Content Browser** and Go to the **Content > FirstPersonBP > Blueprints** folder. Double-click the **FirstPersonCharacter** blueprint to open it.
2) In the **Event Graph**, right-click in an empty space to add the **Event AnyDamage** node. This node will handle the damaged logic for the player.
3) From the white output pin of the **Event AnyDamage** node, pull a wire to add a **SET Player Health** node. This node will update the player's health.
4) From the input pin of the **SET Player Health** node, pull a wire to add a **MAX (float)** node. This ensures that the player's health never drops below 0.

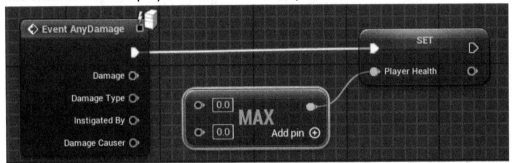

5) Pull a wire from the top input pin of the **MAX (float)** node to add a **Subtract** node.
6) From the top input pin of the **Subtract** node, pull a wire to add a **GET Player Health** node.
7) Pull a wire from the bottom input pin of the **Subtract** node and join it to the **Damage** output pin of the **Event AnyDamage** node. This links the damage amount to the health calculation.

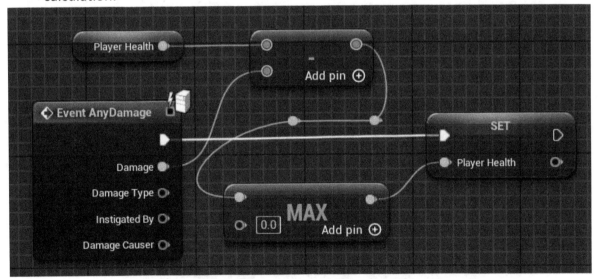

8) Compile and save the blueprint, then press the Play button to test the setup.

When an enemy gets close to the player and attacks, the player's health meter will deplete. Since the enemy can attack the player now, we can explore additional options on how the enemy perceives the player.

APPLYING ENEMY SOUND DETECTION

Enemies that can only chase players directly in front of them are easy to avoid. To make them more challenging, we can use the **PawnSensing** component to enable enemies to detect nearby sounds made by players. When a player makes a sound within an enemy's detection range, the enemy will investigate the location of that sound. If they spot the player, they will attack. If not, they will wait at the sound's location for a moment before resuming their patrol.

ATTACHING HEARING TO THE BEHAVIOR TREE

We will incorporate a sequence of tasks in the Behavior Tree for when the enemy hears a sound. Since attacking the player remains a higher priority, investigating sounds will be of lower priority.

To enable the enemy to investigate the sound's origin, we need to create two keys in the blackboard:

- ✓ **HasHeardSound (Boolean):** Indicates whether a sound has been heard.
- ✓ **LocationOfSound (Vector):** Stores the location of the sound, directing the enemy where to investigate.

Steps to Create Blackboard Keys and Add the Investigate Sound Sequence:

1) In the Content Browser, go to **Content > Enemy** folder and double-click the "**BT-EnemyBehavior**" asset to open the Behavior Tree Editor.
2) Click on the "**Blackboard**" tab at the top right side.
3) Click the "**New Key**" button and select "**Bool**" as the key type. Title this new key "**HasHeardSound**".

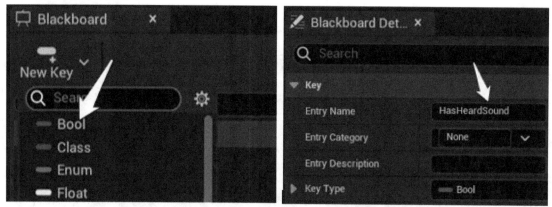

4) Click the "**New Key**" button again and choose "**Vector**" as the key type. Title this new key "**LocationOfSound**".

5) Save the **blackboard** and click the "**Behavior Tree**" tab.

6) Drag the **"Attack Player"** sequence and all its task nodes more to the left in the **Behavior Tree**, leaving room between "**Attack Player" and "Move to Patrol"**. This is where you will add our hearing sequence.

7) Pull a wire down from the "**Selector**" node to add a "**Sequence**" node. Change this node name to "**Inspecting Sound"**.

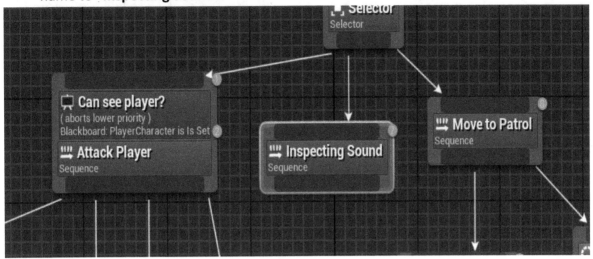

8) Right-click on the **"Inspecting Sound"** node, hover the mouse on **"Add Decorator"** to enlarge the menu, and choose "**Blackboard**" to add a decorator.

9) Click the decorator, and in the "**Details**" panel, set "**Blackboard Key**" to "**HasHeardSound**", "**Observer Aborts**" to "**Lower Priority**" and **"Node Name"** to "**Heard Sound?"**.

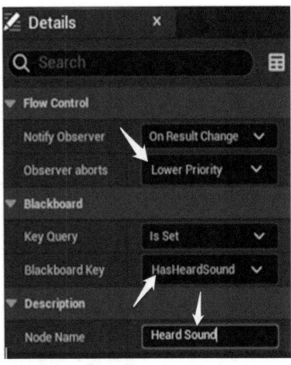

The following screenshot displays the "**Investigate Sound**" sequence node with the decorator. Note that the priority of nodes in a Behavior Tree is left to right:

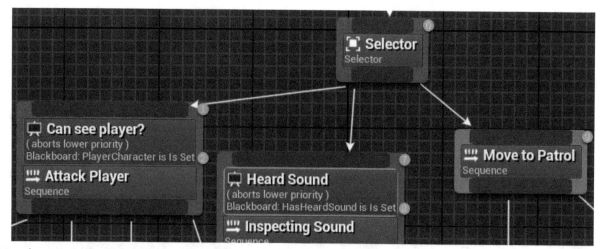

You have created the blackboard keys, the sequence node, and the decorator. Our next step is to create the task nodes of the "**Inspecting Sound**" sequence.

CONFIGURING THE INSPECTION TASKS:

The **Inspection Sound** sequence will function similarly to the **Attack Player** sequence. When an enemy is patrolling and hears a sound, they will move toward the position of the noise.

To add the task nodes, follow these steps:

1) From the **Inspecting Sound** sequence node, pull a wire to add a **Move To** task node. Go to the **Details** panel, and set the **Blackboard Key** to **LocationofSound.**

2) Again, from the **Inspecting Sound** sequence node, pull a wire to add the **Wait** task node. In the **Details** panel, set the Wait Time to 4.0 seconds.

3) From the **Inspecting Sound** sequence node, pull another wire to add a **BTTask-ClearBValue** task node. Go to the **Details** panel, set the **Key** to **HasHeardSound** and the **Node Name** to **Reset Heard Sound**.

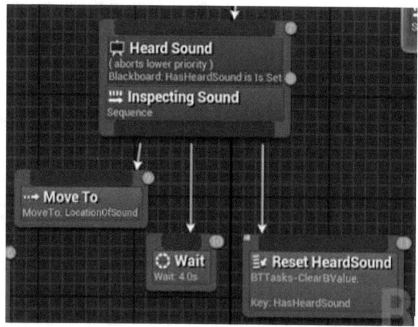

4) Save your changes and close the Behavior Tree Editor.

CREATE VARIABLES AND A MACRO TO UPDATE THE BLACKBOARD

Next, we need to configure the **BP-EnemyController** blueprint to instruct our AI on how to respond to sounds in the game by creating variables and a macro to update the blackboard. Follow these steps:

1) In the Content Browser, go to **Content > Enemy**, and double-click the **BP-EnemyController** blueprint.

2) In the **My Blueprint** panel, under **Variables**, click the plus (**+**) button to add a new variable. In the **Details** panel, title the variable **HearingLength** and set its **Variable Type** to **Float**. Compile the blueprint and set the **DEFAULT VALUE** to **1500**.0.

3) Add another variable in the **My Blueprint** panel. Go to the **Details** panel, title it **HasHeardSoundKey,** and set its **Variable Type** to **Name**. Compile the blueprint and set the default value to HasHeardSound.

4) Create another Name variable named **LocationOfSoundKey**. Compile the blueprint and change **DEFAULT VALUE** to **LocationofSound**.

5) Go to the **My Blueprint** panel, under Macros, and click the **plus** (**+**) button to create a new macro. Name it **UpdateSoundB**.

6) Go to the **Details** panel of the macro, create an input parameter titled **In** of the **Exec** type, another input parameter titled **Location** of the **Vector** type, and an output parameter titled **Out** of the **Exec** type.

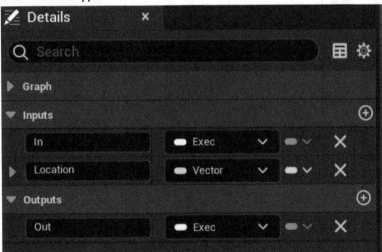

In the next steps, we'll create nodes for the UpdateSoundB macro; Steps 7-10 will be used to store Sound Position:

7) On the **UpdateSoundB** macro tab, right-click in the graph to add a "**Get Blackboard**" function node.

8) Pull a wire from the "**Return Value**" pin of the "**Get Blackboard**" node to add a "**Set Value as Vector**" node.

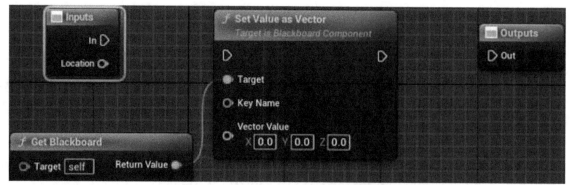

9) Pull a wire from the "**Key Name**" pin of the "**Set Value as Vector**" node to add a "**GET Location of Sound Key**" node.

10) Join the "**Location**" pin of the "**Inputs**" node to the "**Vector Value**" pin of the "**Set Value as Vector**" node. Also, Join the white execution pins of the "**Inputs**" and "**Set Value as Vector**" nodes.

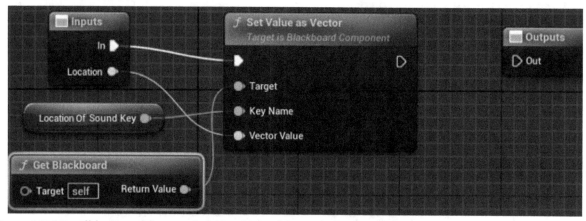

Steps 11-13 will be used for setting Has Heard Sound Key:

11) Pull another wire from the "**Return Value**" pin of the "**Get Blackboard**" node to add a "**Set Value as Bool**" node. Enable the "**Bool Value**" parameter.

12) Pull a wire from the **Key Name** pin of **the Set Value as Bool** node to add a **GET Has Heard Sound Key** node.

13) Join the white execution pins of the **Set Value as Vector**, **Set Value as Bool,** and **Outputs** nodes. Close the **UpdateSoundB** macro tab and compile the blueprint.

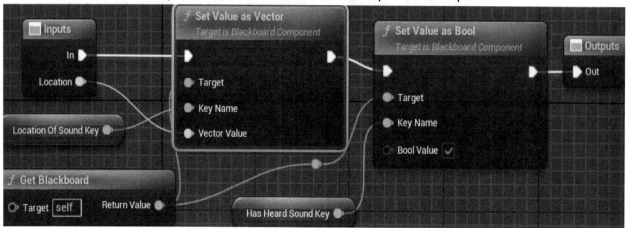

Since we have created the **UpdateSoundB** macro, we will use another event of the **PawnSensing** component to detect sound.

TRANSLATING AND STORING THE NOISE EVENT DATA

The **PawnSensing** component we added to BP-EnemyController provides us the foundation to build both visual and auditory sensing in our enemy AI. You will use the **On Hear Noise** event that activates whenever the **PawnSensing** component discovers a special type of sound broadcast by a pawn noise emitter.

We will need to configure the blueprint so that the enemies only perceive noises that are made a short distance away; else, it would feel biased for the player to shoot their gun from the opposite corner of the map and let every enemy immediately recognize their location. Create the On Hear Noise event with the following steps:

1) Go to the **Components** panel, and choose the **PawnSensing** component. Go to the **Details** panel, look in the **Events** category, and click the plus (+)to the right of the **On Hear Noise** event to add it to the Event Graph.

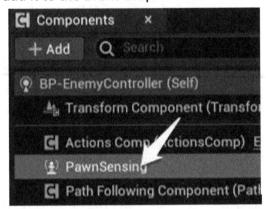 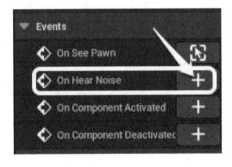

2) In the **On Hear Noise**, we want to call the **Update Sound B** macro if the distance between the sound location and the enemy is lesser than the value of **HearingDistance**:

3) Pull a wire from the white pin of the **On Hear Noise (PawnSensing**) node to add a **Branch** node. We'll be using this setup to calculate the distance between the sound's origin and the enemy's location with the **VectorLength** function. If this distance is lesser than the defined Hearing Distance, the **True** output pin of the **Branch** node will be activated.

4) Pull a wire from the **True** pin of the **Branch** node to add the **Update Sound BB** macro node. Join the **Location** pin from the **On Hear Noise (PawnSensing**) node to the **Location** pin of the **Update Sound BB** macro.

5) Now, pull a wire from the **Condition** input pin of the **Branch** node to add a **Less** node.

6) Pull a wire from the bottom input pin of the **Less** node to add a **GET Hearing Distance** node.
7) Right-click in the empty space of the **Event Graph** to add a **Get Controlled Pawn** node. This will retrieve the enemy instance being controlled by the **BP-EnemyController.**
8) Pull a wire from the **Return Value** pin of the **Get Controlled Pawn** node to add a **GetActorLocation** node to obtain the enemy's location.
9) Pull a wire from the **Location** pin of the **On Hear Noise (PawnSensing)** node to add a **Subtract** node.

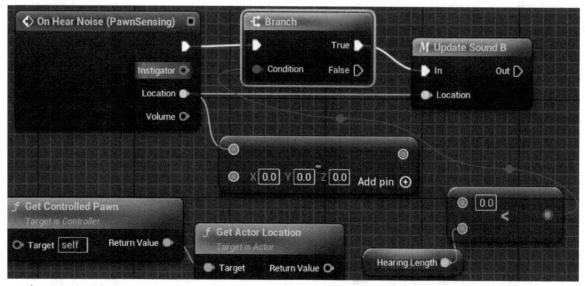

10) Join the bottom input pin of the **Subtract** node to the **Return Value** pin of the **GetActorLocation** node.
11) Pull a wire from the output pin of the Subtract node to add a **VectorLength** node.
12) Finally, Join the **Return Value** of the **VectorLength** node to the top input pin of the **Less** node. The **Return Value** of the **VectorLength** node represents the distance between the sound's location and the enemy's location. **Compile** and **save** your blueprint to ensure all changes are applied.

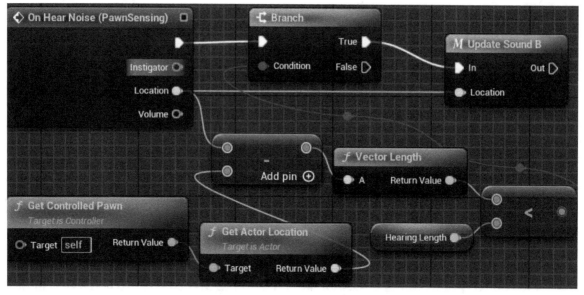

To enhance our enemy AI's ability to detect player-generated sounds, we've modified it to recognize broadcast noises. Now, we need to add nodes in the **FirstPersonCharacter** blueprint to trigger the AI's hearing response based on player actions.

ADDING NOISE TO PLAYER ACTIONS

The **Pawn Sensing** component of **EnemyController** can only discover noise generated by the Pawn Noise Emitter. This means existing sound effects, such as the gunfire sound, won't trigger the enemy's sensing component. It's crucial to understand that the nodes responsible for creating noise for pawn sensing are independent of the sounds players hear. These noises are purely for AI event detection.

To ensure noises are detected by the pawn sensor, we need to add the **Pawn Noise Emitter** component to an actor. We will modify two player actions—sprinting and shooting—to produce noticeable noise by using this component.

Steps to Implement the Pawn Noise Emitter are listed below:

1) In the content browser, go to **Content** > **FirstPersonBP** > **Blueprints** and open the **FirstPersonCharacter** Blueprint.

2) Click the **Add** button In the **Components** panel and search for "**pawn**". choose the **Pawn Noise Emitter** component.

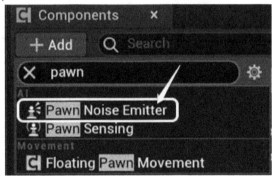

3) Start by adding noise to the sprinting action. In the **My Blueprint** panel, open the **ManageStaminaDrain** macro. Next, you will add the **Make Noise** node after the **SET Player Stamina** node.

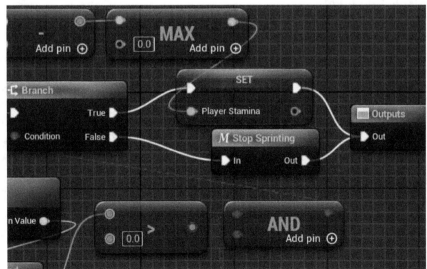

209

4) To make space for another function node, drag the Outputs node to the right.

5) Pull a wire from the white output pin of the **SET Player Stamina node**. Search for the **"Make Noise"** function to add the **Make Noise (PawnNoiseEmitter)** function as shown below.

6) Then, alter the **Loudness** input of the **Make Noise** node to **1.0.**

7) Pull a wire from the **Noise Location** input of the Make Noise node to add a **GetActorLocation** node.

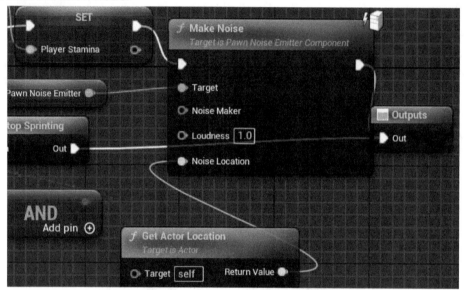

Next, we'll integrate the **Make Noise** node in the **InputAction Fire** event after reducing the **ammunition**. You can find the **InputAction Fire** event in the **Graphs** section of the **My Blueprint** panel.

8) Pull a wire from the white output pin of the **SET PlayerCurrent Ammo node**. Search for the **"Make Noise"** function to add the **Make Noise (PawnNoiseEmitter)** function as shown in step (**11**).

9) Alter the **Loudness** input of the **Make Noise** node to **1.0.**

10) Pull a wire from the **Noise Location** input of the Make Noise node to add a **GetActorLocation** node.

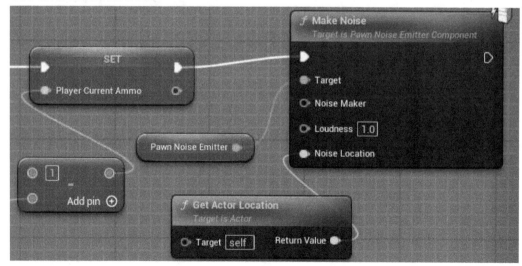

210

11) Compile, save, and then click on Play to test the game.

When you're behind an enemy or outside their line of sight, sprinting or firing your gun should cause the enemy to approach the location where the noise was made. If they see you during their investigation, they will start heading directly toward you.

With enemies now able to detect you through both sight and sound, avoiding detection becomes more challenging. We will now shift our focus to gameplay balance by equipping the player with tools to combat their enemies.

CREATING A DESTRUCTIBLE ENEMIES

In earlier chapters, we designed enemy targets that the player could eliminate with a few hits. Now, we want to extend this feature to our new enemies, giving the player the ability to reduce the threat they pose. To achieve this, we'll add blueprint nodes in BP-EnemyCharacter to manage damage and destruction. Each enemy will require three hits from the player to be destroyed.

To handle a hit in your game, follow these steps:

1) Open the Content Browser and go to "**Content > Enemy**". Double-click on the "**BP-EnemyCharacter**" blueprint.

2) Go to the My Blueprint panel, under the **Variables** section, and click the plus "**+**" button to add a new variable. Name this variable "**EnemyHealth**".

3) Go to the **Details** panel, and change the **Variable Type** to **Integer**. Compile the blueprint, and then set the **Default Value** to **4**. This means the enemy starts with **4** health points.

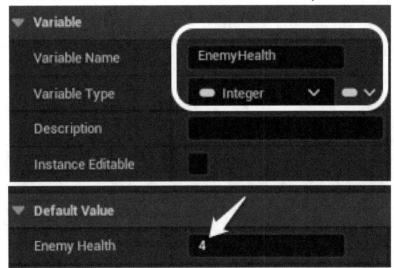

4) In the Event Graph, right-click in an empty space to add an **Event Hit** node. Next, we will be setting up Nodes for **Event Hit** actions.

5) Pull a wire from the **Other** output pin of the **Event Hit** node to add a "Cast To BP_FirstPersonProjectile" node. Join the white pins of **Event Hit and Cast To BP_FirstPersonProjectile.**

6) Pull a wire from the white output pin of the **Cast To BP_FirstPersonProjectile** node to add a **Branch** node.

7) Pull a wire from the **Condition** pin of the **Branch** node to add a **Greater** node.

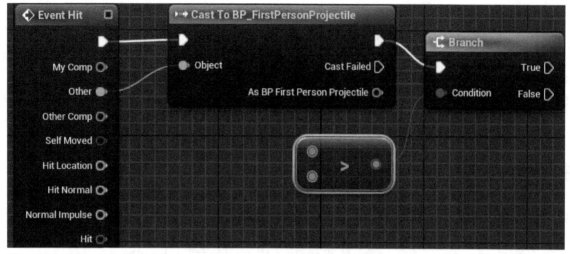

8) Pull a wire from the top input pin of the **Greater** node to add a **Get Enemy Health** node. Enter a value of **1** in the lower input of the **Greater** node.

9) Pull a wire from the **True** output pin of the **Branch** node to add a **Decrement Int** node.

10) Pull a wire from the input pin of the **Decrement Int** node to add a **Get Enemy Health** node.

11) Pull a wire from the **False** output pin of the **Branch** node to add a **Spawn Actor from** the **Class** node. In the Class parameter, select the **Blueprint_Effect_Explosion** class from the starter content.

12) Pull a wire from the **Spawn Transform** parameter to add a **GetActorTransform** node.

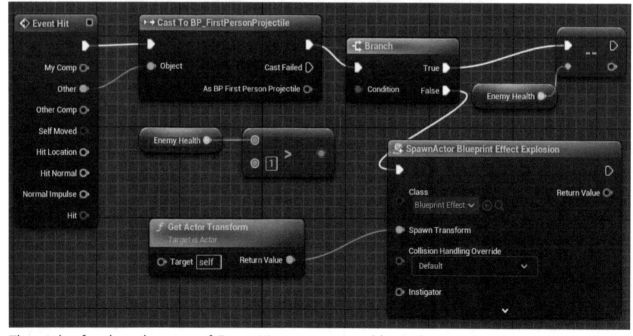

The nodes for the other part of Event Hit we want to add are the same as those used in the **BP_CylinderTarget** blueprint, so we will copy the one in the **BP_CylinderTarget** blueprint.

13) Open the **BP_CylinderTarget** blueprint located in the **Content > FirstPerson> Blueprints** folder.

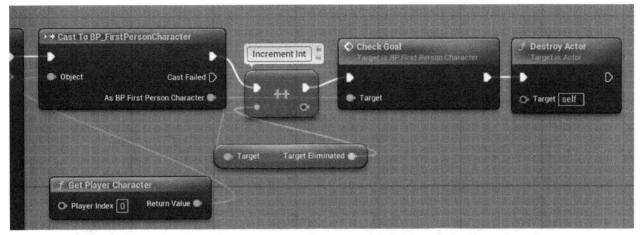

14) Select and copy the nodes displayed above, then paste the nodes into the **BP-EnemyCharacter** blueprint.

15) Join the white output pin of the **Spawn Actor** node to the white input of the **Cast to BP_FirstPersonCharacter** node. Compile, save, and press **Play** to test.

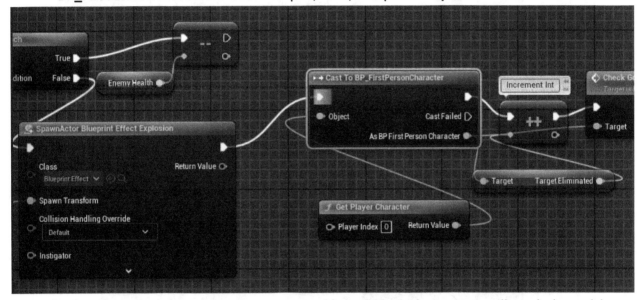

henceforth, when the player shoots an enemy three times, the enemy will explode and be destroyed, similar to the cylinder targets. To maintain the game's challenge, we will increase the difficulty by spawning more enemies.

CREATING MORE ENEMIES WITHIN GAMEPLAY

To ensure continuous gameplay, we will regularly spawn new enemies in the level. This means that if the player destroys the initial enemies too quickly or too slowly, the difficulty will gradually increase with more enemies appearing.

CREATING THE BP-ENEMYSPAWNER BLUEPRINT

We'll create a blueprint that produces enemies at random locations within the level. The frequency of these spawns is controlled by a variable called "**SpawnTime**", and the maximum number of enemies is limited by another variable called "**MaximEnemies**".

213

Create this blueprint using the following steps:

1) Open the Content Browser, and go to "**Content > Enemy**". Click the "**Add**" button and select "**Blueprint Class**".

2) Select "Actor" as the parent class. Title the blueprint "**BP-EnemySpawner**" and double-click it to open the Blueprint Editor.

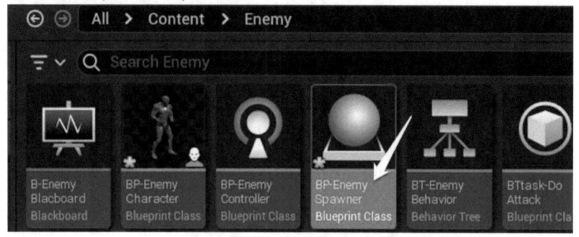

3) Go to the "**Variables**" section of the "**My Blueprint**" panel, click the plus "**+**" button to add a new variable, and title it "**SpawnTime**". Go to the "**Details**" panel, set the **Variable Type** to "**Float**" and activate the "**Instance Editable**" option. Compile the blueprint and set the **default value** to "**10.0**".

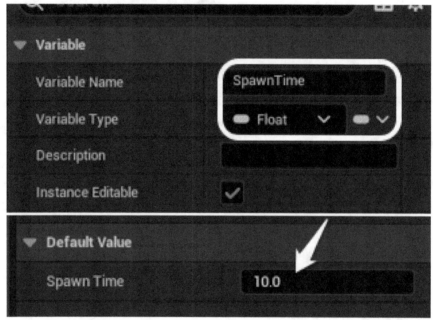

4) Go to the "**My Blueprint**" panel, create a new variable, and title it "**MaximEnemies**". Go to the **Details** panel, set its **Variable Type** to "**Integer**" and activate the "**Instance Editable**" option. **Compile** the blueprint and set its **DEFAULT VALUE** to **5**.

5) Go to the "**My Blueprint**" panel, and click the plus "**+**" button in the **Macros** category to create a new macro. Rename this macro to "**SpawnEnemy**".

6) Go to the **Details** panel of the macro, add an **input** parameter titled "**In**" of **Exec** type and an **output** parameter titled "**Out**" of **Exec** type.

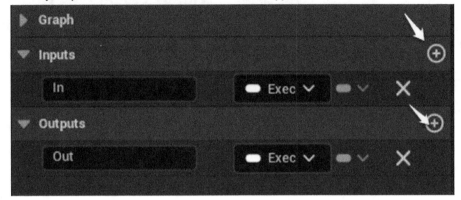

7) Open the "**SpawnEnemy**" macro tab, and add the necessary nodes to spawn a "BP-EnemyCharacter" instance at a random location in the level. Check the subsequent steps.

8) Right-click on the graph to add a "**Spawn AI From Class**" node, and join the white execution pins of the **Inputs**, **Spawn AI From Class**, and **Outputs** nodes.

9) Go to the **Pawn Class** option, and select "**BP-EnemyCharacter**". Then choose "**BT-EnemyBehavior**" in the **Behavior Tree** option.

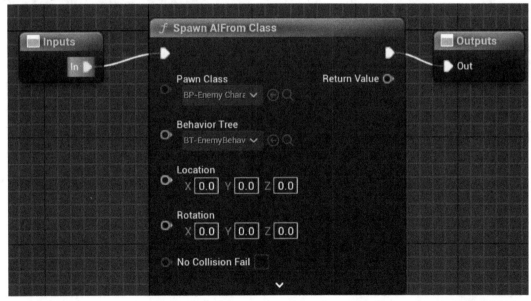

10) Pull a wire from the "**Location**" feature to add a "**GetRandomPointInNavigableRadius**" node. Enter **10000.0** as the **Radius** value. This node returns a random location based on the navigation mesh.

11) Pull a wire from the "**Origin**" parameter to add a "**GetActorLocation**" node.

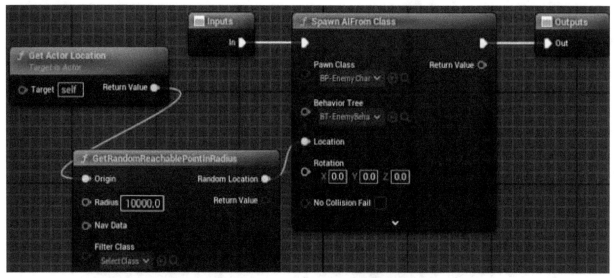

12) Go to the Event Graph of **BP-EnemySpawner,** then pull a wire from the white execution pin of "**Event BeginPlay**" to add a "**Set Timer by Event**" node.

13) Enable the **Looping** option. Pull a wire from the "**Time**" feature to add a "**Get Spawn Time**" node.

14) Pull a wire from the "**Event**" feature to add a custom event. Title it "**TryToSpawnEnemy**".

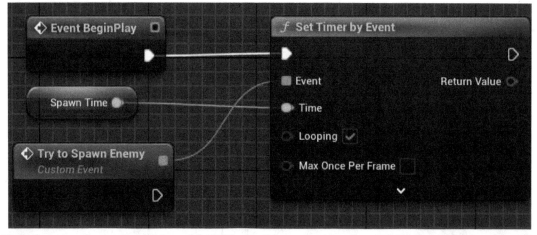

15) Pull a wire from the white pin of "**TryToSpawnEnemy**" to add a "**Get All Actors Of Class**" node. In the **Actor Class** parameter, choose "**BP-EnemyCharacter**".

16) Pull a wire from the white output pin of "**Get All Actors Of Class**" to add a "**Branch**" node.

17) Pull a wire from the **True** pin of the "**Branch**" node to add the "**Spawn Enemy**" macro node.

18) Pull a wire from the "**Out Actors**" pin of "**Get All Actors Of Class**" to add a "**Length**" node. The return value of the "**Length**" node will be the number of enemies in the level.

19) Pull a wire from the output pin of the **Length** node to add a **Less** node. Then, join the output pin of the **Less** node to the **Condition** feature of the **Branch** node.

20) Pull a wire from the bottom pin of the **Less** node to add a **Get Maxim Enemies** node.

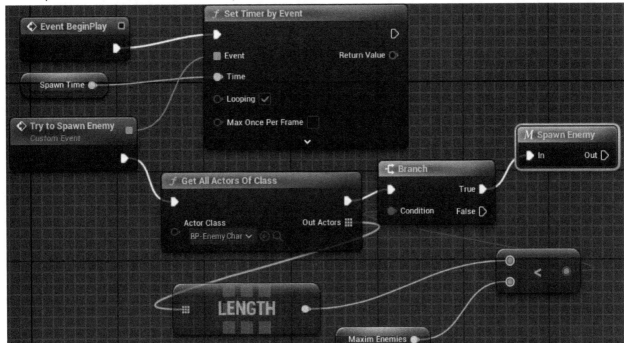

21) After completing these connections, compile and save your Blueprint. Close the Blueprint Editor, then locate the **BP-EnemySpawner** in the content browser. Drag it into your level to create an instance. Click the **Play** button to test the enemy spawning. functionality.

As you run the game, you will notice new enemies regularly appearing. However, these enemies won't move unless they detect the player. This happens because they lack established patrol points to pursue. Instead of adding patrol points, we will introduce randomness to their navigation behavior.

CREATING ENEMY WALKING BEHAVIOR

In Chapter **8**, we set the default enemy behavior to patrol between two points. While this was effective for testing the hearing and seeing components, and suited for a stealth-oriented game, we will now increase the game's challenge by making enemies walk randomly. This will make avoiding enemies harder and encourage more confrontations. To achieve this, we will modify the BT-EnemyBehavior Behavior Tree.

USING A CUSTOM TASK TO DETECT A WANDER POINT

We need to create a key in **B-EnemyBlackboard** to store the enemy's next destination. Contrary to the **PatrolPoint** key, this destination will be represented by vector coordinates rather than an in-game actor. We will then create a task to regulate where the enemy should wander within the level.

create the key and task using the following steps:

1) Open the **Behavior Tree** Editor by double-clicking the **BT-EnemyBehavior** asset in the content browser.

2) Switch on the **Blackboard** tab to edit **B_EnemyBlackboard**.

3) Click on the **New Key** button, choose **Vector** as the key type, and title this new key **WanderPoint**.

4) Save your blackboard, then click on the "**Behavior Tree**" tab to return to the Behavior Tree.

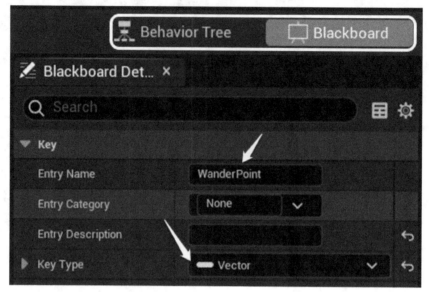

5) Click on the **"New Task"** button on the toolbar and choose the **BTTask-BlueprintBase** on the drop-down menu.

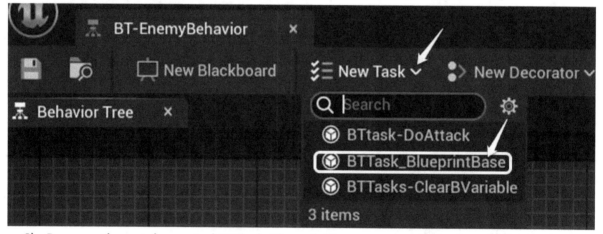

6) Rename the newly created **BTTask-BlueprintBase** asset to **BTTask-DeteckWanderPoint**. Double-click on **BTTask-DeteckWanderPoint** to open it in the Blueprint Editor.

7) The **Details** panel displays the class default. set the **Node Name** field to **DetectWanderPoint**.

8) Go to the "**My Blueprint**" panel, and click the plus "**+**" button in the Variables grouping. Go to the Details panel, title the variable as **WanderKey,** set its type to **Blackboard KeySelector**, and enable the **Instance Editable** option.

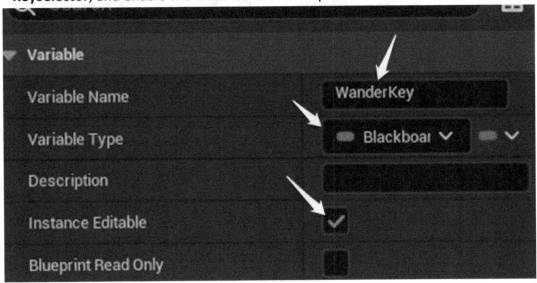

9) Hover over the **Functions** category in the "**My Blueprint**" panel, click the **Override** dropdown, and choose **Receive Execute** to add the event.

In the Event Receive Execute, we will select a random location within the level and store it in the blackboard. Check the subsequent steps.

10) Pull a wire from the white pin of **Event Receive Execute** to add a **Set Blackboard Value as Vector** node.

11) Pull a wire from the white output pin of **Set Blackboard Value as Vector** to add a **Finish Execute** node. Ensure the **Success** feature of the **Finish Execute** node is checked.

12) Pull a wire from the **Key** parameter of **Set Blackboard Value as Vector** to add **a Get Wander Key** node.

13) Pull a wire from the **Value** feature of **Set Blackboard Value** as Vector to add a **GetRandomPointInNavigableRadius** node. Enter **10000.0** as the **Radius** value.

14) Pull a wire from the **Origin** parameter to add a **Make Vector** node.

15) Compile and save the blueprint.

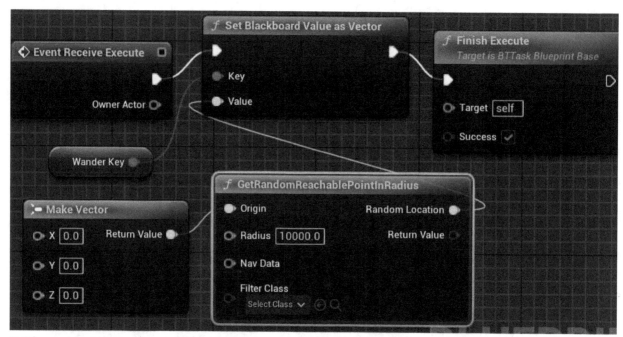

With our custom task set up, we can now modify BT-EnemyBehavior to make the enemy locate and move to the WanderPoint

ADDING WANDERING TO THE BEHAVIOR TREE

We will change the **Move To Patrol** sequence into a **Wander** sequence. The new **Wander** sequence is represented in the Behavior Tree by nodes we will be adding in this section:

To modify the Behavior Tree, follow these steps:

1) Open the **Behavior Tree** Editor by double-clicking on the **BT-EnemyBehavior** asset in the content browser.

2) Locate and select the **Move To Patrol** sequence node. In the **Details** panel, change the **Node Name** field to **Wander.**

3) Select the **Move To** task node and change the **Blackboard Key** to **WanderPoint**.

4) Pull a wire from the **Wander** sequence node to the left of the existing nodes to add the **BTTask-DetectWanderPoint** node.

220

5) In the **BTTask_DetectWanderPoint** node's **Details** panel, set **Wander Key** to **WanderPoint**. Also, set the **Node Name** to **Get Next Wander Point.**

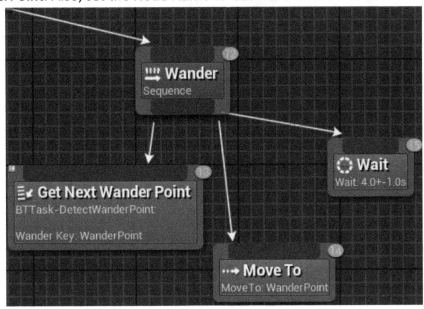

6) Save your changes and close the Behavior Tree Editor.

These adjustments integrate wandering behavior into the enemy's actions. Now, let's make some final adjustments to the blueprints:

FINAL ADJUSTMENTS AND ASSESSMENT

You will remove the **Event BeginPlay** from **BP-EnemyCharacter**, which was previously used to set Patrol Point. This is no longer needed as we now use random **WanderPoints**.

You will then adjust the **Target Goal** value in **FirstPersonCharacter** to ensure longer gameplay. Set this value to **15**, meaning the player needs to eliminate **15** enemies to win the game.

1) Open the blueprint for **BP-EnemyCharacter**. Go to the **Event Graph**, and remove the **Event BeginPlay** node and all connected nodes.

2) After making changes, compile the blueprint, save your work, and then close the Blueprint Editor.

3) Open the **FirstPersonCharacter**. Locate the **TargetGoal** variable in the **My Blueprint** panel. In the **Details** panel, modify the **Default Value** to **15**.

4) Compile your changes, save the blueprint, and close the Blueprint Editor.

5) To test the enemy's wandering behavior, use the **Simulate** option in the menu. You can find it by clicking on the three (...) dots next to the **Play** button.

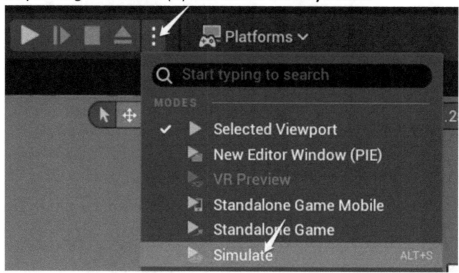

To navigate freely on the level, hold down the right mouse button and use the W, A, S, and D keys along with the mouse. As you explore, you'll notice enemies appearing and moving to different spots across the level.

We've developed a specialized task to locate random wander points and integrated it into the Behavior Tree. This enhancement enables enemies spawned by **BP-EnemySpawner** to navigate the level effectively.

CHAPTER TEN
ADDING THE FINISHING TOUCHES AND GAME STATES

Next, we'll take the concluding steps to transform our game into a complete and engaging experience that truly challenges the player. First, we'll implement player death, which will occur when the player's health is fully depleted. Next, we'll introduce a Stage system that increases the difficulty by requiring the player to defeat more enemies as they advance through each stage. Finally, we'll add a saving and loading system, allowing the player to leave the game and return later to the same stage they were last playing.

MAKING DANGER REAL WITH PLAYER DEATH

In Chapter 9, we made significant progress toward creating a balanced game where enemies pose a real threat, but players can use skill to overcome these challenges. However, one crucial element is still missing: player death. If the player runs out of health, they should not be able to continue progressing through the game. We'll apply what we learned from the win screen we created in Chapter 7 to a lose screen. This screen will allow the player to restart the level with full ammo and health but will erase any progress they had made toward their goals.

SETTING UP A LOSE SCREEN

The loss screen will appear when the player runs out of health, we will introduce options to restart the last stage or quit the game. This is similar to the win screen; we can save time by using our **WinMenu** asset as a template.

Follow these steps to create LoseMenu:

1) In the Content Browser, go to the "**Content > FirstPersonBP > User-Interface** folder. Right-click on "**WinMenu**" and select **Duplicate**. Title the new Blueprint Widget "**LoseMenu**". Double-click the "**LoseMenu**" asset to open the UMG Editor.

2) Select the text object showing **You Won!** Go to the **Details** panel, rename the text element to "**Lose msg**", change the **Text** field in the **Content** section to "**You Lost!**", and set the Color and Opacity to a dark **Magenta**.

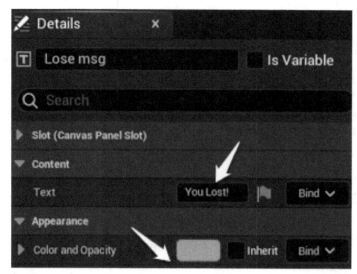

3) Compile and save your work. The two buttons, **Restart** and **Quit**, can remain identical to their WinMenu counterparts in appearance and functionality for now. Next, we need to adjust the FirstPersonCharacter Blueprint to display the lose screen when necessary.

DISPLAYING THE LOSE SCREEN

To create a more immersive experience, we'll set up a custom event titled "**LostGame**" that triggers when the player runs out of health. Create and configure the Custom Event using the following steps:

1) In the Content Browser, go to "**Content > FirstPerson** > Blueprints folder and then double-click the "FirstPersonCharacter" Blueprint.

2) In the **Event Graph**, right-click to add a Custom Event and rename it "**LostGame**".

3) Pull a wire from the output execution pin of "**LostGame**" to add a "**Set Game Paused**" node, and enable the **Paused** checkbox.

4) Right-click in the **Event Graph** to add a "**Get Player Controller**" node. Drag from the **Return Value** output pin to add a "**SET Show Mouse Cursor**" node. Activate the checkbox beside **Show Mouse Cursor** and connect this node to the output execution pin of "**Set Game Paused**".

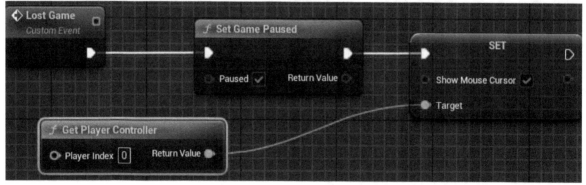

5) Pull a wire from the output execution pin of the "**SET Show Mouse Cursor**" node to add a "**Create Widget**" node. In the Class parameter, select "**LostMenu**".

6) Pull a wire from the **Return Value** output pin of the "**Create Widget**" node to add an "**Add to Viewport**" node.

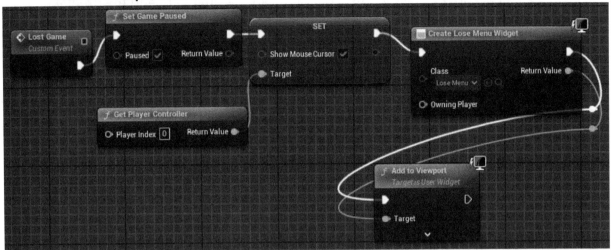

Next, we'll adjust the "**Event AnyDamage**" to call the "**LostGame**" event when the player's health reaches zero. Go to Event Any Damage and:

7) Pull a wire from the white output pin of the "**SET Player Health**" node to add a "**Branch**" node.

8) Pull a wire from the output pin of the "**SET Player Health**" node to add a "**Nearly Equal (float)**" node. Join the **Return Value** pin to the **Condition** input pin of the "**Branch**" node.

9) Pull a wire from the **True** output pin of the "**Branch**" node to add the "**LostGame**" node.

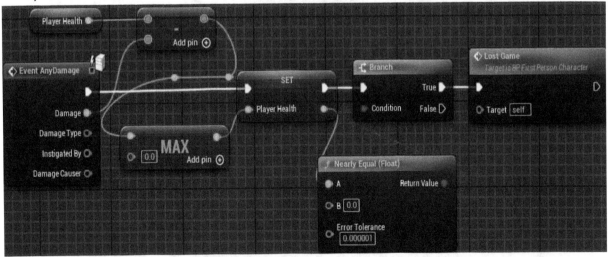

10) Compile and save your work. Click **Play** to test. If you stand next to an enemy long enough for it to drain your health to zero, you should see the "**LoseMenu**" we constructed.

Now, the player needs to be more cautious to avoid losing the game. In the next step, we'll add a stage-based experience to make the game even more engaging. stage

CREATING STAGE-BASED SCALING WITH SAVED GAMES

While our game now offers a full-play experience, it can feel limited due to the fixed number of enemies. To make the gameplay more engaging, we can introduce a stage-based system, similar to arcade games, where the difficulty increases as the player advances through each stage. This approach adds depth and fun without needing extensive custom content creation.

The stage will act as a measure of the player's achievement—the higher the stage, the greater the accomplishment. To ensure players are challenged by their skill rather than the time they spend in one sitting, we'll introduce a save system. This allows players to resume from where they left off, maintaining their progress across sessions.

USING THE SAVEGAME CLASS TO STORE GAME INFORMATION

To create a save system, we first need to make a Blueprint child of the "**SaveGame**" class, which will store the game data we want to save. Specifically, we'll track which stage the player was on before quitting the game. We don't need to store data on how many enemies the player has killed, as it makes more sense for each game session to start at the beginning of a stage.

Create a child of the "SaveGame" class using the following steps:

1) In the Content Browser, go to the "**Content > FirstPerson > Blueprint** folder. Click the **Add** button and select **Blueprint** Class.

2) In the parent class selection screen, search for and select "**SaveGame**" as the parent class.

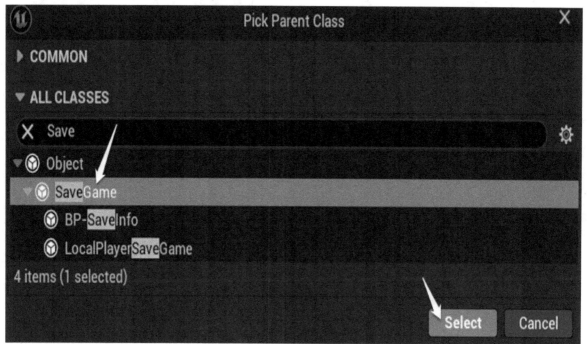

3) Title the **Blueprint** "**BP-SaveInfo**" and double-click it to open the Blueprint Editor.

4) Go to the **Variables** section of the "**My Blueprint**" panel, and click the plus "**+**" button to add a new variable. In the **Details** panel, name it "**Stage**", and change the **Variable Type** to **Integer**. Compile the Blueprint, and then set the **Default Value** to **1**.

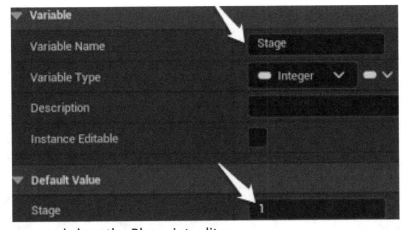

5) Compile, save, and close the Blueprint editor.

With the "BP-SaveInfo" Blueprint set up, next, you will learn how to save and load game data using this Blueprint.

SAVING GAME INFORMATION

To save game data effectively, we need to store it on the player's machine and retrieve it when the player returns. We'll handle this within the FirstPersonCharacter Blueprint, just like our other gameplay settings. Here's how to create the necessary variables and macro to save game information:

1) In the Content Browser, go to "**Content > FirstPerson> Blueprints** and double-click the "**FirstPersonCharacter**" Blueprint.

2) Go to the "**Variables**" section of the "**My Blueprint**" panel, and click the plus "**+**" button to add a new variable. In the "**Details**" panel, title the variable "**CurrentStage**" and set its type to "**Integer**". Compile the Blueprint and set its "**Default Value**" to "**1**".

3) Go to the "**My Blueprint**" panel, add another variable, and name it "**SaveInfoRef**". Go to the "**Details**" panel, and set the "**Variable Type**" to "**BP-SaveInfo**". mouse over "**BP-SaveInfo**" to display a submenu and select "**Object Reference**".

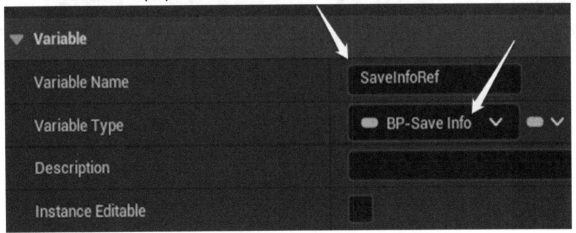

4) Go to the "**My Blueprint**" panel, add another variable, and name it "**SaveSlotName**". Go to the "**Details**" panel, and set its "**Variable Type**" to "**String**". Compile the

Blueprint and set its "**Default Value**" to "**SaveGameFile**". This is used to store the filename.

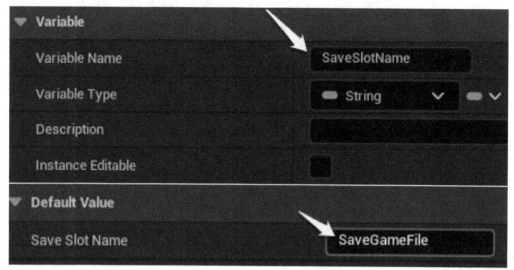

5) Go to the "**My Blueprint**" panel, and click the plus "**+**" button in the "**Macros**" section to create a new macro. Title the macro "**SaveStage**". Go to the "**Details**" panel of the macro, create an input parameter titled "**In**" of the "**Exec**" type and an output parameter named "**Out**" of the "**Exec**" type.

On the **SaveStage** macro tab, you will be adding some nodes. We want to test if the **Save InfoRef** is valid. If it is not valid, you will create an instance of **BP-SaveInfo** and store it in **SaveInfoRef**. You will then update the **Stage** variable of **SaveInfoRef** and then save the contents of **SaveInfoRef**

6) Pull a wire from the "**In**" pin of the "**Inputs**" node to add an "**Is Valid**" macro node.

7) Pull a wire from the "**Input Object**" feature to add a "Get **SaveInfoRef**" node.

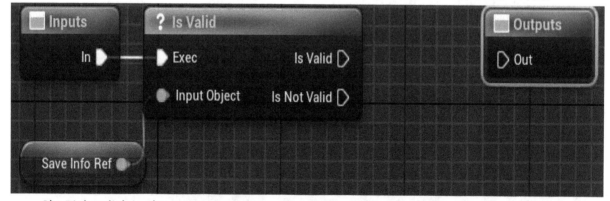

8) Right-click in the **Event Graph** to add another "**Get SaveInfoRef**" node. Pull a wire from the "Get **SaveInfoRef**" node to add a "**SET Stage**" node.

9) Attach the "**Is Valid**" output pin to the white input pin of the "**SET Stage**" node. Pull a wire from the "**Stage**" input pin to add a "**Get CurrentStage**" node.

10) Pull a wire from the white output pin of the "**SET Stage**" node to add a "**Save Game to Slot**" node. Attach the white output pin of "**Save Game to Slot**" to the "**Out**" pin of the "**Outputs**" node.

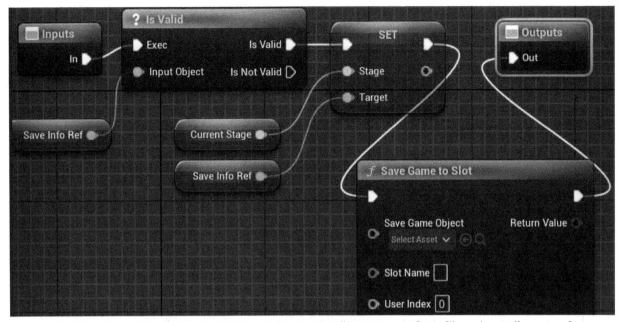

11) Attach the "**Save Game Object**" pin to the "**Get SaveInfoRef**" node. Pull a wire from the "**Slot Name**" pin to add a "**Get SaveSlotName**" node.

12) Pull a wire from the "**Is Not Valid**" output pin to add a "**Create Save Game Object**" node. In "**Save Game Class**", choose "**BP-SaveInfo**".

13) Pull a wire from the "**Return Value**" pin of "**Create Save Game Object**" to add a "**SET SaveInfoRef**" node. Join the white output pin of "**SET SaveInfoRef**" to the white input pin of the "**SET Stage**" node.

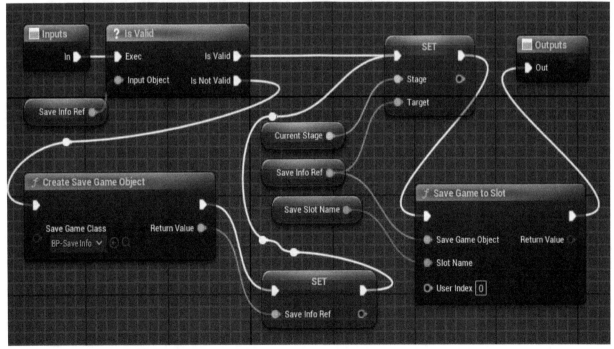

14) Compile and save the Blueprint.

Next, we'll create a macro to load the contents saved using the SaveStage macro.

229

LOAD GAME INFORMATION

To load game information, we will create a macro named "LoadStage" that retrieves the saved **Stage** and stores it in the "**CurrentStage**" variable. Create the LoadStage macro using the following steps:

1) In the "**My Blueprint**" panel of the "**FirstPersonCharacter**" Blueprint, click the plus "**+**" button in the "**Macros**" category to create a new macro. Rename it to "**LoadStage**". In the "**Details**" panel of the macro, create an input parameter titled "**In**" of the "**Exec**" type and an output parameter titled "**Out**" of the "**Exec**" type.

On the "**LoadStage**" macro tab, you will add the necessary nodes, as we will unveil in the subsequent steps

2) Pull a wire from the "**In**" pin of the "**Inputs**" node to add a "**Does Save Game Exist**" node. Pull a wire from the "**Slot Name**" pin to add a "**Get Save Slot Name**" node.

3) Pull a wire from the "**Return Value**" pin to add a "**Branch**" node. Join the white output pin of "**Does Save Game Exist**" to the white input pin of the "**Branch**" node.

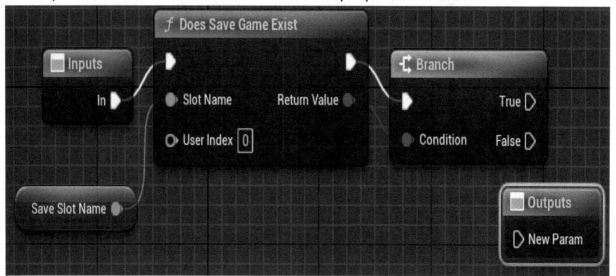

4) Join the "**False**" pin of the "**Branch**" node to the "**Out**" pin of the "**Outputs**" node. To add a **reroute** node, double-click a wire, to help modify the shape and position of a wire.

5) Pull a wire from the "**True**" pin of the "**Branch**" node to add a "**Load Game from Slot**" node. Pull a wire from the "**Slot Name**" pin to add another "**Get Save Slot Name**" node.

6) Pull a wire from the "**Return Value**" pin of "**Load Game from Slot**" to add a "**Cast To BP_SaveInfo**" node. Join the white output pin of "**Load Game from Slot**" to the white input pin of the "**Cast To BP_SaveInfo**" node.

7) Join the "**Cast Failed**" pin of the "**Cast To BP_SaveInfo**" node to the "**Out**" pin of the "**Outputs**" node. Add a reroute node if necessary.

8) Pull a wire from the "**As BP Save Info**" pin of the "**Cast To BP_SaveInfo**" node to add a "**SET Save Info Ref**" node. Join the white pins of "**Cast To BP_SaveInfo**" and "**SET Save Info Ref**".

230

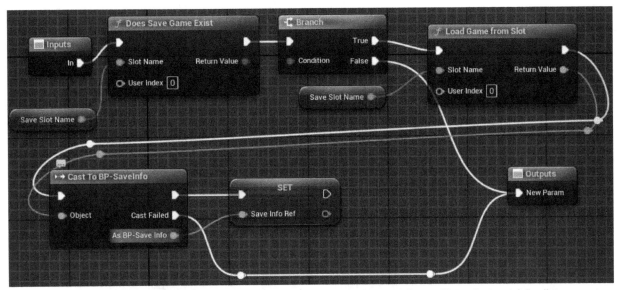

9) Pull a wire from the blue output pin of the "**SET Save Info Ref**" node to add a "**Get Stage**" node.

10) Pull a wire from the "**Stage**" pin to add a "**SET Current Stage**" node. This will retrieve the value of the "**Stage**" variable that was saved and store it in the "**CurrentStage**" variable of the "**FirstPersonCharacter**" Blueprint.

11) Join the white pins of the "**SET Save Info Ref**," "**SET Current Stage**," and "**Outputs**" nodes. **Compile** and **save** the Blueprint.

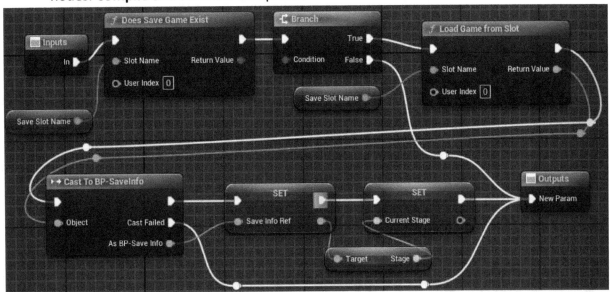

Using the "**SaveStage**" and "**LoadStage**" macros, we can allow the player to resume the game at the stage they left off. To increase the challenge, let's set the "**TargetGoal**" based on the stage.

INCREASE THE TARGETGOAL

To adjust the gameplay as the player progresses, we'll utilize the data stored in the save file. This will involve creating a variable called "**StageScaleMultiplier**" that will multiply the current stage to determine the new "**TargetGoal**". Increase the "TargetGoal" using the following steps:

1) Go to the "**Variables**" section of the "**My Blueprint**" panel, and click the plus "**+**" button to add a new variable. Title it "**StageScaleMultiplier**", set its "**Variable Type**" to "**Integer**", compile the Blueprint, and set its "**Default Value**" to **2**.

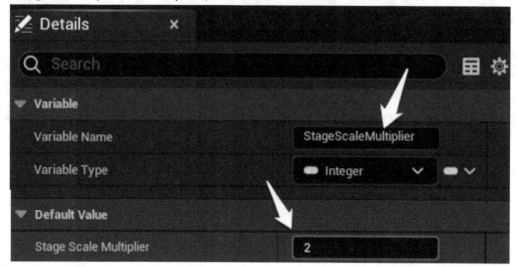

2) Go to the "**My Blueprint**" panel, and click the plus "**+**" button in the "**Macros**" category to create a new macro. Title this macro "**SetStageTargetGoal**". In the "**Details**" panel of the macro, create an input parameter named "**In**" of the "**Exec**" type and an output parameter named "**Out**" of the "**Exec**" type.

3) On the "**SetStageTargetGoal**" macro, add the necessary nodes, as we will unveil in the subsequent steps.

4) Pull a wire from the "**In**" pin of the "**Inputs**" node to add a "**Set Target Goal**" node. Join the white output pin of "**SET Target Goal**" to the "**Out**" pin of the "**Outputs**" node.

5) Pull a wire from the "**Target Goal**" pin to add a "Multiply" node.

6) Pull a wire from the top input pin of the "**Multiply**" node to add a "**Get Current Stage**" node.

7) Pull a wire from the bottom input pin of the **Multiply** node to add a **Get Stage Scale Multiplier** node.

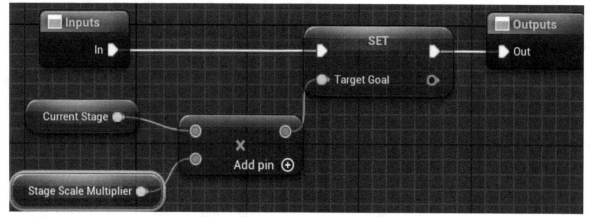

8) **Compile**, **save** the Blueprint, and return to the Event Graph tab.

9) In the **My Blueprint** panel, under the **Graphs** section, access **Event BeginPlay** and add the **Load Stage** and **Set Stage Target Goal** macro nodes. Then connect with Hud on the Screen node.

When a stage starts, the Load Stage macro loads a saved file if it exists. The Set Stage Target Goal macro sets the TargetGoal. When the player reaches the TargetGoal, a switchover screen will be displayed.

CREATING A SWITCHOVER SCREEN THAT WILL BE DISPLAYED BETWEEN STAGES

Now, when the player defeats sufficient enemies to meet the **TargetGoal**, they see the **WinMenu**, which congratulates them and provides options to restart the game or quit the application. With the new Stage-based gameplay, we'll adapt this **WinMenu** screen into a switchover screen for progressing to the next Stage.

Create the switchover screen using the following steps:

1) In the Content Browser, go to **Content** > **FirstPerson** > **User-Interface** and rename the **WinMenu** Widget Blueprint to **StageSwitchover** to better reflect its new purpose.

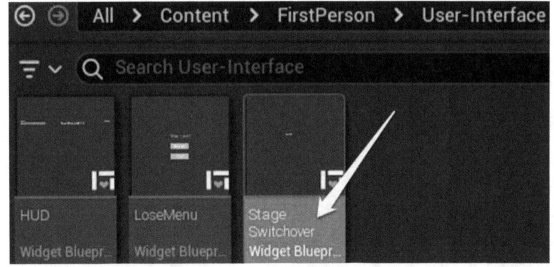

2) Double-click the **StageSwitchover** Widget Blueprint to open it in the UMG Editor. The new **StageSwitchover** screen will include some elements, as we will unveil in the subsequent steps.

3) Go to the **Hierarchy** panel, delete the "**You Won!**" text element and the "**Button quit**" button since we won't need a **quit** option during Stage switchovers.

233

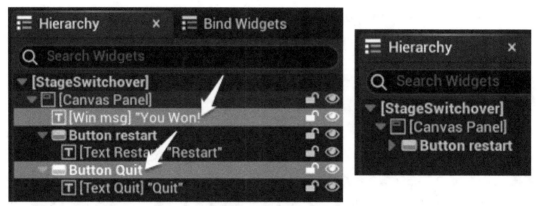

4) Switch to the **Graph** tab. In the **Event Graph**, delete the **"On Clicked (Buttonquit)"** event. Then, return to the UMG Editor by clicking the **Designer** tab at the top right corner.

5) Select the "**Text restart**" element and rename it to "**Text begin".** In the **Details** panel, change the text from "**Restart**" to "**Begin Stage**". Also, rename the "**Button restart**" to "**Button begin**" The feature to reload the level will remain unchanged.

6) Drag a **Horizontal Box** from the **Palette** panel into the **Hierarchy** panel, placing it above the "**Button Begin**" button.

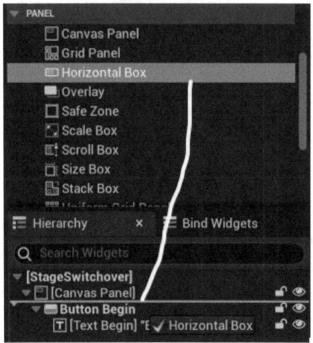

234

7) In the **Details** panel, open the **Anchors** dropdown and choose the **top-center** option. Set **Position X** to -**320**.0 and Position **Y** to **200**.0. Enable the **"Size To Content"** feature, so you won't need to alter the Size of **X** and **Y**. The horizontal box will automatically adjust its size according to its child elements.

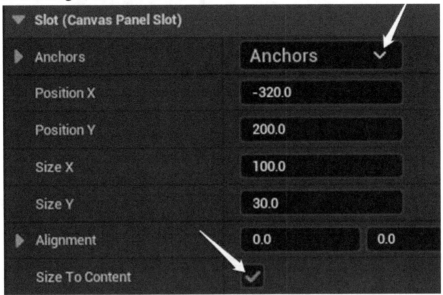

8) Drag a **Text** object into the **Horizontal Box**. Go to the **Details** panel, in the **Content** category, and change the **Text** field to "**Stage**". Then, in the **Appearance** section, set the font Size to **110**.

9) Drag another **Text** object into the **Horizontal Box**. Go to the Details panel, set **Padding Left** to **18**.0, and change the **Text** field in the **Content** category to "**99**" as a reference. In the **Appearance** category, set the font Size to **110**. Your **StageSwitchover** layout should resemble this:

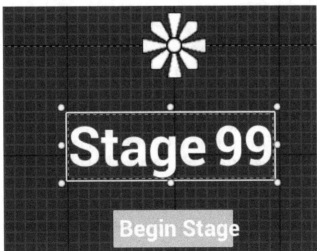

10) Go to the **Details** panel, locate the **Bind** button beside the **Text** field, and create a new binding.

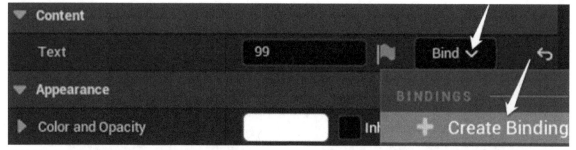

11) In the **Get Text** graph view that appears, add a **Get Player Character** node. Cast it using the **Cast To BP-FirstPersonCharacter** node, and then pull a wire from the **As First-Person Character** pin to add a **Get Current Stage** node.

12) Attach the **Cast** node and the **Current Stage** node to the **Return Node**. The editor will automatically create a **ToText (integer)** node to convert the number into a text format. Compile, save, and close the UMG Editor.

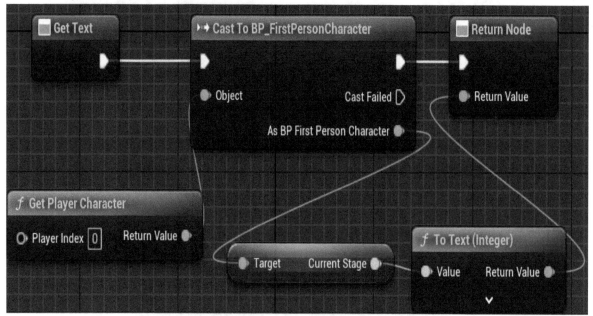

To finalize the Stage-based system, adjust the **End Game** Event.

SWITCHING OVER TO A NEW STAGE WHEN THE CURRENT STAGE IS WON

When the player wins a Stage, the game will switch over smoothly to the next one. This process involves some simple modifications to the End Game Event in the FirstPersonCharacter Blueprint. Specifically, the **StageSwitchover** screen will be displayed, which is a modified version of the **WinMenu**.

Modify the **End Game** Event using the following steps:

1) In the Content Browser, go to **Content** > **FirstPerson** > **Blueprints**. Open the FirstPersonCharacter Blueprint by double-clicking it.

2) In the Event Graph, locate the **End Game** Event. Go to the **Details** panel, and rename the **Event** to **End Stage**.

3) Alter the comment box label to **End Stage: (Shows Switchover Menu)**.

4) Break the wire between the **End Stage** and **Set Game Paused** nodes. Move the **End Stage** node to the left to create space for additional nodes.

5) Right-click in the **Event Graph** to add a **Get Current Stage** node.

6) Pull a wire from the **output** pin of the **Get Current Stage** node to add an **Increment Int** node. Join the white pins of the **Increment Int** and **End Stage** nodes.

7) Pull a wire from the output white pin of the **Increment Int** node to add the **Save Stage** macro node.

8) Attach the **Out** pin of the **Save Stage** node to the white input pin of the **Set Game Paused** node.

9) **Compile** and **save** your changes. Click the **Play** button to test the game.

When you load the game, you'll notice that the target goal counter at the top displays a low number of enemies. Defeat the number of enemies indicated by the goal and the Stage switchover screen will appear, showing Stage 2.

Press the **Begin Stage** button to reload the level with restored health and ammo, but with a higher enemy target. If you quit and reload the game, it will start at the last saved Stage.

Now that we can track player progress, we should also provide an option to reset the save file, allowing players to start the game from the beginning if they want.

PAUSE THE GAME AND RESET THE SAVE FILE

We need to create a **Pause Menu** that allows players to resume the game, restart from Stage One, or quit the application.

BUILDING A PAUSE MENU

To build the **PauseMenu,** we'll use our existing **LoseMenu** as a template. Use the following steps to create the PauseMenu:

1) In the Content Browser, go to **Content** > **FirstPerson** > **User-Interface**. Right-click on **LoseMenu** and choose **Duplicate**.

2) Rename the duplicated Blueprint Widget to **PauseMenu**.

3) In the new **PauseMenu**, locate the text that says "**You Lost!**" and change it to "**Paused**" in the **Details** panel. Adjust the **Color and Opacity** to green for a distinctive look and change the name to msg

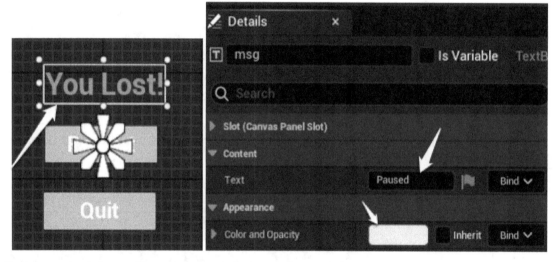

4) Move the "**Paused**" text up to make room for another button. In the **Slot** category, set **Position X** to -170.0 and **Position Y** to -400.0

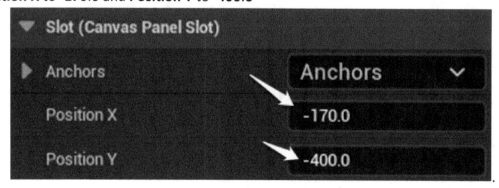

We will add a new button for the "**Resume**" option and rename the "**Restart**" button to "**Reset All**".

5) Drag a **Button** element from the **Palette** panel to the **Canvas Panel** object in the **Hierarchy** panel, positioning it below the "**Paused**" message. In the **Details** panel, rename this button to "**Button resume**". Click on the **Anchors** dropdown and choose the option that centers the anchor on the screen.

6) Set **Position X** to **-180**.0, Position Y to **-250**.0, **Size X** to **360**.0, and Size **Y** to **110**.0.

7) Drag a **Text** object from the **Palette** panel to the "**Button resume**" element in the **Hierarchy** panel. Go to the **Details** panel, and rename the text object to "**Text resume**". Change the **Text** field in the **Content** section to "**Resume**" and set the font size to **50.**

8) Change the name of the "**Button restart**" button to "**Button reset**". Rename "**Text restart**" to "**Text reset**" and update the **Text** field to "**Reset All**".

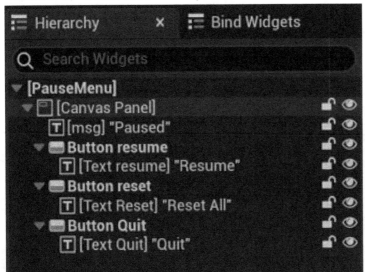

9) Compile and save your changes.

With the visual elements of the **PauseMenu** now set, we can proceed to work on the functionality.

RESUMING THE GAME

To resume the game, we need to perform a series of steps. First, we have to remove the **PauseMenu** from the screen. Next, we hide the mouse cursor, and finally, we unpause the game. Add this functionality using the following steps:

1) Click on the **"Button resume"** element, scroll to the bottom of the **Details** panel, and click the plus **"+"** button beside the **"On Clicked Event"**.

2) In the **Graph** view, set up the following nodes for the **"On Clicked (Buttonnresume)"** event

3) Pull a wire from the **"On Clicked (Buttonresume)"** node to add a **"Remove from Parent"** node.

4) Right-click in the **Event Graph** to add a **"Get Player Controller"** node.

239

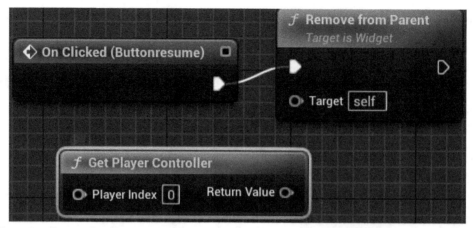

5) Pull a wire from the **"Return Value"** of **"Get Player Controller"** to add a **"SET Show Mouse Cursor"** node. Join the white output pin of **"Remove from Parent"** to the white input pin of **"SET Show Mouse Cursor"**. Ensure the **"Show Mouse Cursor"** feature remains unchecked.

6) Pull a wire from the white output pin of the **"SET Show Mouse Cursor"** to a **"Set Game Paused"** node. Ensure the **"Paused"** feature remains unchecked.

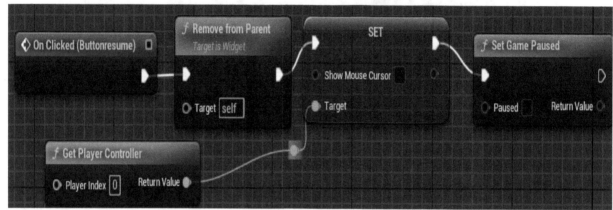

These steps ensure that clicking the Resume button executes the necessary actions. Next, let"s introduce the actions for the **Reset All** button."

RESET THE SAVED FILE

The "Reset All" button deletes the existing save game, if there is one, and reloads the game level. To automate this process, we'll create a macro that handles the save game deletion. Follow these steps for that:

1) In the **"My Blueprint"** panel, click the plus **"+"** button under the "Macros" category to create a new macro. Rename the macro to **"DeleteFile"**. In the **"Details"** panel, add an input parameter titled **"In"** of type **"Exec"** and an **output** parameter named **"Out"** of type **"Exec"**.

240

On the "**DeleteFile**" macro tab, add the necessary nodes as we will unveil in the subsequent steps. This includes retrieving the "**Save Slot Name**" from the "**FirstPersonCharacter**" instance.

2) Add a "**Get Player Character**" node, cast it with "**Cast To BP-FirstPersonCharacter**", and then pull a wire from the **As BP-FirstPersonCharacter** to add a "**Get Save Slot Name**" node.

3) Pull a wire from the white output pin of "**Cast To BP-FirstPersonCharacter**" to add a "**Does Save Game Exist**" node. Attach the **Slot Name** pin to the **Get Save Slot Name**.

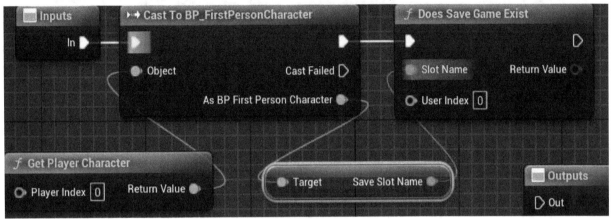

4) Pull a wire from "**Does Save Game Exist**" to add a "**Branch**" node. Attach the **Return Value** to the **Condition** pin.

5) Pull a wire from the **True** output of the **Branch** node to add a **Delete Game in Slot** node. Then, Join the **Slot Name** pin to the **Get Save Slot Name** node. Join the white output pin to the **Out** pin of the **Outputs** node.

6) Attach the **Cast Failed** pin of **Cast To BP-FirstPersonCharacter** and the **False** pin of the **Branch** node to the **Out** pin of the **Outputs** node.

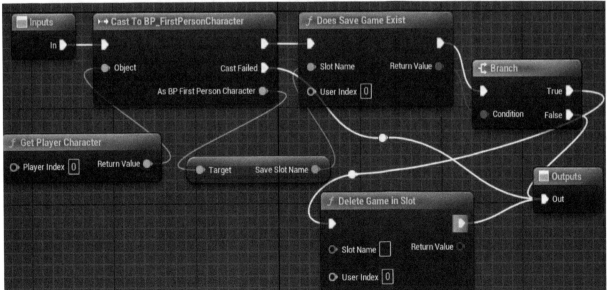

7) In the **Event Graph**, after the **On Clicked (Buttonreset)** Event, add the **Delete File** macro node.

241

8) Compile and save the Blueprint.

ACTIVATING THE PAUSE MENU

We will be using the **Enter** key to pause the game and open **PauseMenu.** Follow these steps to trigger the **PauseMenu:**

1) Click the **Settings** button at the far right of the toolbar and choose **Project Settings.**
2) On the left side of the window that appears, find the "**Engine**" category and choose the "**Input**" option. Click the plus "**+**" sign beside "**Action Mappings**". Title the new action "**Pause**" and choose the "**Enter**" key on the dropdown menu to assign this key to the **Pause** Event.

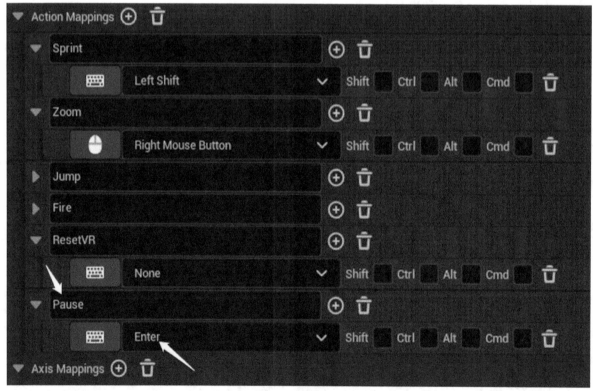

3) In the Content Browser, go to **Content** > **FirstPerson** > **Blueprints** and double-click on the **FirstPersonCharacte**r Blueprint.

4) Right-click in the **Event Graph**, and search for "**input action pause**" to add the **Pause** Event node. Copy all the nodes from the **LostGame** Custom Event and paste them near the **InputAction Pause** node.

5) Join the "**Pressed**" pin of the **InputAction Pause** node to the white input pin of the **Set Game Paused** node.

6) Change the **Class** feature of the **Create Widget** node to "**Pause Menu**".

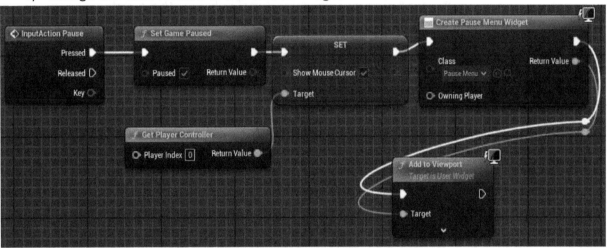

7) Compile, save, and click "**Play**" to test your setup.

Now, when you play the game, pressing the **Enter** key should bring up the pause menu. Clicking the "**Resume**" button will close the pause menu and return you to the game. If you progress through several Stages and then press the "**Reset All**" button in the pause menu, the level should reload, resetting your progress to the first Stage. If this works as expected, congratulations! You have successfully created a save system that can store, load, and reset progress across multiple Stages of gameplay.

CHAPTER ELEVEN
BUILDING AND SHARING YOUR GAME

Part of the effective methods to develop as a game developer is to share your work with others. Sharing allows you to gather valuable feedback, which can help you refine your designs and improve your content. A key early step in this process is to create shareable builds of your game, enabling others to play and experience it firsthand.

Unreal Engine makes this task straightforward by providing tools to build your game for several platforms with ease. Next, you will explore how to optimize your game's settings and guide you through building it for your target desktop platform.

After this chapter, you should be able to get a packaged version of your game ready to share and install on other machines, opening the door to feedback and further development.

OPTIMIZING GRAPHICS SETTINGS FOR YOUR GAME

Before creating a build of your game optimized for a specific platform, it's essential to adjust the graphics settings to match your target machines. In Unreal Engine 5, these settings are known as **Engine Scalability Settings**, and they control various aspects of visual quality. Balancing visual quality with performance is crucial, as games with low frame rates can detract from the overall gameplay experience, even if the game mechanics are strong.

It's important to find the right balance between high-quality graphics and smooth performance on your players' devices. Since PCs and macOS computers have different hardware capabilities, many games allow players to adjust graphics settings via custom menus. However, for our game, which uses simple assets and has a limited level size, we will set default graphics settings before creating the build.

To adjust the **Engine Scalability Settings**, use the following steps:

1) Click the "**Settings**" button on the right side of the Level Editor toolbar.

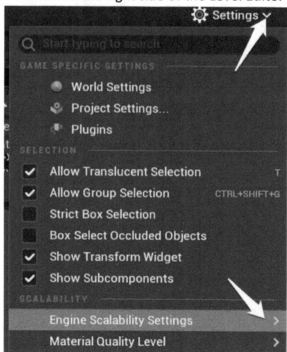

2) When you hover over the **Engine Scalability Settings**, a pop-up will appear showing various **Quality** settings that you can adjust, as illustrated in the screenshot below: These steps will help ensure that your game looks great while maintaining a good performance level on your target platform.

Scalability Groups						
	Low	Medium	High	Epic	Cinematic	Auto
View Distance	Near	Medium	Far	Epic	Cinematic	
Anti-Aliasing (TSR)	Low	Medium	High	Epic	Cinematic	
Post Processing	Low	Medium	High	Epic	Cinematic	
Shadows	Low	Medium	High	Epic	Cinematic	
Global Illumination	Low	Medium	High	Epic	Cinematic	
Reflections	Low	Medium	High	Epic	Cinematic	
Textures	Low	Medium	High	Epic	Cinematic	
Effects	Low	Medium	High	Epic	Cinematic	
Foliage	Low	Medium	High	Epic	Cinematic	
Shading	Low	Medium	High	Epic	Cinematic	
Landscape	Low	Medium	High	Epic	Cinematic	

3) At the top of this menu, you'll find buttons labeled from **Low** to **Epic**. These serve as preset configurations, allowing you to select a balance between performance and visual quality for runtime. Selecting the "**Low**" option will adjust all quality settings to their minimum, optimizing performance at the cost of visual appeal. On the other end, the "**Epic**" setting maximizes all quality settings, providing the best visuals but potentially impacting performance based on the assets you're using.

4) The "**Cinematic**" button switches all settings to cinematic quality, ideal for rendering high-quality cutscenes. This setting is not meant for gameplay or runtime use.

5) By clicking the "**Auto**" button, the Editor will automatically assess your machine's hardware and adjust the graphics settings to achieve an optimal balance between performance and visual quality. This is particularly useful if you're developing on hardware similar to your target audience, as it can help you quickly establish appropriate graphics settings for your build.

6) If you want to adjust the game settings individually, here's a brief explanation of each option:

   ✓ **Resolution Scale:** This setting allows the game engine to render the game at a lower resolution than the target resolution, and then uses software to upscale the image. This can improve performance but may result in a slightly fuzzy appearance at lower scales.

   ✓ **View Distance:** This specifies how far from the camera objects are rendered. Objects beyond this distance won't be shown, which can improve performance but may cause objects to suddenly appear when they enter the visible range.

   ✓ **Anti-Aliasing:** This smooths out jagged edges on 3D objects, enhancing the visual quality of the game. Higher settings reduce jagged edges more effectively but can decrease performance.

   ✓ **Post Processing:** This controls various visual effects applied after the scene is rendered, such as motion blur and light bloom. Adjusting this can affect the overall visual quality.

- ✓ **Shadows:** This setting influences the quality of shadows in the game. Higher shadow quality can significantly enhance visuals but often comes at a performance cost.
- ✓ **Textures:** This affects how textures are managed by the game engine. If your game uses many large textures, reducing this setting can help manage graphics memory usage and improve performance.
- ✓ **Effects:** This setting adjusts the quality of special effects applied to the game, like material reflections and translucency. Higher-quality effects can enhance visual fidelity but may affect performance.
- ✓ **Foliage:** This affects the quality of foliage in the game, impacting how detailed plants and trees appear.
- ✓ **Shading**: This setting influences the quality of material shading, affecting how realistic surfaces look. Adjusting this can impact both visual quality and performance.

To optimize your game's performance, it's essential to regularly test it on the target machines where players will experience it. Pay close attention to any areas where performance slows down. If you notice that your game consistently runs slowly, consider reducing some postprocessing effects or anti-aliasing settings. However, if the lag occurs only in specific parts of the level, you might need to decrease object density in those areas or lower the quality of certain game models.

since we've covered how to adjust graphics settings, let's look at customizing some project settings before building your game.

SETTING UP YOUR GAME FOR OTHERS TO PLAY

Unreal Engine supports a wide range of platforms, allowing you to build games for Windows, macOS, Android, iOS, and Linux. The engine also supports content creation for various virtual reality platforms, such as Oculus Quest, and 8th and 9th generation consoles. However, developing for consoles requires you to be a registered console developer with the necessary development kit.

Every platform has its own unique requirements and best practices for game development. For instance, mobile games often require more rigorous optimization to perform well.

To adjust how your project appears on the target machine, follow these steps:

1) Click on the "**Settings**" button in the Level Editor toolbar and select "**Project Settings**" from the menu.

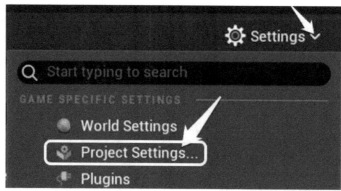

2) In the **Project Settings**, you'll find a range of options on the left panel that let you customize various aspects of the game, the engine, and platform interactions. Initially, you'll be directed to the **Project - Description** page. Here, you can set the project's name, choose a thumbnail image that will appear in the Unreal Engine project selector, and write a brief explanation of the project along with details about its creator as illustrated in the screenshot below.

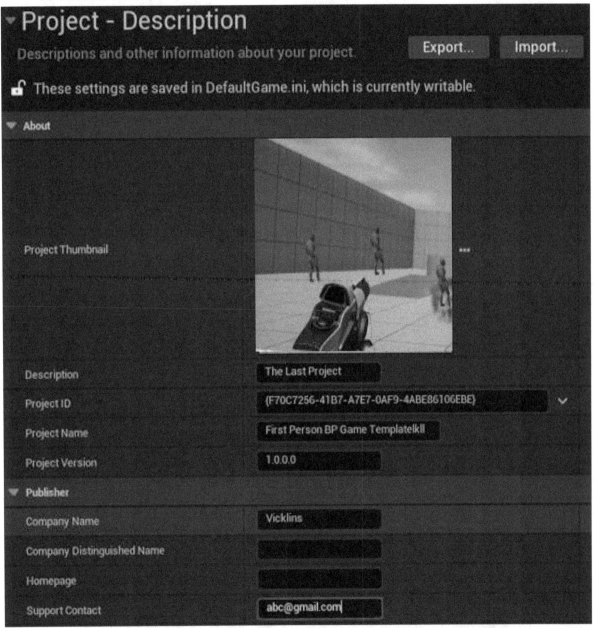

3) When you click on **Maps & Modes** in the left panel, you'll be taken to a page where you can specify which map the game should load by default. Since our game only has one map, this decision is straightforward. However, it's common to set a dedicated map for the main menu to be the first one to load. In games with several maps, it's essential to ensure that the initial map can manage the loading sequence for subsequent maps during gameplay.

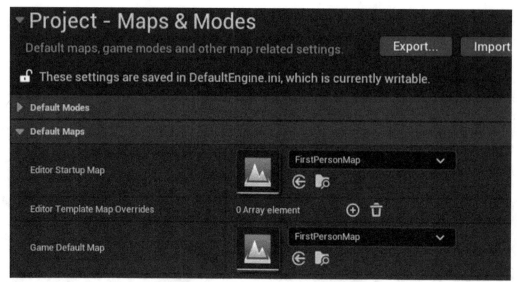

4) Lastly, clicking on the platform you're targeting for this build will direct you to a page where you can customize settings specific to that platform.

5) In the **Windows** section shown in the screenshot, you can change the **Splash** screens and image **Icon** for the game. For mobile and console platforms, there will be additional options specific to each platform.

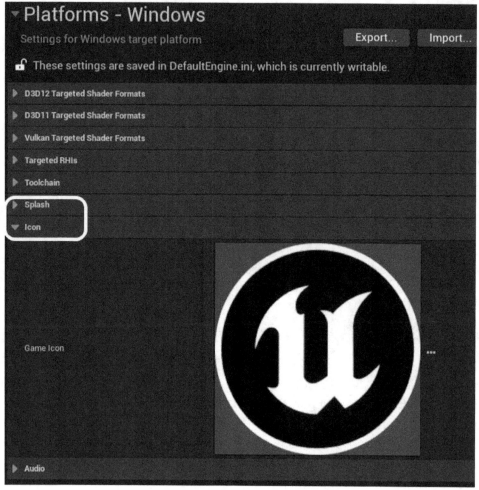

6. To customize your game, replace the default splash and icon images with the ones you prefer. You can use a simple edited screenshot from your game or a custom piece of art created precisely for the icons and splash screens. Once you're happy with your project settings, close the **Project Settings** window to begin packaging your project.

PACKAGING YOUR GAME INTO A BUILD

Creating a build of your game involves packaging it into a format that can be distributed and played on a specific platform, like Windows or macOS. This process gathers all your game's code and assets and sets them up correctly for the selected platform. In this guide, we'll focus on preparing a release for Windows or macOS.

Important Note: Unreal Engine 5 can only create Windows builds on a Windows system and macOS builds on a macOS system. This means that the platforms you can target are somewhat limited by the system you are developing the game on. If you're working on a Windows PC but want to make a macOS build, you need to install Unreal Engine 5 on a macOS machine, transfer your project files there, and build the macOS version without any further adjustments.

Use the following steps to package your game to be played on a specific platform:

1) In the toolbar, click the "**Platforms**" button, mouse over your desired platform, and select "**Package Project**".

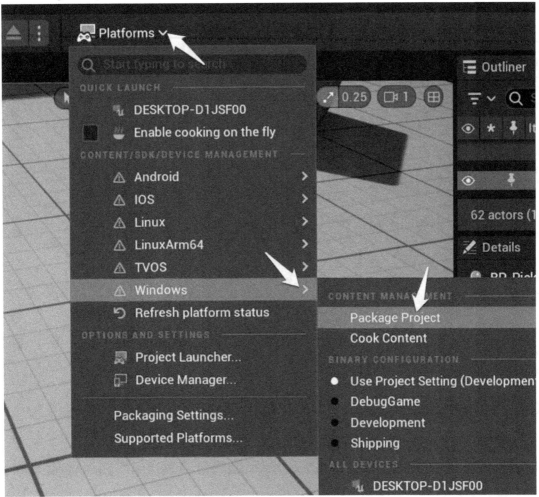

2) You'll be prompted to choose a location on your computer to save the build. Once selected, a popup will notify you that the engine is packaging your project. If there are any issues, you'll see an error message in the output log window. Packaging time varies based on the project's size and complexity. If successful, you'll receive a notification that the packaging is complete. Cheers, you've created a packaged version of your game!

3) Locate the folder where you saved your build. On Windows, open the **"WindowsNoEditor"** folder and double-click the executable to run your game. On macOS, open the **"MacNoEditor"** folder and double-click the application to launch it   - Take a brief minute to explore your game in its finished form and appreciate the mileage achieved. You have just created a functional game for others to play and appreciate. Creating even a simple game is a significant achievement, and you should be proud of your work!

This project is packaged using the default settings, but there are several options that you can adjust in the packaging.

BUILD AND PACKAGING SETTINGS

Next, we'll explore some settings available for build and packaging. The "**Platforms**" submenu includes the "**Packaging Settings**" option, which opens the "**Project - Packaging**" page where you can adjust configuration options.

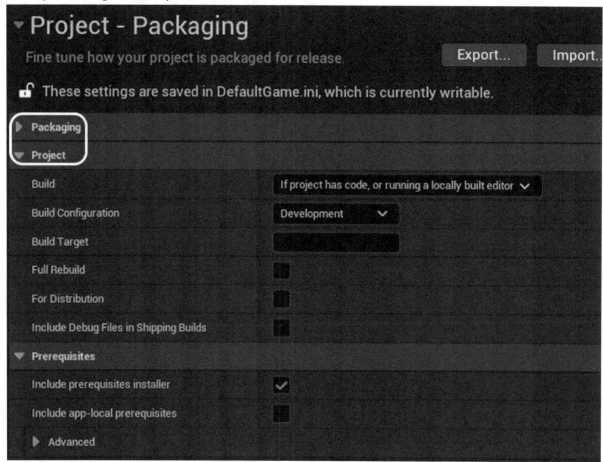

The "**Packaging**" category contains various technical options for optimizing packaging. The "**Build Configuration**" setting determines how the build is executed. For Blueprint-only projects, you can choose between two options: "**Development**" and "**Shipping**". Development builds include debugging information to help identify errors. In contrast, Shipping builds are streamlined and lack debug information, making them ideal for creating the final version of your game for distribution.

The "**Staging Directory**" property specifies the folder where the packaged build will be saved. The "**For Distribution**" option is necessary when submitting a game to the Google Play Store or App Store.

When you're finished adjusting settings, you can close the "**Project - Packaging**" page.

If you need to transfer your project to another computer or share it with someone else, use the "**Zip Project**" option in the **File** menu of the **Level Editor**. This feature copies and compresses the essential project files, making them easy to transport.

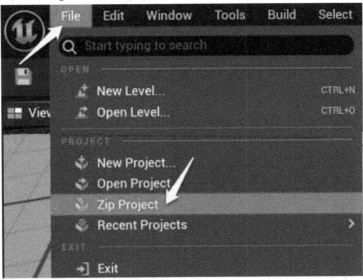

There are several packaging options, some of which are platform-specific. Take your time to explore and understand the various packaging options available for your game's target platform.

CONCLUSION

Unreal Engine is a mainstay of the game and virtual production development sectors (which also includes technologies for other industries like digital twins. The extent to which you can make the most from Unreal Engine is how far you dedicate yourself to practice with Unreal Engine User Interface using this amazing user guide.

This user guide must have taught you how to create variables, functions, and macros. You must have learned how to create a first-person shooter (**FPS**) using the Unreal Engine application.

If you are in the concluding part of this impactful user guide, you must have seen the reason why Unreal Engine is unique and needed in the world at large.

If this user guide has helped you in one way or the other, do well to tell others by dropping positive reviews to enable other users to explore the same advantages in this impactful user guide.

INDEX